Beyond Paris

Beyond Paris

A young man sets off to work in Paris but goes beyond to discover the world, finding the man he would become along the way.

An Adventure Travel Memoir By
Paul Alexander Casper

∞INFINITY
PUBLISHING

ISBN 978-1-49-990552-6 (Paperback Book)
ISBN 978-1-49-990632 (Hardcover Book)
ISBN 978-1-49-990553-3 (eBook)

Library of Congress Control Number 2019008752
Classification: LCC G226.C37 A3 2019 | DDC 910.4--dc23 LC

Book Design by Jane Dixon-Smith & Paul Casper
Front Cover Photography by Joyce Casper

First Printing Edition 2019

INFINITY PUBLISHING
1094 New DeHaven Street, Suite 100
West Conshohocken, PA 19428-2713
Toll-free (877) BUY BOOK
Local Phone (610) 941-9999
Fax (610) 941-9959
Info@buybooksontheweb.com
www.buybooksontheweb.com

The information in this book is true and as complete as possible after fifty years to the best of our knowledge. The author and publisher disclaim any liability in connection with the following pages.

www.BeyondParis.info

For my mother, Inez,
my beautiful wife, Kathy,
my sons Nicholas & Christopher
and
for all the other
Road Knights
around the world

*Is the end
of one journey
just the beginning
of another?*

Author's Note

This book is a memoir.

It reflects my present recollection of the experiences I had in 1970.

Every adventure in this book is true.

Every conversation is my best memory after almost fifty years.

I have changed the names of some people in this book

after not being able to locate them around the world.

I have compressed, contracted and subtly rearranged

time and events in several instances.

Otherwise,

this book is a true account

of my experiences as I remember them.

Foreword

Things to remember about 1970...

- The cost of a gallon of gas was $.36
- A pair of men's leather shoes cost $6.97
- Richard Nixon was President
- The average house price was $4,975
- The cost of a postage stamp was $.06
- The Dow Jones was 631 in 1970. In January 2018, it broke 26,000
- The 1970 Song of the Year was "Bridge Over Troubled Water," by Simon & Garfunkel
- The most popular 1970 TV Comedy was *All in the Family*
- The top college football team was the Nebraska Cornhuskers
- The number-one fiction bestseller was *Love Story* by Eric Segal
- The median household income was $8,734/yr
- MLB's MVP was Johnny Bench of the Cincinnati Reds
- A cyclone in Bangladesh killed 500,000 people
- 1970 popular films: *Catch 22, Patton* and *Hello Dolly*
- The minimum wage was $2.10/hr
- Average monthly rent was $140.00
- The Isle of Wight concert in August in England drew 600,000 attendees

Preface

After pledging Theta Chi Fraternity at Drake University and then,

of course, not making grades,

I was put on academic probation in 1965,

my freshman year.

The threat of dismissal inspired a dramatic comeback, however,

and I graduated in 1969 with a Bachelor of Fine Arts Degree—

on time and on the Dean's List.

Immediately I was hired by an internationally known Chicago graphic design

firm, after competing against almost a hundred other applicants.

A year later, I felt I knew everything there was to know about life.

The obvious next step, it was clear to me, was

to quit my job and get a one-way ticket to Paris,

where I would work on the Champs Elysées as an art director

and chase French women.

Contents

Cincinnati

Although a soft wind had brought a
misty rain
a little earlier in the day,
the grass was almost totally dry now.
Everyone's skin was warm and sticky again
on this predictably hot Cincinnati July
summer night.

And as usual,
fireworks were in the air.

1.

Escape

10:30 PM, July 3, 1959

Carl handed me another bottle of Pabst Blue Ribbon beer while I rummaged around on the coffee table for a cigarette. "Dream Lover" by Bobby Darin started to play in the background as lights of a passing car skipped past the basement window. Earlier in the evening, we had been talking about the usual things: the Reds, girls, life and the fact that grade school was finally almost over for both of us. Carl's parents were out for the night, and we had recently just finished listening to the end of the Phillies vs. Reds game, which the Reds won 6-1. It didn't look like it was going to be a very good year for the 1959 Reds, but the games were always interesting, especially when you had an outfield consisting of Frank Robinson, Jerry Lynch, and Vada Pinson. Even though he was new to the Reds, my favorite player was Leo Cardenas at shortstop. Like him, I had the hands to grab any ground ball close to where I was. Now if both he and I could just learn how to pull the ball at the plate, we both might turn out to be dual-threat players.

Watching Carl walk over to the radio to change the channel, I lit up, and as I blew out the match, I thought about an incident earlier in the day. At eleven years old and too young to buy cigarettes myself, I had to be clever and a little devious. One scheme I used often and had today was to wait outside Frisch's Restaurant, not far from Western Hills High School, where I would soon go, and ask people as they came out if they could give me a quarter to call my mother. Now, sometimes it became sticky trying to get a quarter when all anyone needed was a dime to make a call, but I had the face and a little bit of that cute blond kid hustle to get the quarter. Then it was a matter of waiting a couple of minutes to let the moment clear, walking into the entryway of the restaurant, between the two sets of doors, nonchalantly putting the quarter into the cigarette vending machine, pushing the right button, picking up the pack of Winston's and moving easily to my bike around the corner and off.

"Let's get out of here, I need to get some air," Carl yelled. He was halfway up the stairs before I got a chance to ask why. The street was quiet. I'm not sure what time it was, but probably most of our neighbors were either watching TV or in bed. We shuffled slowly over to a parked car in front of the Collins' house. After a minute or two of blowing great smoke rings that seemed to mystically come alive and linger in the night air, staying close as if to wait for something out of the ordinary to happen, I motioned to Carl about lightning in the distance that could be coming our way. Just then he reached into his pocket and brought out four ominous but enticing-looking cherry bombs.

"Cool. Did you hitch to Kentucky again to buy a bunch of fireworks?"

He and his friend had this history, of course without their parents knowing, of thumbing across the river each year and buying a lot of big-time and big-noise-making bombs of different kinds. It was quite an adventure to do that and especially dicey at our age.

"You know, old man Collins really is a dick; he's been a thorn in my side for I don't know how long," Carl spit out as he handed me two of the red, round jewels.

Now, this was not a one-sided story. You really couldn't tell who the biggest loser might be when Carl moved in across the street from a guy who was a real tyrant about the cleanliness and protection of his yard. He yelled at everyone all the time; you could barely walk on the public sidewalk in front of his house without feeling you were trespassing. You always felt a pair of eyes watching you as if he were waiting to jump out of his house and start yelling. And Carl living so close must have filled him with tension each time he left his house. On the other hand, Carl made sure there was retaliation, especially on days or nights around Halloween or Damage Night each year. He could be quite creatively mischievous.

"Are you ready?" he asked.

"What…what do you mean… ready?"

There was no answer; he just motioned my cigarette to each of his hands, to light the fuse on each bomb. "Now light yours, Paul," he said as the fuses began to sparkle and hiss. It crossed my mind—Now what? It was late; the street was quiet; most people were asleep or getting there; what were we going to do with these things? There were only houses close together as far as the eye could see. Just exactly as I was wondering where these cherry bombs were going to go now that they were lit, Carl yelled, "Throw 'em now," and I watched him hurl his two towards the roof of Collins' house. Who knows why people do the things they do? Who knows why after that fleeting moment of sanity, of thinking, no, that's probably not a good idea, I lit mine and threw one and then the other as hard as I could towards the same roof? For a moment I was hypnotized, watching the twirling, sparkling bombs flying in an almost coordinated dancing movement as his first thrown hit the house, quickly exploding just above the front door, another hit the roof and bounced a couple of feet before also exploding in a bang louder than the first. My two went farther, the first soaring over the roof and falling down the back of the house, which I'm sure sounded to the inhabitants like they were being bombed from front and back. My second one almost magically stuck for a second on the very pinnacle of the roof, defying gravity until it decided its time had come. That one made the loudest explosion of the four.

I stood there admiring what we'd done like someone admiring a painting he had just finished. Our type of art was mischief of an almost a spiritual quality; it was pure; we couldn't have done it any better, and it was loud. I'm sure half the neighborhood was thinking what the hell was going on.

Just then Carl grabbed me and pulled me to the street, mouthing, "Quiet, it's old man Collins!" Not more than a second or two later we were crawling under the car, thinking he'd never see us here, as we were in the dark, and his front porch was a distance away. There was a streetlight nearby, but its light was only hitting the back end of Collins' Chevy. My heart was racing, but I knew it would calm down in a moment. He wouldn't be able to see us under the car from that distance.

Funny and scary at the same time, Collins bounded out the front door on to his porch and started yelling, "Marchetti, Carl Marchetti, I know that was you! You are really in trouble now. I'm calling the cops! You are going to jail." I guess all these years of monkey business had finally caught up with Carl. Funny, I thought, how suddenly his yelling was either getting louder or he was getting closer... closer!

Yes, he was now moving to the front of the car. All we could see was his feet and, man, were we watching his feet. I don't know about Carl, but my heart was pumping like wildly; I'm sure old man Collins could hear it. As he continued to yell and slowly move around the car, we nudged ourselves quietly to scoot over in the opposite direction.

Just as he had made one revolution around the car and was back on the grass, Carl tugged on my sleeve and whispered, "We gotta make a run for it."

I didn't say it, but I thought it, WHAT! Are you crazy? He's right there. Before my thought was even finished, Carl was out from under the car. What else could I do—with that commotion, Collins' next move would be to look under the car. If I was going to get caught, I wanted to get caught with someone. I slid out quickly and saw Carl running up the street, into the dark and away from the streetlight. Took one quick peek through the car window and just as I thought I saw Collins start to bend down to look underneath, I immediately started running towards the dark. Within a few steps, I saw Carl stop to wait for me. However, three seconds later, Collins was yelling and running after us with the ferocity and mad zeal of an angry bull.

I yelled, "Head for Wynn's." It seemed invitingly dark on the side of their house.

Old man Collins was gaining on us as we approached the huge honeysuckle hedge running between Parks' and Wynn's yards. Without thinking, without talking, intuitively I went left of the approaching long hedge, and Carl went right. Both of us hoped to disappear into the black backyards.

Just as I was about to reach the end of the yard and another perpendicular part of the six-foot hedge, I thought I heard Carl yell, "Oh no!" But I had no time to ponder what that meant; I worried Collins was right behind me. All I could do was take a leap as big and as high as I could over the hedge, hoping I could clear it and that nothing would be waiting for me on the other side.

Thankfully, although I landed hard, I landed on flat ground. I froze, lying still and not even breathing. My heart was pounding like a locomotive.

As I was lying there, I could hear old man Collins yelling and calling Carl's name, but the yelling was fading and moving away back towards the street. After a few minutes to make sure Collins was giving up and going back home, I called for Carl, hoping he wasn't lying in the next yard beaten to a pulp.

"I'm OK, Paul, are you?" Carl replied. "You know, as we split up, Collins came after me. I jumped up on the stone grille by the hedge, and the only thing I could see was long pointy sticks looking back at me. I closed my eyes and hurled myself into them, hoping I'd get lucky and miss all of them. I'm lying amongst them now and still checking to make sure I haven't impaled myself. Who would create something as evil as this?"

I responded, "It's old Tony's tomato garden, and those sticks have the tomato plants tied to them."

We lay there motionless for a while in the dark. My breathing was almost back to normal as I pulled a pack of Winston's from my pocket and lit up. Just about then I started to feel a raindrop or two hitting my face. As I took two deep inhales, I savored the by-then-familiar sensation of having gotten away with it. I was too young—and too cocksure—to imagine that there would ever come a time when I might not.

***

Eleven years later, in 1970, I was again lying on my back pulling a pack of cigarettes from my pocket, this time on foreign soil. Lying in the dirt of that backyard seemed like it was just yesterday but also felt like a million years ago. It was not so dark this time. It was more like dusk, except it was artificial; there were no windows in this cell.

It was a big cell. I think jail cells in foreign countries tend to be bigger than in the United States. Certainly, the conversation was different. I was the only American there, and from what I could hear, at best there were a couple of my fellow inmates who could speak some English—very deficient, broken English.

With no windows to guide my sense of day or night, I could only guess, and my guess was that it was night. Everyone has his own internal clock, and mine told me the meal cart should be coming soon. The cell—partly in light and partly in shadow, purposely I'm sure for the different whims of the variety of characters it held—was unusually noisy, almost as if it were starting to have a little heartbeat.

I was thinking about luck and what life is. Is a person's life good or bad depending on his decision to go through this door or that door, down this street or another, or speak to this person and not the next? It's certainly curious how life happens. Why we do the things we do? Is there a rhyme or reason to our decisions and experiences?

Carl and I seemed to have avoided a terrible outcome all those years ago. I can't even imagine what would have happened if we had been caught. How lucky were we to have made that split-second, almost magical decision to run on separate sides of the huge hedge?

I began to ponder what a good friend told me about two months prior as we were going to go to sleep on a deserted beach off the coast of Spain. As I had found myself doing more than ever on this journey, we had been talking about the elusive meaning of life. We had both read some philosophic books recently; bumming around Europe lends itself to such luxuries. He had read more than I had. I remember one of his quotes from the French philosopher and writer, Albert Camus: "You will never be happy if you continue to search for what happiness consists of. You will never live if you only are looking for the meaning of life." So many of us seem to want to find—or feel they must find—the meaning of life. Is there one? Is there a script we all follow or is life haphazard? Where are the answers? As I traveled, I wondered, do I even know the questions yet? I was wondering about a lot of things, wondering how I got here, wondering how this time would be different—because this time I did get caught.

How many split-second decisions does one make in one's life? How many turn out OK and how many don't? Are those moments the moments of being and feeling… lucky? Sometimes you escape, but sometimes you don't.

Out of the corner of my eye, as I started to put out my cigarette, I saw movement towards me. The figure eyed the guard on the other side of the bars, straining to be nonchalant as he walked in my direction. He started to mumble something in German. But as he slowed down just a bit to walk by me, he half-whispered in stilted English, "We have plan; we break out of here tonight."

Even though my mouth was closed, my eyes popped wide open and my mind yelled an earthshaking... "WHAT?!"

Paris

With great expectations in the spring of 1970,
on my flight from JFK through Iceland,
landing in Luxembourg,
I wrote in my travel journal:

**"My life will change this year
and it will never be the same again"**

When or how I wasn't sure,
but I knew the process would begin in Paris.

2.

Enchanté Paris

7:30 PM, April 8, 1970

The rain had been unrelenting, but at this moment I was dry and huddled alone under Café Le Select's dripping awning. There were a couple of people inside, but as I looked down Boulevard Montparnasse and then over to Boulevard Raspail, it was quiet. Everyone was afraid of and fed up with the rain. It was the second time that I'd been in this famous café, dodging the rain, feeling each day more and more confident and Parisian.

"S'il vous plait, un Pernod," I said and nodded to the waiter. I had only been here a couple of days, but almost instantaneously I sensed this was my city. I had never felt as excited, or for that matter as afraid of finally living in my own skin. As I flipped the collar of my corduroy sport coat up to protect me from the cool breeze, it was clear the waiter didn't trust me to pour and make my own drink. As only a French waiter can, he made me feel inadequate and eager at the same time. I watched him place the cube of sugar on a petite spoon delicately resting on the rim of a small glass. There was no doubt he was being rude, but I could also see this was an art to him as he poured the Pernod over the cube and lit the sugar as carefully as Picasso would have added a dash of color to one of his paintings. After a long minute or two, he gently poured some ice-cold water, filling the glass halfway. And as I took a sip, that soothing licorice taste brought a smile to my lips. I gazed at the rainy mist slowly but persistently falling. I felt the nearby presence of Jake Barnes from Hemingway's novel *The Sun Also Rises*, and I also imagined Larry Darrell from W. Somerset Maugham's *The Razor's Edge* quite possibly ordering a Pernod here or up the street at Le Dôme or La Coupole. Even though I'd tried to read Maugham's book several times and failed, if I'd watched the movie *The Razor's Edge* on TV once, I watched it a thousand times. That film was one of the most important inspirations for my international adventure.

Jake in *The Sun Also Rises* was a correspondent for *The New York Herald* in Paris. His life, in the movie version, looked wonderful. Paris looked wonderful. As I watched him on his Paris streets, I started to envision myself there also. My vision, how I pictured myself, was very different from a lot of other young travelers coming to Europe at this time. I didn't see myself as a hippie. I wanted to be the Tyrone Power of 1970.

I imagined myself always in suits. My Parisian friends would be also dressed to the nines. My acquaintances would probably be successful creatives in art, words and fashion. I would work for a prestigious ad agency. I'd create great ads. I'd probably be around beautiful French models so often that I would get to know most of them and date some. If you wanted to find me, you'd check Paris's best restaurants, cafes or nightclubs. I would have a great apartment with views of the Seine and the Île de la Cité. I saw myself at sunset, as Notre Dame was bathed in a mystical yellow and orange glow, sipping a glass of perfectly balanced Cabernet as I opened my gold-stamped cigarette case with one hand and paused for a moment to decide whether to pick a Marlboro or one of the French Gauloise, for I always kept both on hand.

But Jake didn't only know Paris. He traveled often. Most importantly, he traveled to Spain. I wondered about Spain. Yes, Paris had to be my first stop, but I didn't know any French, while I did know some Spanish. I wondered, was Spain very different from France and especially Paris? Jake was so carefree, in control of himself and his city. He had fun wherever he went, whatever he did. I didn't know if I would ever find out about Spain; I was just finding out about Paris, and the more I delved into the city, the way of life and the history, I realized that what I wanted to learn might take me not days or weeks but frankly (and I worried about this) years and years.

Larry Darrell's Paris was different. His Paris was more serious. As the 1960s were ending, many felt an impulse to look back and analyze what different movements had accomplished and what more needed to be done.

The youth of the world was a group moving and flowing, not in one direction but many at the same time. During my college days, I witnessed the unrest of the nation that seemed to have had its start on college campuses around the country. Many of the firsts were at the University of California at Berkeley, student demonstrations that soon would hit directly or indirectly many colleges and universities from coast to coast. My campus activity was peaceful, but many were not. The end of the 60s not only flashed protests over the airwaves nationwide and internationally but also inundated us with almost daily news about the Vietnam War, the rise of the counterculture, and fashion being turned upside-down by the mini-skirt. Drugs were an ever-increasing topic of conversation, with LSD especially fascinating. The world was seeing once and for all that the Civil Rights Movement was not going to go away. Rock music was exploding and piggybacking on all the subjects in the news. The young all over the world were being affected by the experiences of those who lived through Woodstock, those who changed Haight-Ashbury—the hippie world was now global.

Many people were saying many things, but one brilliant line hit the nail on the proverbial head when Dylan sang, *"The times they are a changing."* As 1970 opened, many young people from various parts of the world began traveling, especially to Europe and parts east, to find themselves. Most were coming to loaf, to find cheap drugs and to avoid responsibility. I knew who I was and what I wanted. My plan was all laid out. It was good, and it was going to happen. I was different. After college and after a year of working in a nationally known graphic design studio in Chicago, I decided I knew most of what I had to learn about advertising/design–and about life. Quite an accomplishment to think so, let alone believe it, at that point. I was just twenty-one years of age.

Nothing was happening in Chicago, and I needed adventure. As seemed to happen often with me, I was sitting in a bar late one night with Steve Stroud, a Theta Chi Fraternity brother, fellow artist and good friend, and an idea was hatched. Our plan was to get jobs in advertising on the Champs-Élysées and have great adventures. Shortly thereafter, we quit our jobs, bought one-way tickets to Paris and were ready to go when Steve was drafted. It was only a couple of weeks before our travel date. I didn't want to go at that point, but Steve never wavered. He said, "You have to live the dream for both of us; I might never make it back." He put his money where his mouth was, drove me to New York and put me on an Icelandic flight departing JFK.

The flight was both eventful and uneventful. We were packed like sardines in, it seemed, one of Icelandic's oldest jet props. It felt like we were flying in slow motion. The noise was deafening, and of course, I was anxious and antsy with the anticipation of shortly stepping foot on foreign soil for the first time. But the drudgery of the flight was broken by the announcement upon landing that there were problems with the aircraft. Apparently, our scheduled stop in Iceland—because the jet-prop couldn't carry enough fuel to make it all the way across the Atlantic—was very lucky because somewhere over the deep blue sea all kinds of lights were going off in the cockpit…we needed to land, and quickly. Our short-planned layover lasted over twenty-four hours, with us passengers permitted to only walk around the airport.

I kept imagining what Europe would be like: would I be able to talk to anyone, would anyone understand me, how would I get to Paris from Luxembourg, would I be able to deal with French francs? What type of job would I obtain? So, when a fellow passenger, Doug Richmond, who was about my age and from New York, seemed to be interested in and curious about my plans to get a job in advertising and start a new life, I took the opportunity to explore why he was traveling. Doug was what I thought of as a New York type—not very tall, longish dark hair, bold and kind of mouthy. He had attitude and was worldlier than I was. As the day and night passed, and finally the flight continued, he decided he had to see if I could really get a job. He was just bumming and was intrigued. It seemed luck was with me again; my new acquaintance had taken French for many years in school, so we would be able to communicate. As he took care of one of my biggest concerns, I also took care of one of his. He was worried about finding an affordable place to stay. As Steve Stroud and I spent a couple of days in NYC before my flight, we had happened to start a casual conversation with a guy at the Museum of Modern Art. It so happens he had just returned from traveling himself, and he had a lead on a great small cheap hotel in Paris. He wrote the info down on a matchbook cover, and I put it in my pocket. But as we all know, luck can go both ways. As I talked to more people on the plane who lived in Europe and particularly Paris, the prospects for getting a job were not looking promising. A hard-to-get-your-hands-on work permit was apparently going to be a problem.

Our flight eventually landed, and Doug and I collected our heavy and way too many bags and found a night bus to Paris. It was 3:00 or 4:00 a.m. when we exited the Paris bus station. There was no one around and no taxis or any other type of transportation. We didn't know the exact address of our destination, The Hotel Namur, but it wasn't far from the intersection of the Luxembourg Gardens and St. Michel. Unfortunately, we were a block or so away from the Louvre and nowhere close to our destination. After crossing the Seine, always looking for non-existent taxis, and walking for literally four hours in pouring rain, we gave up on finding the Hotel Namur and talked our way into a seedy little place that didn't even have a name but was dry.

It'd been a couple of days, and unbelievably it was still raining.

We did eventually find the Hotel Namur, which was great and cheap. Unfortunately, the couple of local government offices I visited to find out about the process of getting a job were complete dead ends. It could take up to six months to get a work permit. I encountered a good number of smiles and giggles when I admitted I really didn't know any French. What did I expect? But I was twenty-one and naïve.

It just wasn't fair. I'd flown all this way just to be snickered at, laughed at and left on the street with not even a whisper of a hope of getting a job. One very nice French woman pointed out that not only was my dream of working in an ad agency in Paris caput, but I probably couldn't even get a job as a street cleaner because I wouldn't be able to understand my boss when he told me to go to a certain part of Paris to clean a certain street.

Although crushed by my recent findings, I discovered and got to know Paris, sometimes with Doug, sometimes alone. We went to the Louvre and saw the *Mona Lisa* and *Venus de Milo*—amazing; walked and people-watched along the Seine—hypnotizing, visited Notre Dame and The Luxembourg Gardens—ancient greenery and captivating; The Eiffel Tower—beautifully arranged steel to the sky; The Arc de Triomphe—majestic at the end of The Champs Élysées. These are places that once seen can never be forgotten.

One night we went to The Olympia, a famous theater on the Boulevard des Capucines in the 9th arrondissement, to see a French variety show. I didn't understand most of the evening's entertainment, except for a French female singer, Marie Laforêt. Other than back in 1963, when I first heard "Sukiyaki" by Kyu Sakamoto, I had never really heard or been enticed by any foreign language song. But that night, when she sang "Paint It Black" by the Rolling Stones in French, I was mesmerized. Besides falling in love with her immediately, that entire experience of being captivated by mystical foreign music forever etched itself in my mind. I knew then I would have to find that kind of music, wherever or whenever; it would now be part of my life forever.

In recent days I'd been walking back to the Hotel Namur by myself, as Doug turned in somewhat earlier than me. It was now around 9:00 p.m., and I still hadn't eaten dinner. At least it had stopped raining. I'd been sitting too long and needed to stretch my legs. Down Boulevard Raspail to Rue Leopold Robert, looking down a small, quiet street, I saw a warm ochre light breaking the darkness. Just a nondescript small café, but it looked empty and inviting. I entered and slid into a small table beside the front window, a perfect spot to write down some of the happenings of the day, as I tried to do every night, in my travel diary.

As I was finishing my bowl of boeuf bourguignon, a group of people arrived, a hodge-podge of unknown nationalities. One of the guys sat in a chair next to me, smiled, and in what appeared to be a South African or Australian accent, asked, "American? Francais? Oder sind Sie Deutscher?" Before I could answer, he continued in English. "What's your story, mate?"

I wasn't sure what he meant, so I said, "I'm not sure I have a story."

If he meant what was I doing here, that was a good question. It certainly looked like I wasn't going to get a job. If anyone needed a story, I did and quick. Right now, I was stuck in neutral in Paris. Quite literally up the Seine without a paddle.

"Maybe you will, if not today or tomorrow, maybe very soon," came his reply as he got up and walked over to his group. One of the girls brought out a guitar and started strumming.

Paris at Night

Untouchable women, eyes that stare
All the signs tell you to beware
Sky liquid pours at suspicious times.
Heels on broken sidewalks rhyme
Foreign menus move up and down.
The only talk is a foreign sound
Wicked women are your only friends.
You might pick one or two, but do they pretend?
Moving red dots glow on a damp lonely street
Who knows what a stranger will meet?
Frequent looks are but foreign stares
And one who hesitates is one who dares.
Dark streets can be an inviting sight
But how can a traveler measure where there is no light?

Written April 12, late one evening in Paris while walking alone

I ordered another beer as a guy in his sixties walked through the door and sat in the midst of the group. He was different somehow. Longish hair, deep tan and wearing casual, almost Mexican-looking field worker clothes but with a sport coat, a look I'd never seen. I thought, remember that look. I sensed right away that maybe I didn't have a story, but this guy certainly did. He had lived. There was an ambiance. This was someone who had traveled; this was a man with presence. Maybe he didn't have wealth, but he had experiences and the results of those experiences. I thought, when I grow up, I want to be him. I want to exude that kind of presence.

One of the group handed him a beer, and after a sip, he started to hum in unison with the guitar player. Then, in a soft voice, he started to sing in French words that fit and flowed perfectly with the tune. I would have given anything to know what those words were and what he was singing—singing almost as if to himself—but everyone in the restaurant was now straining to hear him.

I was just about to give up on knowing what he was singing about when the guy who had asked me about my story earlier motioned me over to where they were gathered around a small fireplace. Beer in hand, I sat down next to him.

After a minute or two, my tablemate leaned over and whispered, "My name is Marcos. That's Caesar singing, and Christa is playing the guitar."

"Hello, I'm Paul."

"Where are you from, Paul?"

"Chicago," I responded and asked softly what the singer was singing about.

"He's singing about some of the journeys and the places he's seen as he has traveled throughout his life, and about certain types of knowledge and wisdom he's long been searching for but still hasn't found." Just then Caesar stopped singing, and Christa started singing in a different language—Spanish, I think.

After a couple of swallows of beer, Caesar, almost on cue, started singing again but this time in English as Christa continued softly singing some lines in Spanish. I wondered if he could be translating what he had been singing earlier. Marcos was right; this man had traveled around the world many times. And the places he sang about were the most exotic and dangerous places.

My mind started to drift as I listened. I wondered if I could do that. I was already away from home, already on the road. My initial hesitancy upon landing in Europe and during those first days in Paris was quickly fading. I was becoming much more confident in my ability to maneuver, navigate and communicate in a foreign land.

"Who's your friend, Marcos?" Caesar said, turning towards me.

"Caesar, this is Paul. It appears you've enticed him with your tales. I sense he could be a traveler also if given a chance."

The next couple of minutes were spent updating Marcos and Caesar on my current predicament and what I had been doing the last five years.

"He says he doesn't have a story as yet, Caesar."

"I don't know about any story, but I came to Paris to work. And that now looks dead. I really don't know what I'm going to do. Maybe I'm at a dead end?"

"You can come with us. We're on our way to Morocco. But I'm not sure you would find your story there, especially going with us. My feeling is you need to walk alone for a while to truly discover your story," Marcos suggested as he looked to Caesar for additional guidance.

"I don't know. Usually I do get a feeling about people and what they should be thinking and maybe even doing, but honestly, I don't get any vibe from Paul. Maybe Paul needs—well, maybe, metaphorically speaking, he needs to venture deeper into the woods. Paul, have you ever heard the saying—*if you don't get lost, there's a chance you may never be found?* That can mean different things to different people. I know you feel trapped right now with your initial plan gone awry. But maybe Paris wasn't the end of your journey but the beginning."

Now that thought was interesting. Was this problem meant to happen? If this was the beginning, where would I go next? So, did I want there to be a next, and how much would it cost?

Another hour passed listening to Caesar tell stories, real stories, stories that seemed to hold you on the edge of your chair, one right after the other. Stories that now were becoming much clearer to me, stories I didn't have and frankly had never really wondered about.

"It's getting pretty late, everyone; I think I should be going. I guess I'll just have to wait and see what tomorrow brings. It was a pleasure meeting you, Caesar. Morocco sounds exotic, but I don't think that's my road right now."

"Paul, your road will find you. Don't worry or try too hard to discover your path. I believe all of us come into this world with a purpose. Some have called it a road, others a story, and many more refer to that something, that enlightenment, by other names. If I'm not mistaken, as you leave this café tonight and make your way back to your hotel, you'll have a lot to think about. Maybe a direction will reveal itself. Peace be with you, Paul; maybe we will meet again. I hope so."

After walking for a while, I realized there was no way I'd ever fall asleep with all these thoughts bouncing around in my head. I had made my way down Boulevard Montparnasse and saw it was late enough that I could get a cozy outside table at La Coupole. I sat down and ordered a beer. And almost immediately a young Parisian couple wearing amazing coats sat down beside me.

"Excusez-moi, monsieur, vous avoir une cigarette," came a request in French with a German accent.

"Would you like a Marlboro?" I responded as he held up two fingers and said thank you in almost perfect English. With only a week in Paris, I was certainly jealous and surprised at how many Europeans spoke two or three languages. It was so different from the States. It was an ability I'd like to have myself someday.

"Where are you from?" he asked as we moved a little closer to each other.

"Chicago," I answered as I lit all three of our cigarettes.

"Danke," came his reply in German. "Have you been in Paris before?"

"No, my first time. I love it. Unfortunately, it's very expensive. I had hoped to get a job here, but that's not going to work out. Do you live in Paris or do you travel here often?"

"We live in London. We're just stopping in Paris for a day or two on our way back from Moscow."

"Are you traveling for fun or business? I've seen some people here wearing the same kind of coats both of you are wearing. So different, where did you buy them?"

"Well, we just like to travel. We travel, really, just to travel. We make some money here and there along the way. The coats are sheepskins from Afghanistan. I'd like to have fifty more of them; they are beginning to be the thing in Europe, and they are so hip. We bought our coats in Moscow from this guy who just came back from Kabul in Afghanistan. He was honest with us; he bought each one for $5-$10, and he sold them to us for $200 each. I could sell them for more than that to my friend Freddie who owns the Granny Takes a Trip boutique on Kings Row in London."

It didn't take long to have the proverbial light bulb go berserk, blinking wildly in my head. This was interesting, this was more than interesting, and this was exciting. I could do this; I could be rich. Afghanistan! Wow, of all the places as I thought of the world, I'd have to say Afghanistan had never come up. Where was that in relation to India? It seemed like a long way away, a very long way away. At that moment I blurted, "Afghanistan? How would you ever get there?"

"Well, there might be a number of ways to get there, but if I were you, I'd take The Orient Express," my new acquaintance responded. "That would be so cool. I've never ridden on it, but you can catch it right here in Paris. Are you thinking about buying some coats and selling them?"

I think he kept on talking for another minute or two, but immediately upon hearing the words "The Orient Express" I was gone, again starting to daydream about sitting in a luxurious train car streaking through Eastern Europe on my way east to the exotic, to adventure, to halfway around the world, to Asia. Now that just might be the start of what could be "My Story." How in a million years could Caesar have known that I would find my story so soon?

Back to reality and answering my new friend, I said, "Could I? I mean, can someone with no experience just go to some far-off place and buy some things and sell them and make a lot of money?"

"Well, there are people already starting to do just that. Maybe you could also."

"Maybe I could."

Not long after, they left. I ordered another beer and watched it begin to rain again as I let my mind drift. What was happening? Was I really thinking about going to Afghanistan? Was I thinking I could buy some coats and drag them 1,000-2,000 miles across the earth and then sell them? This was exciting, but was it also crazy? Was this me? Was I thinking about, well…I guess, maybe some would call it…an adventure? Was I just a regular guy? I don't think regular guys wake up most mornings and say to themselves, "I'm going to have adventures." Regular guys get up in the morning and go to their jobs, pick up some groceries on the way home and then spend the evening looking at a baseball game on TV, take the dog out for a quick walk and then go to bed watching Johnny Carson. Remember, I'm the guy who wanted to get a job, albeit a pretty neat job, in Paris and live here and do the things most would do living in a large international city. Hopping on one of the world's most glamorous trains and traveling halfway around the world to negotiate and buy pounds and pounds of exotic coats and then lugging them back to London, a city I had yet to visit, was not regular-guy stuff. As the rain continued to fall, I tried to look through the raindrops for some clue…some hint of what I should do. Was this thinking just too wild? Who was I to think I could start a business out of nowhere with no research? My dad was a corporate guy; we weren't an entrepreneurial family. The more I thought about it, the more I realized I did not know the clothing business at all, I didn't even know how to begin to find out. This was feeling more and more half-baked.

Then I remembered. *Paul, you've already experienced half-baked with your plan of coming over to Paris in the first place, cold, unprepared and thinking you could end up with some great advertising art director's job and have a life out of a Hemingway novel. Remember how well that has gone so far.*

How could I ever decide? And if I decided that any idea like buying coats in Afghanistan should be way off the table and decide against it, then what? Do I just give up and go home? I had miscalculated on how much French I would have to know. It seemed I'd never learn the language quickly enough to get a job. My savings wouldn't last that long. So, what then? Stay a couple more weeks here or maybe travel a little to one or two more countries and then go home? Is that what life is? Daydreaming about big things, big adventurers, but ultimately coming back to reality and letting those ideas disappear in puffs of smoke? Hmm? I continued to daydream as I watched the rain fall.

Twenty minutes later I was bounding up the stairs in the Hotel Namur and knocking emphatically on Doug's door. Yelling, "Get up, fucker, I've got it; we're going to be rich!"

Opening his door and looking somewhat annoyed but intrigued, he said, "What is going on? How much wine have you had tonight? And what do you mean rich?"

"OK, sit down and give me some of that wine you're drinking and hold on to your hat; I've come up with the idea of ideas. If you are up for it, tomorrow morning we are going to get tickets on The Orient Express headed for India. When we get to India or maybe Afghanistan, we are going to—now hold on to your socks—we're going to buy as many sheepskin coats as we can. Then we are going to lug them back to London, sell them and then we are going to be rich."

"You are incredible. You come knocking on my door with not one outlandish idea, but three out-of-this-world ideas. Why in a million years do you think we could do that? But I'll give you credit, you've got a mind-blowing kind of wild imagination. Did someone give you some pot or hashish on top of your wine tonight?" Doug shook his head.

"I met this German guy and girl, they were coming back from Moscow, and they had these beautiful coats that you and I have been noticing here in Paris. He told me this guy who sold them the coats had recently bought them in Afghanistan and that he only paid about $5 for each of them. The German guy then says he knows he could sell them in London for about $250 each. Listen, we could pool our money and buy, say, 200 coats, sell them and pocket $50,000!"

We stayed up the rest of the night. With no plan of his own going forward, Doug eventually saw the enlightened wisdom of going to India and Afghanistan to buy coats. He started to get very excited. I don't know how much wine we were drinking; we were getting loud, and there seemed to be empty bottles rolling around the room everywhere.

"The first thing we have to do is buy a map. How are we ever going to find our way to the East, to Afghanistan to India or even maybe 'to meet the Czar?'" I finally put forth.

"It's easy, we just go to the Champs-Élysées and turn right and ride the rails towards the rising sun."

"Imagine," he said. "The Pyramids, Mecca, Masada, and then to the shores of Babylon. Think of the mystery, the adventure of it all."

"That's right. Then after that, all that's left is to climb a mountain and look down the other side to Afghanistan just sitting there waiting for us…it will be easy, you'll see," Doug related, nodding and handing me another bottle of wine to open.

As I continued to drink into the night long after Doug dozed off, I was concerned with my financial situation. I boarded my Icelandic flight with exactly $900. I'd watched my spending in Paris, but this city was a killer; everything cost more than in the US. I wasn't sure how much the Orient Express would cost, but it didn't matter—we were going, end of story. But the reality was that we better strike it rich quickly with this idea. I knew that not every city was as expensive as Paris. But every city would cost something. I was guessing I'd leave Paris with $600-$700 in my pockets. Afghanistan was a long way away and probably an even longer way back, as we would have to find a way to transport all those coats.

From meeting on a plane a matter of days ago, to going into international business together, my relationship with Doug had evolved quickly. My companion, a writer by trade, also had the feeling that it was his time to see Europe. As New Yorker, his manner was much more aggressive than mine. He was one of the over 500,000 who had lived through and been deeply affected by his experience at Woodstock in August of 1969. It had been great to have a companion in my first days overseas. I was incredibly lucky to have someone to commiserate with, laugh with, eat and drink with, and, of course, someone to translate until, day by day, I got more comfortable with communicating—sort of—in a foreign land. We got along and were both wide-eyed about all we had seen so far.

We rose the next morning to a sunny day and made our way through the French Quarter to buy our Orient Express tickets. Nothing seemed to be easy, even with my companion's ability to speak some French. It took forever, and at the end of the experience, I was hoping more than knowing that we were scheduled for the right train. What I did know was that we were now set to leave Paris in a couple of nights and, implausible as it may sound, we were going east. *"Going east to meet the Czar"*, as Jim Morrison would say, voyaging to some of the world's most exotic and unknown lands. And I couldn't help but imagine the trip, journeying through many of the capitals of Europe to those somewhat secret lands of Eastern Europe, then to Constantinople with its history and then the land of the Crusades and the Middle East and eventually, I could barely say it, Asia, and adventures halfway around the world.

And those adventures started on the world's most interesting train, The Orient Express.

I wondered if I would be in a train coach with European royalty, or possibly a movie star from Italy. Might I pass a spy from Berlin as I walked down the hallway to what I was sure would be a fabulous dining car filled with some of the most interesting people in the world?

The day passed slowly as we walked the Champs-Élysées, that avenue of avenues that ends with Napoleon's Arc de Triomphe, so massive and beautifully positioned. Along the way I bought a map, what would be the first of many maps, I thought, as this one only showed Europe to Istanbul. I say "only" a little tongue in cheek, as the map, laid out, covered a large café table and made Istanbul look thousands of miles away, even though, as best we could discern from the ticket agent, the ride from Paris to Istanbul was only about a day and a half. Buying a train ticket in a railroad station is one thing, but to now have this map to look at—this was adventure; this was really the start of something exciting. Doug eventually got bored with my insistent opening and looking at *"The Map"* as we made our way from one café to another. As it was now late, he said he'd meet me back at the hotel. I walked for a while and again ended up near the Black Jack Discothèque.

I had stopped the other night for a while talking to the doorman or at least trying to in some broken French. We had spent an hour that night watching a young French prostitute soliciting possible clients walking by, laughing and shaking our heads at the success and failures she experienced.

My friend was there again. He greeted me, "Bonsoir, Chicago," and I called out "Hey, Jack, how's it hanging?" I'm sure his name wasn't Jack, but that was the name on the sign above the door, and he seemed to understand my intent. Even though I was running out of Marlboros, it was an obvious choice to hand Jack one. An hour passed as we talked and watched an unbelievable assortment of unusual late-night characters walk past us. Michelle, as Jack had named the prostitute, was not having much luck. As he had the other night, Jack attempted to get me to spend some time with Michelle. At one point he even went over to her and seemed to argue with her. I think he was trying to get her price down for me.

Even though he was a doorman, Jack didn't seem to care who came in and out until a big limousine pulled up in front, and several guys in black suits got out. He rushed over to them quickly. I was left alone, trying to imagine who these guys were. Were they hoods, were they celebrities, were they French or from some far-off land?

Just then there was a tap on my shoulder. Michelle was standing almost right on top of me. "Ainsi, vous avez peut-être comme moi. Cet homme affirme que nous devrions faire un deal." I wasn't sure what she had just said. Of course, she said it very fast and again, with my almost nonexistent French, I could only guess. However, as I was starting to be totally captivated by her perfume, I noticed Jack, still holding the door for the limousine occupants, motioning to me with one hand, rubbing his thumb and forefinger together in a circular motion, indicating, I believe, "negotiate with her." With Michelle now standing so close, I noticed how young and attractive she was. I asked, "Combien?" As a new world traveler, I had learned how to ask how much for a bowl of soup and now, you see, I knew how to ask a prostitute her price. By now she knew I was American and probably able to speak very little French. She saw the doorman motioning to me and made a face in his direction, mumbling surprisingly in English, "Screw him" and proceeded to say, "Il vous en coûtera 250 francs pour être avec moi." I only understood the 250, which she said in English. My quick math told me she probably wanted $50.

"No, no—no way" was my instantaneous response. She again made one of her faces and started to walk away. But after only five or six steps, she turned around and started to look me over, head to toe, seemingly trying to judge what to do next. I took out a pack of Marlboros and motioned would she like one. She smiled for the first time and walked over to me, taking one from the pack. "Merci."

As she turned against a slight wind to cup her hands over my lighter lighting her cigarette, I again began to feel hypnotized by the fragrance coming off the back of her neck. I took the opportunity to put forth, "One hundred francs."

"Non, ce n'est pas possible" came her quick reply. She turned up her nose and started to quickly walk away.

But then, again, she stopped and turned toward me. Quickly, sensing hesitation on her part, I immediately began a hopefully pity-producing monologue that went something like this.

"Mademoiselle, I have been on a long trip. I've had great

adventures, met lots of interesting people and have seen many beautiful things around the world, but never have I seen anything like you. You are truly the most beautiful thing I have ever seen. I leave tomorrow to fly back to America, and I have spent all my money."

I'm not sure I looked sincere enough in my lie about leaving tomorrow, especially trying to fool a probably experienced and skillful, if young, working girl. I'm not sure how much she understood of my speech, but she seemed to grasp the essential meaning. Again, her facial movements and hands lifted in exasperation. Even at one hundred francs, about $20 US dollars, I was splurging. But I thought twenty dollars was doable, especially since I was shortly going to be a wealthy fashion entrepreneur. Although I had never thought about having a sure-to-remember experience with a French prostitute, some things just happen, and as they do you have to make decisions.

I continued, "All I have is one hundred francs, no more."

She again stood there looking at me and then looking around, seemingly to check if there was anyone else, anyone with more money. I looked around also; there was no one.

She started talking to herself as she looked around. The more she talked, the more the conversation with herself became agitated. I wish I knew what she was saying, but on the other hand, I kind of did know.

After a minute or two she more pointedly vocalized in my direction, "Est-ce que je peux avoir un autre Marlboro cigarette?"— accompanied by raising two fingers to her mouth and intimating taking a puff. I didn't have to understand French to know she wanted another cigarette. I took one out for both of us and struck my lighter as she put her hands over the flame to let us both inhale our protected first puffs. She was calmer now. All of a sudden, the atmosphere surrounding us turned from confrontational to relaxed. She even smiled a little as I blew a smoke ring or two, and the late-night breeze floated them past her and up into the air.

"OK, oui, one hundred francs," she whispered and motioned for my hand. She took it in hers as we turned and walked down the avenue.

Orient Express

Could life get any more interesting?

Hanging on the handrail of the steps leading up to our train compartment on the world-famous Orient Express,
I searched for the exotic and fascinating characters
I hoped to meet in the days ahead.

Next stop, India and beyond.

3.

Going East to Meet the Czar

10:15 PM, April 13, 1970

Our excitement and anticipation levels were off the scale as we dragged our bags through the train's hallowed hallways. Funny, I thought, not the hallways or compartments that I had been imagining. "How ya doing, Doug? I've had enough; these bags sure don't get any lighter the longer you carry them, do they? We've gone through about a thousand cars so far. I'm tired and, by the way, haven't seen any of your movie stars or anyone who might look like a spy. I can't go another step—how about this compartment?"

"Okay, why not," Doug responded.

We collapsed into ornate-looking couch-sized seats facing

each other. As we were about to experience repeatedly, even though our Orient Express was supposed to depart Gare de l'Est at some time in the early evening, we didn't leave until closer to 11:30. For the last couple of hours, we had tried to check out more of the train. We just weren't finding any interesting characters—as I saw it, we were the most interesting people on the train.

Unfortunately, at 3:00 a.m., as I was finally starting to fall asleep, a non-English speaking conductor didn't find us interesting at all.

What was supposed to be a simple ticket and passport check as we crossed into Germany almost had us thrown off the train. Our conductor was furious and wildly throwing his arms around, making it known this was not a compartment for us as he threw our baggage into the hallway. We finally understood; we were in a first-class compartment, and we most certainly were not first-class travelers. We followed him through numerous train cars until he finally stopped at one containing a young German who looked somewhat like a fellow traveler.

The remainder of the night went fast, with hardly any sleep. Early the next morning we entered the huge main train and switching stations in Munich, Germany. We had to exit the train with all our baggage for an eight-hour layover. After changing some money, we bought some food and walked around Munich for a while after we put our baggage in a rented locker.

Back at the station in one of its many cafes, having a regular beer in a glass that looked a foot tall, we met a student from Denmark. He was trying to decide whether to go back to the university or keep traveling. He'd been gone six or seven months. We were on our way to Istanbul; he had just been in Istanbul. His English was fair, sometimes hard to understand. But what caught our attention was his warning about traveling from Turkey east to India. India was great, he said, but watch out for Iraq and Iran; gun battles seem to spring up in every town. He also alerted us that because the conditions were so miserable in those desert countries, many of the gangsters were moving west to exactly where the Orient Express was headed next—Yugoslavia and Bulgaria.

We bought him another beer in hopes of finding out more about—I couldn't believe I was saying this: "Gangsters!"

Before we could continue to give him the third degree, we heard an announcement over the public address system, luckily in English, that our train was going to be leaving shortly from track 27.

And again, we had no sooner picked what seemed to be a very nice and cozy compartment when a conductor was at our door asking to see our tickets, motioning us to follow him as he shook his head from side to side mumbling to himself in German. Many cars later, there was no doubt in my mind that not only were we leaving first-class accommodations, we were apparently not stopping in second class either. In each car, the compartments looked worse. Finally, he stopped and signaled us into a beat-up compartment already occupied by what appeared to be an elderly Yugoslavian couple with a ton of luggage.

Okay, I thought, we had gotten used to having the space to ourselves, but why not, this was more interesting. We could manage, we could do this, it was how the compartment was designed. Two people on one side, two on the other—but why did they have to have so much baggage?

As we got closer to the Yugoslavian border, the train started making many more stops. Doug and I scouted some other cars. Many of the compartments were filling up; some, it appeared, were too full. I started to wonder, could—and before I finished that thought, we turned the corner to our compartment. A new German guy was sitting on our side.

It was now kind of uncomfortable, but tomorrow morning we would be in Istanbul. We could manage this, even though now it had been thirty-something hours with very little sleep and sitting up the whole time. But in talking to the German guy, we discovered to our disbelief that no, not tomorrow morning, but not until sometime the day or night after tomorrow would we arrive in Istanbul. The feeling was indescribable. I laughed to keep from crying.

Another hour passed. The farm couple had opened some bags of food that seemed by their odor to be way past their expiration dates, assuming they even had such things in the small villages and towns where we stopped. By now, there was no room for many of the villagers, and they just dropped their bags in the corridor and sat next to or on them. Walking between compartments had become nearly impossible.

A hulking Turk suddenly barged into our compartment, very drunk and wanting to befriend anyone who would look his way. The German couldn't take it anymore and fled.

Not long after the Turk also left, and we thought we had caught a break. But no. He came back with three of his friends, a teenage girl and two guys—and all had been drinking heavily.

Now we had eight instead of the recommended four people in our compartment. The girl sat across from us, and two of the more sinister-looking Turks bookended Doug and me, with the original Turk, Mehmet, sitting on a suitcase in front of the window.

"Swede...no, English," remarked Mehmet as he cut pieces from a rotten-looking piece of fruit he had taken out of a bag.

Was he cutting it with a knife? Nah, more a machete.

Confused, Doug and I looked at each other, and I answered, "No, American."

"Oh, Americano," Mehmet said with a sly smile. The two bookend Turks nudged us and nodded their heads and grinned.

"Tourists, how you say, para? Money? Tourists," he said, rubbing two fingers together on the other hand not holding the very big knife. "Where you from?"

"Chicago and New York," Doug whispered, hoping not to encourage this line of questioning.

Mehmet smiled. "Very much money. Tourists, I think."

"No, no, we are just students—just poor students."

The conversation continued, but I was starting to notice the young girl sitting directly across from me. Her body was swaying, and her hand frequently came up to rub her eyes or hold back belches, as if a hand could do that. She—we'll call her Jane for lack of a better name—was starting to be in trouble. Her eyes were roaming, moving up in their sockets. She had been drinking, of course, but the odor wafting from our passengers and their food was enough to make anyone nauseous.

I thought, how can this be? This was not the prisoner train from *Dr. Zhivago*; this was the Orient Express! Where was Sean Connery; where was 007; where were the beautiful heroines or evil-but-gorgeous female foreign spies? This was the Orient Express; I should be having dinner in the club car, sipping expensive wine and listening to furtive whispered conversations at the other tables. And my dinner partner should be Greta or Ursula, not Mehmet.

And as I was starting to fantasize about Ursula—think Ursula Andress, the 1960s movie star—Mehmet changed places and sat beside me. He put his arm around my shoulder as he said, "You

Americanos should come with us. We Gypsies. We take you for…I mean, we, bok"—that was clearly an expletive—"how you say… we show you a good time. No problem, we have money; you have money. How much money you have?"

At that moment, much to my relief, Jane jumped up, screamed three words in Turkish, and dove for the door, barely managing to slide it open before she heaved her guts into the hallway. The contents of her stomach landed between two huge Yugoslavian ladies, who seemed to not only not notice but not care. They continued arguing with anyone who would speak to them.

Somehow, one of the conductors cleaned up the mess. Before he could disappear, Doug and I begged him for relief, any relief. He motioned again with his fingers, as many Europeans seemed to do in our company, signaling, *It'll cost you, but get your bags and follow me*. He took us to a sleeper with two English girls. Morning was almost upon us, and we were just falling asleep when a new conductor burst in asking for our passports and visas. The train was entering Communist Yugoslavia.

He stood in front of us, yelling and gesturing. "I know, I know," I said. "No visas." Having gained wisdom from recent experience, I thought it appropriate to hold out my hand and rub my thumb and forefinger together as I repeated the word "visa" in pigeon Yugoslavian. We walked into the hallway, the conductor negotiated payment with the border guard, and we were given two slips of paper with stamps on them—they looked official.

The conductor indicated we were lucky. We could have been taken off the train and even jailed: we were lucky to get that guard. As we were walking away, we heard the conductor talking to himself, "Bulgaria won't be as easy, and I will not be here to help you; you'll have another conductor."

Back in our compartment, I think we would have started to do some major worrying if we weren't so tired—but within ten seconds, we were out cold.

We woke up mid-morning to the girls holding hot pastries under our noses. They had jumped off the train and gotten food items from vendors like those we had seen on the platforms as we passed through so many small, dismal-looking Eastern European towns.

The girls, Chelsea and Alice, were on holiday to meet one of their grandmothers in Istanbul, a woman whose late husband had been a British attaché to Turkey about thirty years earlier. They were going to travel south along the seacoast for a couple of weeks.

The train wound through the dreary Yugoslavian countryside slowly, but we were grateful to have a day so calm after the chaos of the night before.

Doug and I jumped out a couple of times when we stopped—what seemed like fifty times, in every town we passed through—to buy food from a vendor. Most of the vendors were selling the same indeterminate meat between slices of the same stale-looking gray bread.

The drinks were all takeoffs on American soft drinks like Coke and Pepsi, but the tastes were very different and highly suspect. The endless hours looking out our windows as we chugged up hills and rolled down the other side were so desolate, they prompted me to write a poem about the very mysterious Orient Express.

As I continued to draw our travel line on my map, starting in Luxembourg, then to Paris and now leaving the large Belgrade station, it became clear to me that I had to find another map. This one, although perfect and large, only went as far east as Istanbul.

The Orient Express

Bells clang, whistles ring,
Doors slam fast, steam shoots out, up with the mast.
The Orient Express is now sailing East
Into the past...

The train magically wrapped in a foreign tongue,
Thin hallways filled with mystic music sung.
Baggage packed high in compartments so small,
Inside now is the air for all.
The pace is slow with numerous stops
All the peasants crowd in with most of their crops.
Some are thieves, some villains, this cannot be right,
And to take a chance is to turn out the light.
Originally thought I'd be traveling with Kings & Queens,
Now it seems that was only in my dreams.
No more winding roads or unpaved streets,
Only train tracks to lead me to my life's complete.
Does adventure await, can I live to see another day's explore?
And when I think I just can't take any more,

Bells clang, whistles ring,
Doors slam fast, steam shoots out, up with the mast.
The Orient Express is now sailing East
Into the past...

Written April 15, while stopped in Belgrade, Yugoslav

I needed one showing Iran, Iraq, Pakistan and Afghanistan—the entire route to India. As I read my map and scratched my face something else became clear: I was growing a beard. This was a first for me.

Yes, it wasn't much of one, but after more than a month not shaving, I had more than stubble. I glanced at my reflection in the window and decided I liked it. It looked rugged and adventurous, appropriate for this time in my life. The idea of a different look appealed to me, and I had started to comb my hair, which I had grown considerably since I left the States, straight back. My new life would be devoid of modern bath facilities and mirrors, I guessed, and low-maintenance would be best. I reminded myself of a blond, younger Barry Gibb, think early Bee Gees. My hair was more than creeping over my collar, but I managed to control it by frequently dampening it with water, often raindrops. No matter where we went in what country we passed through, it was raining. When we did a food run, it inevitably poured more heavily. It had rained all or part of every day we'd been in Europe—hopefully, the gateway to the East, Istanbul, would have some sunshine for us.

The rain finally did end; it began to snow. For some of the afternoon and into the evening, that consistently gray landscape was slowly but surely whitening with falling snow. It looked so cold outside. I sure hoped Istanbul was far enough south that we wouldn't have to worry about snow. I consoled myself by thinking about all the sheepskin coats we would buy in India. We would have plenty of furs to protect us from any degree of chill—and plenty of money to put in our pockets, which would also shield us from the cold.

As we turned in, we all talked about Istanbul. Incredible, we thought, the gateway to the East, the jumping-off point of the Crusades. Historic Paris was different from anything I had ever experienced—it had been the thrill of my lifetime. But now we would be going even further back in time, to the land of warriors of old and the sultans of the desert.

It seemed we had no sooner fallen asleep when we heard that familiar, "Attention! Attention! Messieurs and Mademoiselles, passport inspection." It was three o'clock in the morning. I could hear the train puffing outside the window; the metal beast was impatient. It didn't want to stop; it wanted to run. I could feel that restlessness vibrating in the compartment. Our new conductor agreed; he wanted to make this border stop a quick one. I was impressed with Doug's ability to stay asleep while he found his passport and passed it to the conductor without opening his eyes. As I lay there waiting for the conductor to return with our passports, I did wonder if we had taken the prospect of last night's calamity happening again seriously enough. This was a Russian territorial partner; we were in the grasp of the Communist empire.

My worry was not unfounded; whatever last night was, this was starting to feel much worse. Moments later numerous guards, conductors and even passengers were crowding into our compartment and yelling at us to get up and follow them. They took Doug and me out onto the platform. There was no negotiating. This was rough; no one was speaking English, and there were many more guards coming from around the corner, all with machine guns. I watched our conductor as all this was happening. He was quiet and showed no emotion. Some passengers tried to come out onto the platform, but a few guards pushed them back, with everyone yelling in multiple languages. The guard who looked to be in charge was talking on a hand-held radio device, I assume to his superiors. He kept saying what sounded like "American CIA." That may have been my imagination. As he talked he pointed towards the station house. I looked inside and saw bars on the window—and in a dark corner of the room what looked like bars from the floor up to the ceiling. Was their next move to put us behind bars? The border guards had an entrance far down the line from the station door entrance. I muttered to myself, *This is it, and it is bad.* We are in Bulgaria; these guys are probably meaner than the Russian guards. This is a dark country; not good. I bet Bulgarians don't even like other Bulgarians, let alone foreigners. The one guard kept on saying, "Net visa, net visa!" I wondered what the word for spy was. Had he said it many times already?

I wondered what nationality our conductor was. I hadn't heard him speak at all since Doug and I had begun pleading for leniency. Doug never stopped trying to get us out of this; he even got down on his knees. It was impressive; I believe he tried words in languages he didn't speak, to no avail. Just then, the border guard leaned his semi-automatic against a pillar. I was sure he was in the process of getting a pair of handcuffs out, to cuff Doug. Okay, it had just gone from bad to very bad to no way; we were going to be arrested in Bulgaria. My mind started to fly—jail, then what—do they even have a judicial system, or do they just throw people immediately in dark, dingy Communist prisons? My imagination was out of control. Were there places worse than bad prisons where they lock up the spies and throw away the keys?

A second border guard ran up, yelling and motioning for the guards harassing us to come quickly. I couldn't understand what the problem was, but it appeared to be more serious than the need to detain the two American spies. At that moment, our previously silent conductor jumped in and handed one of the border guards our passports, apparently saying he'd take responsibility for the two spies, making sure they would never touch Bulgarian soil again. He appeared to ask his friend Borislav if he could okay us quickly, as the train had been held up way too long? The guard looked at the conductor, looked at us, looked at his partner, looked at the new, approaching guard and threw up his hands. Swearing up a storm in Bulgarian, he stamped our passports and ran off to solve whatever the new crisis was.

As we boarded the train our conductor admonished us in perfect English: "You fools are very lucky; they were going to transport you up to Sofia (the capital of Bulgaria.) They have a terrible prison there. Who knows when they would have remembered you were even in there!"

Yes, we were lucky, but the unpleasantness wasn't over yet. Over the sound of my heart racing, I heard furious comments from other passengers and saw the dirty looks aimed at Doug and me. The train was very off schedule now, and the two American idiots were to blame.

Sleep was out of the question. Eventually, I couldn't take it anymore and quietly moved out into the hallway, where I sat down on the floor next to a dim hallway light. It was the middle of the night, but the huge train was just now quieting down. It had been an hour or so since the Paul & Doug Spy Variety Show.

I fell asleep in the passageway, waking when I was gently kicked by our friend and savior, the conductor. We had another border check as we crossed into Turkey.

At our stop in Edirne, the border town, I woke up Doug. We ran out to find something to eat on yet another train platform. Folded dough sandwiches stuffed with something unidentifiable was the best we could do, but we were hungry, and they disappeared fast.

Standing in the hallway next to the open windows, Doug and I talked about getting off this hell on wheels and onto, we hoped, a much better sister train that could take us east to Afghanistan and India. We would stay overnight in a hotel and leave again the next morning, arriving in India, hopefully, in a few more days.

About an hour away from Istanbul, I stood in the hallway smoking my cigarette, watching camels, unbridled and wandering free, dotting the landscape. The wonder of that made all the trauma with the border guards almost worth it. Yeah, I was entering another world for sure.

My reverie was interrupted by Doug, who came around the corner and asked if he could have a couple of cigarettes for himself and a guy he had just met. Introductions were made. "Assalamu alaykum," nodded the nicely dressed gentleman as I lit their cigarettes. (I only had two Marlboros left. Would I have to start smoking foreign cigarettes?) Our new smoking buddy, Dr. Sevim, was a doctor, of what I did not know. He was about forty years old and better dressed than anyone else I had seen on the train. Born and raised in Istanbul, he had traveled extensively east and west during and after schooling. He was much more interested in us than he was in talking about himself and was especially interested in Doug's updates on New York City, where he had studied ten years ago.

After a few minutes, the conversation still on NYC, I started to drift, wondering what the next couple of days would bring. I almost wished we were planning to spend more time in Istanbul, one of the world's oldest and most mysterious cities.

I raised my hand. "Doctor, pardon me, if I may, you greeted us just before with a phrase I've heard numerous times on this train. I believe it was something like 'salum alaken.' What does it mean, and should we be using it as we make our way into Muslim lands?"

He responded, "The Muslim greeting 'As-salamu alaykum' means 'Peace be upon you.' And then the usual response would be 'Wa-Alaikum-Salaam,' which means 'And unto you peace also.'" I seemed to have hit an important chord with this question, and he continued. "Islam is a wonderful way of life; the way of it is so wonderful. The norm of specifying how it should be put forth: 'As-salamu alaykum' meaning 'peace be upon you' or more perfectly: 'Assalamu alaikum wa rahmatullahi wa barakatuh,' meaning peace, mercy and blessings of Allah be upon you.' In this regard, Allah says in the Qur'an: 'And when you are greeted, greet (in return) with one which is better than it or (at least) return it (in like manner).' For Allah is ever taking account of all things. The greeting Allah is referring to here is generally understood to be 'As-salamu alaykum.'"

I asked about the hand movements he had previously used addressing us and he explained "salaam," which he described as "a greeting from Allah, blessed and good." He clarified how it is done: "The full salaam is a traditional greeting in Arabic-speaking countries and Islamic countries. It is made by sweeping the right arm upwards from the heart to above the head. It begins by placing the hand in the center of the chest over the heart, palm to chest, then moving upwards to touch the forehead, then rotating the palm out and up slightly above head height in a sweeping motion. In the abbreviated salaam, the head is dropped forward or bowed, and the forehead, or mouth, or both, is touched with the fingertips, which are then swept away. Now having just said that, the gesture is losing popularity. I prefer it and always have. I will always use it myself as a sign of respect."

The doctor asked where we were headed after Istanbul. Doug explained our plan to continue to India and get rich by becoming clothing industry entrepreneurs. He thought the idea had merit; he knew of the burgeoning popularity of sheepskin coats in the West, but his voice trailed off as he turned and looked out the window. He said, "I sure don't envy the journey you have left." That caught my attention.

"What do you mean—we heard it was only another couple of days."

And so, before he left to pack his belongings a couple of cars ahead, he proceeded to demolish our best-laid plans.

Yes, he said, to India was about two days but only by airplane. For the last six months there had been not only no direct train but no continuous train travel at all between Istanbul and Baghdad, which was close to the border with Iran. He had heard from some relatives that just as you entered Iraq, all train tracks were out. Now, that might sound ridiculous, he cautioned us, but not if you knew the government in Iraq. You had to travel by bus and, he warned, this was not a bus like any we'd ever ridden or that he'd ever want to take. Even worse, as you reached the eastern edge of Iraq and started to make your way into Iran, you had to watch out for gangsters. Unfortunately, he added, human life is not what it is in America, so beware. Warming to his theme, he implored me to dye my hair. A blond would stand out...my golden locks would be like having a spotlight following me wherever I went. Blond would mean I was either English or Swedish or—even more mouth-wateringly inviting to the bandits—a rich Americano. These gangsters thought nothing of shooting people just to shoot them. As a final warning, he added, if I were you, I'd figure between five and seven days to get there, depending on the weather, because we're getting close to the sand-storm season in Iraq.

Seven more days of traveling in much worse conditions than we had experienced for the last three and a half days.

There was no way, both of us exclaimed after Dr. Sevim left.

We couldn't even begin to imagine seven more days of sitting up day and night in trains and buses and God knows what else before we got there, if we ever got there. And what did he mean, gangsters? It was 1970, but he had warned us that many parts of these two huge countries, Iraq and Iran, were lawless. He explained that sometimes they come on horses, sometimes in trucks and sometimes they just appear out of nowhere. There definitely was no sheriff in town or evidently anywhere in either country.

These were our choices? Give up our perfect plan of getting to India, going into the clothing business and becoming rich, or spend the next week traveling in who-knows-what type of conditions? And experience had taught us that there would be much more time required to get all the proper visas and papers and special inoculations we would need.

Well, the worst that could happen were about a million and one things and all of them very bad. Yes, Dr. Sevim had said I would always be greeted with a smile if when meeting anyone in the East I first greeted them with "As-salamu alaykum," *Peace be upon you.* I planned to do this, but I was afraid that if someone addressed me first with 'As-salamu alaykum' I would completely forget what to say in response.

Doug touched my arm and looked at the skeptically and I tried to read his mind: *If we are really stopped somehow by middle-eastern gangsters do you think what we say to them will mean anything? And before we even opened our mouths, they would probably have already taken all our clothes and gone through our pockets looking for anything of value. I remember you talking earlier on our trip about how much you liked those old black & while road movies with Bob Hope & Bing Crosby. Well I'll tell you, we are not on the* Road to Rio—*we could be on our way to the* Road to Big Long Knives. *Could there be anything worse?*

And then, of course, there were the gangsters. What would be the worst that could happen?

Doug cut to the chase: "The worst is we get drilled with holes or worse, that's the worst and forget it—forget all of it." I agreed. That was that; we would not be going to India. We would not be going into the clothing business. We would not be getting rich, at least not that way. But as the train slowed down, coming into Istanbul station, I wondered, if not that, if not there, then what? We were almost halfway around the world—what would be next?

Istanbul

Nasty communist border guards hovered to
the left of me, still looking, I'm sure,
for those spies from America without visas.

Middle-Eastern gangsters lurked on my
right, just waiting for those rich, blond, blue-
eyed tourists.

I was stuck in the middle, in of one of the
most historic crossroads of history,
a city of the Crusades,
the old city of Constantinople.

4.

"English…maybe you want a Kalashnikov?"

11:55 AM, April 18, 1970

It was late morning when we arrived in Istanbul and, of course, it was pouring rain. After asking around on the train we had gotten a lead on a place to stay, the Pera Palas Hotel. It wasn't a short hike from the Sirkeci Train Station, but the rain did stop for a brief while as we made our way through some of the most crowded but interesting streets I had ever walked. We had crossed from West to East, geographically and culturally. At the hotel we arranged for our baggage, left at the station, to be picked up the next morning.

Istanbul was a world away from American everyday life, with the sounds, smells and landscape utterly foreign. I had made some

69

progress in Paris with the French language, but there was no way to begin to get comfortable with Turkish. But the people were friendly, and there were certainly a lot of them.

Doug and I explored from morning until night. We saw the amazing Hagia Sophia, which once was one of the most significant mosques of Islam but was now a museum. The Hagia Sophia was the largest church in the world until Michelangelo built Saint Peter's Basilica in Rome.

We were also able to go into the Blue Mosque, one of the largest and most prestigious mosques in the Middle East. It is almost impossible to visit when the call for prayers is not going on. But we lucked out and were transported to another world, amazed by the design and architecture of a Muslim mosque, so different than a Western church. Nonbelievers, as we were, were only permitted to enter through one special door, our shoes deposited at the entrance. (I did worry that we would ever be able to find them again, and it took a while to search through all the shoes, but we did eventually retrieve them.)

Upon leaving, we went to the Topkapi Palace, home to the Ottoman sultans for hundreds of years. The Palace was not far away, and as we began to walk, a sign informed us that we were walking on the same bricks and stones that Roman soldiers did a millennium ago. The Crusaders had also trod this road, using Istanbul as a jumping-off point in their bloody campaign to take back Jerusalem, a city that has changed hands half a dozen times over the last 1000 years.

As we walked along some of the old streets of this city, with its exotic smells and sensuous music everywhere, we came to one of the largest, most confusing and mysterious covered markets in the world, the world-famous Grand Bazaar. Almost 400,000 visitors a day passed through the market's almost one hundred covered streets with over 3000 shops. We were completely fascinated. Some of the shops were no bigger than a closet, with everyone trying to negotiate price with us before we even showed interest. It felt like we could have bought anything in the world somewhere in that huge and colorful place. I imagine it is the same way today—you can buy anything, even if you may need to go to a secret backroom for privacy. We often saw suspicious characters ducking into dark corners as we explored.

The Grand Bazaar houses two mosques, four fountains, two Turkish baths, and several cafés and restaurants. In the center is the high-domed hall of the Cevahir Bedesten, a jewelry market, where the most valuable items and antiques could be found during our visit and still are today: furniture, copperware, amber prayer beads, inlaid weapons, icons, mother-of-pearl mirrors, water pipes, watches and clocks, candlesticks, old coins, and silver and gold jewelry set with coral and turquoise. The Bazaar has always been known for its hand-painted ceramics, carpets, embroideries, spices and antique and clothing shops. Many of the stalls in the Bazaar were grouped by type of goods, which ran the gamut from simple necessities to priceless jewels. The Bazaar has been an important trading center since 1461, and its maze-like vaults feature two domed buildings, the first constructed between 1455 and 1461 by order of Sultan Mehmed the Conqueror. The Bazaar was vastly enlarged in the 16th century, during the reign of Sultan Suleiman the Magnificent, and in 1894 underwent a major restoration following an earthquake.

Doug and I spent a spent most of the day exploring the Bazaar and sitting in one of the cafés. We bargained with shop owners and watched the crowds pass, savoring the romantic ancient atmosphere of old Istanbul. Doug lingered over hashish pipes, some of the most ornate I have ever seen. While he was negotiating, I wandered the streets nearby, where I came upon a very young Turk, maybe thirteen years old, with a medium-sized live elephant.

He greeted me: "As-salamu alaykum." Then he bowed.

Proud of myself, I nodded my head and replied, "Wa-Alaikum-Salaam."

He looked surprised for a second but continued in very good English, "Only $25, this elephant is for you. You can ride it out of here today." I have to say I thought about it for a minute; it would be cheaper than the trains I had been taking. I was tempted, just to be able to say I'd bought an elephant in Istanbul for less than a pair of good boots would have been worth it. And I would have liked to have experienced riding one, but reality got the better of me and I declined, even after I got him down to $19. We had been told to watch out for black market items, and it was obvious the elephant was black market—and could I really ride this elephant in the streets of Istanbul? The young man, Emre I believe he was called, did give me a lead on where to buy black market American cigarettes, which I desperately needed.

He also described a restaurant shop I should go to. He said a lot of golden-hairs like me hung out there. Emir indicated that if I was a traveler, I needed to talk to some of the other travelers who gathered there daily. Doug was still set on buying pipes and wanted to see if another store might offer better wares or prices, so he took off in one direction as I left the Bazaar to look for this "meetings" shop.

It wasn't far. Though small and with few patrons, Tale Pastanesi, just as Amir had said, did have some European patrons.

The funny little shop turned out to be the historic and iconic starting point of the famous *"Hippie Trail,"* the travel route taken by young European and American travelers, eventually called "hippies," from the mid-1950s to the late 1970s between Europe and South Asia, through Iran, Afghanistan, Kashmir, India and Nepal.

In later years, this place would change its name for a most unforeseen reason. It seems many travelers could never remember the restaurant's foreign name, but because many of them remembered and liked the various puddings offered, they started calling it "That pudding shop in Istanbul." Finally, the ownership gave in and put up a sign: *The Pudding Shop.*

Although their puddings played a large role in the recognition of the spot, it also became known as a place for travelers to get information. There was a large bulletin board with news about the comings and goings on the hippie trail, with information about destinations including Afghanistan, Pakistan, Kathmandu, India, and even farther east to Thailand and beyond. Many, if not most, who ventured east had to make their way through this important hub for travel ideas, shared rides, personal connections, advice, country news and alerts.

The hippie trail was the name given to a migration of young people from across the globe who felt a need to go east and find something different. Typically, it was an overland journey from Europe to India and or beyond. Most of the journeys passed through Istanbul. There were a few routes from Istanbul east. One took travelers through Iran, Afghanistan and Pakistan to India. Another route could take people to Syria, Jordan, Iraq and Iran and then to Pakistan and eventually India and Nepal. By far the most travelers stopped in India, but some continued east farther into Southeast Asia and even the Far East.

Young people's desire to travel to the east was greatly influenced by the Beatles, who famously spent time in India in the 1960s. That eastward flow stopped rather abruptly in the late 1970s with the Islamic revolution in Iran and the war between Russia and the Mujahideen in Afghanistan. Many also traveled for access to drugs such as hashish. Others looked for spiritual enlightenment, and many more wanted and needed a type of freedom in everyday life that wasn't available in the United States or Europe. Some went just because other people were doing it, and a few simply had adventure in their blood and were curious to see more of the world.

Most traveled the 6,500 miles by bus. Some of those bus trips were organized by young entrepreneurs who took a few or many per ride, depending upon whether the bus was a VW van or a large, fifty-person vehicle. Others traveled by car or motorbike; some even tried to hitchhike. Planes were too expensive and trains scarce and unreliable. There were many horror stories about all these forms of transportation breaking down at different parts of the journey. And often the outcome was either sit a month in the desert waiting for parts or, if the driver just-gave up and walked away, walk however many miles to a town and wait for someone to pass through who would give you a ride east.

Years after I was there, The Pudding Shop did get a lot of international attention when it was included in the scary, based-on-real-events movie, *Midnight Express*. Billy Hayes, a young American played by actor Brad Davis, was initially caught with drugs in Turkey. The police gave him an opportunity to help his cause by wearing a wire and going to The Pudding Shop (where he had made his original drug connection) to see if he could identify those involved or shake out any others. Unfortunately for him, he didn't succeed, and he ended up spending a long harrowing time behind bars.

One night, at about 10:30, Doug and I were sitting in the bar of the Istanbul Hilton after a pleasant American dinner of hamburgers, fries, Pepsis and apple pie. It cost us more for this meal by far than any other Turkish meal we'd had, but that hamburger was my first American meal in two weeks and it was worth it. It also helped that after fourteen days of straight rain, it was sunny.

Earlier that day I had gotten my hands on some recent copies of the *International Herald Tribune*, the English-language paper readily available when you were traveling overseas (It was renamed *The International New York Times* in 2013.) I was happy to get news about the States, especially sports news, but a comic strip called "Rip Kirby" also caught my eye. Kirby was an adventurer/detective looking for the elusive Elysian Fields—the mythological home of an afterlife where Greek heroes were given immortality and vast treasure—Rip was looking for the treasure.

Should I look for the Elysian Fields? At dinner, Doug and I tossed around possible new travel plans but becoming a Rip Kirby didn't make the list. Going east was out; we had already decided that. Traveling north looked almost as bleak, since we would have to cross Bulgaria again. We couldn't risk meeting our border guard, Borislav again, giving him another chance to lock up those two American spies. Going back the way we had just come seemed so "been there, done that." That left south, down to Athens, one of the most historic cities in the world, then perhaps on to the Greek Islands. Then maybe I could become a Rip Kirby—my own Elysian Fields adventure could be waiting for me in Greece.

But I had no money. I had arrived in Paris with about $950, enough, I thought, to last me a month or so before I started collecting a paycheck. I had figured if Jake Barnes could get a job, so could I. That was the plan, and there was no Plan B. It never crossed my mind that I would fail. With only a one-way ticket to Paris, there was no room not to succeed. It was becoming apparent that I was kind of naive—stupid—to have made a bet on myself like that.

Well, Paris was history, as was my brilliant (I still think it was brilliant) idea to become a clothing entrepreneur, letting me extend my stay in Europe indefinitely. Although I had been frugal, Paris is one of the most expensive cities in the world. And although our accommodations on the Orient Express were, for the most part, less than satisfactory, the trip from Paris to Istanbul had taken almost a third of the cash I had come with. After some quick calculations, I realized that if we decided to take another train south to Athens and stayed for even a few days there, I would have barely enough to get to an Icelandic departure city and buy a cheap ticket home.

My plan had been to live in Paris; the more likely scenario was I that would be returning to the States after a month in Europe. With failures at every turn, going back the same person I was when I left was looking inevitable, I was going back with no adventures and no stories to tell about them. No living the life of Jake Barnes or Larry Darrell, no apartment overlooking the Seine, no path to India and enlightenment. I was in this world of crusaders and hippies, running out of money, with few prospects. I could've bought an elephant, but what would I do with an elephant...?

As I drank my beer and continued wallowing in self-pity, I glanced over the shoulder of a patron at the next table who was

reading a Turkish newspaper. I got Doug's attention and pointed—
incredible! On the front-page were pictures of what looked to be
the safe landing of Apollo 13. We couldn't read the paper, of
course, but there sure were a lot of smiling faces in those photos.
Just the wonder of it cheered me up and sent me back to trying
to figure out a plan.

Doug and I ordered more beers and went back to planning
our next move. Doug felt Monday would be the best day for us to
head south. He had decided which guy in the Grand Bazaar had
the best hashish pipes, and he was sure he had negotiated the best
price. But the Bazaar was closed on Sundays, so we had to wait two
days to leave. We would buy our tickets Monday morning, then go
to the Bazaar and buy some pipes. Doug had been urging me to
buy a couple. Hashish was not my thing, but I could see they were
unique. If I could get them home in one piece, I could probably
sell them for a lot more than we had paid.

Before we returned to our hotel, I questioned Doug again
about our decision not to try to get to India. I filled him in on
some news I had gathered at the Pudding Shop. We could possibly
get a ride in a truck or a Volkswagen bus to India, I had learned,
although a couple of people indicated it could take three weeks
to two months for the trip. And that was if whatever vehicle we
started out in made it all the way. One couple from Spain, just
back, said they were stranded in Baghdad for a month waiting for
a truck part. Doug was intrigued: "Maybe we should reconsider?"

I believed Doug had it in him to travel like that. He had spent
about a week at Woodstock, dealing with that craziness, the year
before. When I had seen the pictures on TV of that miserable
mess they gave me the shakes. How could those people stand it, all
packed together, dirty, smelly, hungry, drugged-out day and night?

And it rained most of the days the music was playing! I didn't have the desire to go anywhere near that. Give me a nice suit, a crisp, collared shirt, and good leather shoes, worn in a nightclub with a drink in hand instead.

And so, in the end, after even more beers, we made our final decision. Forget India and go south to Athens. I'm pretty sure Rip Kirby would have gone for trekking to India and adventure, but, maybe, just maybe, adventure was waiting for me in Athens.

We slept until noon the next day. Doug needed to find some things for the next leg of our trip. I had decided that besides the handwritten journal I was keeping about my trip, I should buy a sketchbook so I could draw some of the wonderful things I was seeing. After I bought one at the Bazaar, I wandered into a beautiful hidden park with benches offering a clear view of the Blue Mosque. Before I started drawing, I copied a couple of poems I had written on scrap paper while on the train. The sketchbook's graph paper background was perfect for both.

After an hour or so of sketching the mosque, I had begun to draw a crowd. Maybe as many as ten to twelve men, women and children had decided to stay a while and vocalize their opinions, good and bad, on how I was representing one of the great masterpieces of their city. Two women brought chairs over and sat right beside me, engrossed in a conversation, knitting, but stopping to check my work, either nodding and smiling in with approval or making faces, obviously thinking the opposite. The afternoon went quickly until the Muslim call for prayers echoed from some of the mosque towers close by and my audience left. I was alone as the sun started to slowly set in the west.

I met up with Doug after lunch and we spent a couple of hours talking with several pipe vendors in the Bazaar. Doug finally picked one and began serious negotiations. I enjoyed the banter so much that it was impossible for me to keep composed while negotiating. I inevitably started to laugh at some point; the whole experience was so different from buying something in the States. I had to walk away occasionally for fear of having our Turkish pipe dealer kick us out. I let Doug continue the battle while I looked for something to drink. I finally found something in a bottle, presumably safe to consume, and sat down on some folded rugs being readied for shipment. A Turkish teenager sat down beside me.

He leaned over and said, "English, my name is Zeheb. I am like golden for you; I have just what you want; you need to come with me, and I'll show you."

Caught off guard, I asked him, "And what do you think I want? We've never talked before."

"English, you like the women, don't you? I have a woman for you. She is just right, perfect for you."

"Really, right here, in the middle of the bazaar, you have a woman? What are you trying to sell me? No, no."

"English, this girl is beautiful; you won't be sorry."

"Listen, Zeheb, I'm leaving Istanbul later today on my way to Athens. So sorry," I replied, trying to end the conversation.

"Not just for an hour, English. This girl is yours forever for the right price. I want to sell her to you; she is my sister."

"Are you crazy? You can't sell your sister." I thought with horror of my sisters at home.

"Yes, English, I can. I already sold one sister last week. Now, do you have $50? I will show her to you."

"No, I don't want to buy your sister! I have to go and meet my friend, sorry," Exasperated, I got up to leave.

"How about your friend, would he want a woman? Or if not, English, maybe you want a Kalashnikov?"

"Do you mean a Russian machine gun?"

"Yeah, English, just like brand-new with many, many ammo for you."

By the time I was able to extricate myself from Zeheb, I was offered four different kinds of animals, three of which I believed were on the endangered list. One of them needed a cage, which he said he didn't have, but if I bought right then all I needed to do was just give him twenty minutes, and he'd find one for me in the Bazaar. Zeheb was persistent; you must give him that.

Doug had found me and handed me a bag with a couple of pipes he had bought for me, and even returned some of my money. Doug was apparently a very good negotiator.

As we walked through one of the huge doors leading out of the Grand Bazaar, I turned around and stared for a minute or two. This truly was a different world. I couldn't imagine another place as interesting, exotic or potentially dangerous. For thousands of years, some of the most fascinating characters in the world had bought, sold and stolen almost anything and everything inside those walls.

We rushed back to our hotel to pack for our trip to Athens. Looking at the pile in front of me I knew I had to decide about my clothes. I still had two bags I was dragging around on my shoulders. I had abandoned a few things in our Paris hotel room, but it didn't make any sense to carry around what was left. I again had to make some tough decisions as I departed my hotel room, to discard another sport coat, some dress slacks and more than a couple of starched dress shirts. Although my big duffel bag was now considerably lighter, I still grimaced when I had to carry it for any length of time. My smaller carry-on also had gotten a little more awkward with the purchase of the 14" x 8" sketchbook

After checking out we taxied to the train station. We got some good news when we bought tickets; apparently, we could even get our own compartment. The bad news was we had to hang around until 9:30 p.m. when the train was scheduled to depart.

Athens

I have always dreamed of going back in time,
to a point in history where I could see
what all the words in all the history books
I've ever read really meant.

Now I was truly traveling back in time to
Greece; home to Athens, Sparta,
the Trojan Horse and
Helen of Troy, by chance?

5.

The Night Train to Thessalonica

9:30 PM, April 20, 1970

The Athens Express streamed through the Greek countryside as I gazed with wonder out my open window. In the thick darkness I could feel the pulse of history throb in this ancient land. By now we were far from the oppressive bleakness of Yugoslavia and Bulgaria. We had left Istanbul the day before, and although our compartment was full, the trip had been, thankfully, quiet so far. The calm was a much-appreciated change from our days on the Orient Express.

While having a cigarette in the hallway, I heard a conversation that was somewhat concerning; our days of peaceful travel were in danger of ending. There had been another coup in Greece, and the military was in charge again. I wondered what that might mean for us.

Despite my new worry, I was feeling reborn, remembering my joy earlier in the day as I watched the sun-drenched landscape glide past. The morning had flown by as I surveyed the small, white, sun-drenched buildings peppered among pale ancient ruins, winding in and around picturesque olive and fig groves.

I called our train the Athens Express, but it was in no hurry. Distinctively highlighted with unusually colorful markings, its flamboyant exterior was in stark contrast to its very sluggish route. We stopped, it seemed, at every small town on the way, and although Istanbul to Athens isn't that far, our trip was expected to take thirty-six hours. But there was an unexpected peacefulness to the slow train heading south and I enjoyed the relaxed pace.

Perhaps it was because I had made my peace with the inevitability of deciding, once in Athens, that my great adventure was over. I would explore options, but with my diminished funds, those options were few. Without a plane ticket home, I'd have to make my way to Luxembourg and then home from New York somehow soon.

One of the conductors walked by, announcing something in Greek. I glanced at him, confused, and he stopped and turned to look at me. He gazed at my face, sizing me up, deciding whether I deserved a translation. After two seconds he turned away and walked down the corridor. Whatever nationality I was, I wasn't worth his time of day.

Although I didn't understand most of what he called out in the car, I did hear the name of the Greek city of Thessalonica. Our map told us it was one of the biggest cities in Greece, so Doug and I assumed we would stop there.

I felt the train slowing a little. As Doug woke up from a nap, I told him I thought we were pulling into a station.

"Good, we can exchange some money. The heck with these Turkish lire; let's get some Greek drachmas."

Just about then, our conductor, let's call him Zeus, came back, and Doug stopped him to ask how long we'd be in Thessalonica. Well, Zeus didn't want to be interrupted, and even though Doug was obviously English-speaking, Zeus immediately started waving his hands above his head and yelling unintelligible words that sounded like Greek numbers. Doug asked him a couple of times, "You're saying a two-hour layover, right?"

I thought Zeus was agreeing, yes, two hours. But Doug was unsure as the train pulled to a stop in the very large modern station.

We walked one of the long platforms to the stairs going down to a level below. Several minutes later we finally, after numerous turns, made it to the pedestrian area with shops. Unfortunately, it was now almost midnight, and everything was closed. We started back to our train, starving and unhappy we were not able to exchange our money. Just as we started up the stairs, I saw a rumpled *International Herald Tribune* tossed on the stone walkway floor. I picked it up to see how Rip Kirby was doing—had he found the Elysian Fields? Doug, also a fan of Rip, read over my shoulder and then started up the platform stairs.

I threw the newspaper into an odd-looking Greek garbage can, frustrated. Why couldn't I have adventures like Rip? I didn't need to look for ancient buried treasure, but I needed something, just something to make this trip a little more interesting. I was about three-quarters of the way up the stairs, still mumbling to myself, when I heard Doug yell, "Come on, our train is leaving!"

When I reached the top, I found him already on the train

tracks, jumping over them to get to our train, which was definitely leaving. It began to pick up speed.

I panicked: *Fuck! Are you kidding me, all my stuff is on that train; I'm dead.* And again: *Fuck! Really, now I have to jump down on those tracks, too, to catch that train?*

Now, I wasn't married to Doug or anything. If the fucker wanted to act crazy and try to jump on a moving train, well, good fucking luck. But hey, I thought, he's been a damn good partner so far. If he gets on the train and I'm left here without my stuff or my traveling companion—I'm dead in the water. And during these very few seconds I had a last stupid thought: *What would Rip Kirby do?* I didn't know, but without further thought, I decided: *go for it!*

As I jumped down two or three feet and maneuvered over tracks, I looked up and saw Doug hanging on one of the exit door railings of the train car just ahead, his feet dangling as he tried to get stable footing on the door's footpad.

Everything was happening so fast, with only seconds to react. I saw only one option: jump on the next car. I took a tentative step forward, the train was already moving along. If you have ever seen a guy jump a moving train in a movie, you know you must move with it. But I had run out of time—the stair rail was right ahead of me, it was almost gone. There was no choice: I jumped up from an almost standing-still position. Suspended in midair, I thought of Rip. Hell, he would never have tried this; it would be incredibly stupid to jump on a moving train without a running start. Any adventurer would know that; any class like Adventurer Jumping 101 would teach you on the first day of class at any credible Adventurers College to never do that.

I saw two metal handles above my head and grabbed. I thought, *If I miss them, I'll be bounced off the train and thrown under its wheels.* To this day, I can remember the shock of the enormous force of that moving train as I latched onto one of the handles. As it pulled me sideways I held on, my boots barely on the doorstep edge. When I looked up, heart pounding, I saw a wide-eyed conductor staring at me through the door window. He got over his shock quickly, and started yelling, identifying me as a bandit or worse, and pushing the door in and out to try and knock me off. I shouted, "Athens! Athena! Athens!" But he kept swinging the door back and forth while bellowing furiously in very angry Greek.

He eventually succeeded in dislodging one of my hands from its handle, and by now the train had picked up speed. I bounced on and off the train car step as the Athens Express changed tracks, rumbling forward through the station. I held on for dear life and looked ahead. We would be out of the station soon, speeding into the pitch-black Greek countryside. That would be even more dangerous than my present dilemma. Panic was rising in my throat as I contemplated being knocked off the train as we sped into the dark Thessalonian night, landing on my head in some bush-and-rock-infested ditch. I'd probably never be found, or maybe in a hundred years, I'd be misidentified as a Greek warrior or, as my current conductor, let's call him Phi, would imagine, a bandit.

My focus on the darkness at the end of the station was interrupted by the shock of seeing Doug bounce and roll on the platform pavement alongside our charging train. I could only assume a conductor had knocked him off, and I would be next. I didn't think; I just dropped. There was no time to orchestrate a planned jump; we were at the end of the platform. My feet landed first, but only for a second. The brute force of the moving train plunged me uncontrollably forward. I started to roll wildly, thinking, *Protect your head!* and reached out to stop the tumbling, sliding to a halt with my hands stretched out in front of me, ten feet from the end of the platform.

I turned over onto my back and looked up to see passengers from another train gathering anxiously around Doug and me. Everyone was talking at once, asking the same thing in multiple languages: "Are you alright?" "Estás herido?" "Es-tu blessé?" "Are you hurt?" And from the wisest among them: "You fools, you could have been killed!"

I lifted myself up to catch a glimpse of Doug, checking on his condition after the fall. I mouthed, "Are you OK?" He nodded and pointed to the other side of the platform, five to six sets of tracks away. There was our train, just where we left it. *What!* I could only laugh. Then it hit me. Distracted by the adventures of Rip Kirby we had gone up the wrong stairwell. Idiots, we were idiots.

We hadn't run over tracks to leave our train for the stairwell when we disembarked the train, so why would we think we needed to do that to get back on? And one idiot is bad enough, but wouldn't you think the other clown would hesitate and think, *Stop, this doesn't make any sense!* After all these years, I still don't have an answer, a good one anyway. I guess you just do things in life, and you either get away with them or you don't. Would I do it again—no way! I'm not crazy. As I said, we were traveling together; where he goes, I go; where I go, he goes.

A couple of people helped me sit up, inspecting the bloody scrapings on both hands and pointing to the blood dripping down the side of my face. I felt surprisingly okay, as I patted myself down checking for broken bones or body parts gone missing when I catapulted onto the platform.

Doug and I were still assessing our medical condition when we heard one passenger above the rest. Looking up, we saw a big, loud, ostentatious Texas-ranch-owner type with a southern drawl holler, "I would have given $10,000 to have had a film of that, boys! You both are fools, but it was worthy of film. Y'all couldn't do that again, could you?"

Very funny, I was glad someone enjoyed it. All I knew was that my body ached everywhere and Doug and I needed to wash up and find bandages.

As we started to walk to the stairwell again, looking for medical attention, I felt the inside upper pocket of my sport coat, a kind of subconscious tic I had developed since leaving New York. I was checking for my passport—*and it wasn't there.* Terrified, I yelled, "I lost my passport!" Everyone on the platform started looking. We searched desperately, until, about 20 minutes later, we heard that someone had found a passport and taken it to the police office downstairs.

We rushed back down the fiendish staircase, through excruciatingly long hallways and out to the shopping area where we eventually pointed to a lighted sign reading *Αστυνομία (Police.)* As we approached, followed by a group of concerned—or amused—travelers from the platform, numerous others surrounded us. Out of the corner of my eye, I saw three foreboding black-leather-coat-clad figures approaching us. The other spectators automatically parted to let them through. Just as the guy apparently in command reached aggressively for me the *Αστυνομία* door opened and two Greek officers came out, pushing themselves between Doug and me.

It was scarily obvious: this was the old Greek regime and the new militaristic challengers competing for what just might be valuable spoils. The conversation between them escalated quickly; the yelling and hand-waving were getting more aggressive by the minute.

I couldn't wait for a break in the action, so I periodically shouted, "I've lost my passport; do you have my passport?" They would stop for a second, look at our bloody hands and faces and go back to arguing. I feared they were negotiating about who was going to drag us away, the leather-coated secret police guys or local law enforcement, and I wasn't sure which was the better option. The secret police could take us away to some godforsaken prison where we would rot indefinitely, and while I hoped the local guys wanted to protect us or briefly throw us in jail, it didn't look likely. One officer especially—let's call him Vladislav, he reminded me of our recent border guard, Borislav, they could have been brothers—looked eager to lock us up and throw away the key.

Suddenly, the other guard turned to me and said clearly, "Paul Alexander Casper." I almost swallowed my cigarette. "Yes, yes," I pleaded. They just kept arguing.

Finally, the three secret police guys threw up their hands, turned abruptly and walked away. There was some faint applause from the audience; apparently, this was a win for the old regime. I'd like to think the station passengers were on our side and understood we weren't spies or bandits.

We entered the station and sat down, waiting while an officer filled out numerous multicolored forms. The phone rang and another officer answered, smiling occasionally during the ensuing lengthy conversation. A general feeling of victory in the station confirmed that this was an encouraging triumph of old over new.

The officer returned my passport and they took Doug and me to a different office to get first aid for our wounds. While they patched us up another officer was having a fine old time talking to some guy taking notes. The two of them laughed and gossiped like old friends, and I guessed the guy with the notepad was a reporter. Later we learned that the whole story was going to be in the local newspapers the following day. I hope they spelled my name right.

By the time we got back to our correct train, we had become minor celebrities. Our fellow passengers asked about our health and my passport, and you could see from the small waves and constant looks our way that our train-jump-and-roll had become the top subject of conversation. Everyone was kind, treating us with equal amounts of concern and pity as they discussed the two Americans' physical and mental health and lack of common sense.

We arrived in Athens at about 8:00 a.m. Wednesday morning and found a great hotel with a reasonable daily fee that included two meals. After much-needed baths, we enjoyed a late lunch at a charming outdoor café with a view of the Acropolis. This will undoubtedly be remembered as one of the greatest outdoor cafes I'll ever eat in with on one side the beautiful shimmering Aegean and the other side the magnificent Parthenon high on the hill.

Doug and I baked in the warmth of the Greek sun and reminisced about the night before. Imagining all the terrifying things that could have happened, we congratulated ourselves on our good luck There were numerous tracks entering and leaving that huge train station, but few abutted any platforms before they took off into the night. I still cringe at the thought of what might have been our fate.

We rose early the next morning, grabbed a quick breakfast and got directions to the Acropolis from the concierge. Then we walked. And walked some more. We not only walked endlessly, we walked *up*, on and on. Exhausted, we needed a good rest when we finally reached the Acropolis plateau. In retrospect, it felt like part of the plan, as if God wanted all who set foot on the Acropolis to stop and take in the magnificence of this ancient structure before entering. The hilltop on which the Acropolis was built is one of the most remarkable settings in the world. There are multiple buildings on the site, with the Parthenon as the centerpiece. When at the top looking to the north you see modern Athens. Look to the south, you see the shimmering blue Aegean Sea and the harbor.

The flagship building of the Acropolis of Athens, the Parthenon served as a temple to Athena and was built about 440 B.C. In Athens, the fifth century B.C. was called the Golden Age or The Age of Pericles. Pericles (494-429) was a brilliant orator, statesman, and general who ruled Athens from 443 to the end of his life. Other famous structures on the Acropolis include the Erechtheum, a temple dedicated to Athena and Poseidon; the Propylaea, which was the gateway entrance to the Acropolis; and the sanctuaries of Pandion and Zeus. The Acropolis served as the preeminent sanctuary of the ancient city of Athens; according to the Hellenic Ministry of Culture. Its primary purpose was to provide sacred grounds dedicated to Athena, the city's matron deity. The Acropolis played host to festivals, cults, and historically significant events during the peak of Athens' power. Today, it serves as an architectural masterpiece and source of national pride: it is the most famous site in Greece.

Doug and I explored all the buildings on the Acropolis, filled with awe as we tried to imagine 450 BC. With every step I took, I felt like I was walking in history. No place I have visited since has been as inspiring; it was magical. I spent hours sitting in one location after another, trying to savor the rich history. There were many tourists on the site, and I was saddened by watching these tourists, regardless of nationality, rushing around taking endless pictures of each other by this statue or that pillar. Sad for those who had come but, in reality, were never there.

I was enjoying a stunning view from the cliff going down to the Aegean Sea when I saw an American or European girl approached by two young Greek boys on the make. Within a few seconds, they had positioned themselves at the very edge of the cliff, ready to make their introductions.

"Senora," one said, "You are the most beautiful woman. I never see an angel before; now I do. They should have one more of these statues here, a statue of you," he said longingly in broken English. She stopped to look at them and he continued: "Please take me; I live for you…I will fall down there only for you." He pointed to the bottom of the 200-foot cliff. He picked a flower. "This is for you because you are the beauty of Spring."

I wish I could remember more. The boy had the patter down; he had done this before. The scene was classic, out of a novel or a European film, but the heroine didn't know her part, I guess. The young woman walked away without a word and within a few steps she dropped the flower onto that ancient soil. The boys shook their heads in silent defeat and walked away. What a shame; it appeared that I, the observer, was the only one to find pleasure in the exchange.

Doug returned from his exploring, tired and ready to go back to the hotel. I stayed, not ready to leave, and was finally kicked off the Acropolis at 7:30 p.m. On my walk back to the hotel, I found a little hole-in-the-wall café and had lamb for dinner, washed down with three or four beers. What a long day; what a great day.

Two days later, I was back up on the Acropolis; history called to me. My favorite subject in grade school was history. Whether studying the Vikings, Rome, the Spanish Conquistadors or the warring cities of Sparta and Athens, there was magic for me in those ancient times. I always read more than was expected. I also loved to draw and had talent, I was told. I was always sketching something or getting compliments about my coloring in coloring books of different kinds. My mother saw that and wanted to fan the flame. When I was in grade school, she would enroll me in art classes where my classmates were all adults at the local YMCA. They pretended to like me and fuss over me a bit, but even then, I got the feeling they were jealous and hoped I'd go and play ball rather than come to the next class. So with my budding art talent, my love of history and drawing eventually came together, and I began to draw interesting people and things of days past.

Another day flew by. I continued to be drawn to the Acropolis. Walking inside the Parthenon during yet another return visit, I met a Japanese husband and wife. We talked about the inspiration we found there, and they urged me to visit Japan; home to some of the oldest and most significant historical monuments and sites. We parted, both saying Αντίο, good-bye in Greek. I walked down the steps of the Parthenon and thought, yes, maybe I will go to Japan someday, perhaps adventure awaits me there.

I drew and drew all I saw on the Acropolis, then went down another level of the plateau where I sketched an ancient outdoor theater not far from the beginning of the Agora, the main center of old Athens. I was gone all day, drawing and writing, the writing inspired by the history all around.

Doug and I spent our last couple of days in Athens enjoying the rich pageantry of the Greek Easter celebrations. I had thoroughly experienced the history of ancient Athens, loving every minute of it. Unfortunately, I had yet to come up with a brilliant idea to extend my stay in Europe. Doug, who didn't have the same money concerns, had loved the idea of starting a business selling sheepskin coats, but now that plan had failed, and I sensed him trying to decide what his next move was. He was tired of me complaining about my dwindling bankroll and the prospect of having to give up and go home.

I knew a plane ticket to the USA from Luxembourg was probably somewhere between $180-$250, depending on the country and the difference between European currency and the US dollar. It had cost me just shy of $200 to fly to Europe. The cost of my stay in Athens would be around $100 by the time I left.

Our current plan was to go to Rome. It only made sense for me to move closer to Luxembourg as I searched for any creative way to extend my stay. A month had been interesting, but not world-changing. Maybe six months or a year would be a different story, But that seemed totally out of reach.

It would take us six to eight days overland to get to Rome. I guessed by the time I arrived in Rome, I'd have about $10 left to my name and no way home.

It was also possible to get almost all the way to Rome by boat. We could take the bus to Patras, then a boat for a day or two to the Italian port of Brindisi, and then another bus to Rome or, if Italy allowed it, we could hitchhike to Rome. But we figured the boat might cost more than would be wise for me to spend. Even with a short stay in Rome, I'd have to hope the currency markets were going my way because I would barely have enough to pay for an Icelandic plane ride home. And no money after landing in New York City.

The more I thought about it, the more I hated my predicament. I wanted to stay; I wanted to explore; I wanted adventure. By now I had been seriously bitten by the travel bug. I wondered, *Should I go for glory or play it safe?* I'd met several travelers from Australia, and they talked glowingly about their beautiful country. Australia would be adventure with a capital A. I'd been told that the government there would pay your way and set you up in some profession or another. Being almost halfway around the world was impressive; Australia would be almost *three-fourths* of the way around the globe. Maybe I could get a job on a boat, sail the Mediterranean, around Africa and India to Australia. Unfortunately, these prospects were based on specific things happening, and if they didn't, I'd be stuck with no money and no way home. Europe was cheaper than the US, but staying in hotels and traveling in trains was not. If I stayed, I'd have to cut my travel costs down to nothing.

But you never know what a new day can bring. That previous night I was in despair, but the next evening I stood on our ship's bow, exhilarating in the ocean spray on my face. I was elated. I had a new lease on my travel life.

Doug and I had been having a late outdoor café lunch before we bussed to the port for departure when I had two conversations with people at the next table.

The first was a Dutch guy, who quite frankly looked pretty drugged out, but was obviously a traveler. He tapped me on the shoulder as I yet again loudly lamented my predicament. He proceeded to tell me that all I had to do was get to London and go to the American Express office there. Behind the door, he said, was a bulletin board where American travelers to London who decided to stay forever, or at least a long time, would put notices about their cheap return tickets for sale. These tickets, he explained, were well under $100.

That was music to my ears, it was the solution I had been searching for. If I could save maybe $150 on my flight home, I could continue my adventure. Most people, smarter people, wouldn't have given that spaced-out, long-haired hippie a second thought, but I not only listened, I created a whole new itinerary based on his information. Now, instead of Rome being the stepping-stone to Luxembourg and the States, I was thinking Cannes and the Cannes Film Festival. What a perfect reversal of fortune—from embarrassed return home to consorting with movie stars. Who knows what could happen there?

My second conversation that afternoon was with an American girl who was adamant that I continue my adventure. She had heard that any American who runs out of money and can't get home has a lifeline. Just go to the American Embassy, she said, and they'll get you home for free. I didn't know if she knew that for sure, but it sounded good. I could just imagine thousands of drugged-out young Americans flooding embassies every week, all around the world, saying, "I spent all my money. It's time to get me home."

It didn't seem plausible—but I pocketed the thought.

Regardless, I had a new lease on life. We'd see what Rome would bring, but I had new capital in the game.

Rome

We were kicked out of the Piazza di Trevi, home of the legendary Trevi Fountain, at 3:30 a.m.

The irritated Polizia scolded us:

"This is not a hotel to sleep; it is only for Italian movie producers!"

I was relieved; it was too cold out there anyway.

6.

Me & Michelangelo

10:00 AM, April 30, 1970

The morning sun was scorching when we landed in the Italian port of Brindisi. Our boat trip had lasted about twenty-four hours, and half of those were spent trying to sleep sitting up in a hard-backed chair. We wanted the cheapest ticket possible, and we got what we paid for. The boat ride was miserable but interesting, however.

First, I had discovered duty-free cigarettes. I could buy a carton of ten packs for what two or three packs cost. I bought one carton immediately and planned to buy another before I left the ship.

Next, we weren't the only ones traveling economy, and our

long boat ride gave us the opportunity to talk with young travelers from around the world. I was surprised to hear that most of those I spoke to were traveling without a plan. Some were students with time constraints, but many appeared to be wandering aimlessly with no goal or date set for their return home. Drugs—where to find them, who was selling and for how much—was a constant topic of conversation. I was not opposed to them, but I didn't go looking for them either. Marijuana had been abundant in college, but it didn't do much for me. For me, smoking pot was just a way to be social. I had never bought drugs and did not plan to. Other things were more important to me.

It was captivating to hear the stories these fellow travelers told. I had only been in Europe for three weeks, most of the time spent on trains or buses and now boats. There had not been many opportunities to socialize with young people from other countries, but now I was learning more about traveling and the life of travelers than I had in the weeks since I had arrived. There was good news and some most definitely bad. It was a condensed course in World Travel 101, and certain lessons required reading between the lines, especially when discussing hitchhiking and changing money when crossing into new countries.

It was clear young people in Europe were worldlier than their American counterparts. The size and proximity of European countries to each other makes it much easier to travel internationally. I was amazed to find that nearly all these young people spoke at least two languages. I'd enjoyed attempting the language of the countries we had visited so far and wanted to learn another language as soon as I could. Something besides Spanish, which I studied in high school with minimal success.

Little by little I was feeling more comfortable as I traveled:

Europe was so different from my hometown, Mount Prospect, Illinois, a suburb of Chicago. I was becoming a traveler, and a pretty good tourist. I had visited so many sites that many only dream of seeing in Paris, Istanbul and Athens. And now I would soon be in Rome—the Coliseum, the Roman Forum and St. Peter's awaited me. It mystified me that many of my fellow passengers on the boat were more interested in finding drugs than exploring the historic sites of these wonderful countries. I was proud of all that I had seen; I was not a novice anymore. I'd seen Paris, I'd crossed the bridge from Europe to Asia in Istanbul, I'd walked the Acropolis in Athens. I refused to believe that Rome was where my travels would end.

Significant decisions would have to be made in Rome. My calculations about my remaining funds generated great concern. I was way too often pulling out a traveler's check to cash it. If Rome was the end—well, my heart went much further than Rome, but how could I travel any further on so little?

Besides dealing with my financial worries, I had to decide how I might travel on my own. Whatever my next destination would be, I would go there without Doug. I could sense he thought it was time for us to part, he was being more distant—it was the money thing. He had been a good traveling companion; two heads really had been better than one. I could not have been luckier than to have been able to start my travels with him, and for the rest of my life he would be my "jumping-off-the-train buddy." When we got to Rome we would have to take a hard look at expenses. I imagined Rome was a very expensive city, and Doug had more resources than me.

The rest of the night and most of the next day passed uneventfully. I had more conversations with fellow passengers as bored as I was, and spent many hours wondering about Rome, hypnotized by the continuous rolling waves of the open sea outside my window.

Just before disembarking at Brindisi, Doug and I met a Swedish guy, Liam, who was also going to Rome. He was returning from playing a small part in a movie being filmed in Athens. His plan was to hitchhike to Rome and then eventually home to Sweden, and he insisted we hitchhike with him. He knew some people in Rome; it could be good for us.

We quickly created a sign, "Roma," and tried to get lucky with the cars and trucks driving off the boat. It didn't take long; an Italian guy took all three of us. He said he wanted some company on the six-to-seven-hour drive to Rome.

We reached Rome at 1 o'clock a.m., when our driver left us off at the Piazza di Trevi, by the legendary Trevi Fountain, because it was too late to check into a hotel. As uncomfortable as it would be, I loved it. I had seen the movie, *Three Coins in the Fountain*, I had heard the song! Now here I was, my first night in Rome, and I was sleeping at the most famous fountain in the world.

My elation was short-lived. After an hour or two trying to sleep and freezing our asses off, we were abruptly awakened by the local Polizia. The irritated officer scolded us: "This is not a hotel to sleep; it is only for Italian movie producers!" I was relieved; it was too cold out there anyway. We started walking, and after almost two hours, we found a barely-hole-in-the-wall hotel and finally got to sleep about 5:00 a.m.

Six hours later Doug, Liam and I were up and ready to take on Rome. We made our way to one of the city's most popular meeting places, the Spanish Steps, where Liam told us to wait while he searched for the people he had mentioned to us. While we waited, we looked around and soon found out our first day of exploring Rome was doomed. It was the 1st of May, May Day, and everyone was on holiday. Everything, and I mean everything, was closed.

Our spirits were lifted when, a couple of hours later, Liam returned with good news. He had found his friends, three American girls who worked for one of the English-speaking newspapers in Rome, *The Daily American*. These girls, Maria, Penny and Karen, had just moved into a new apartment, and though it was sparsely furnished, there was room enough for all of us. And as a soon-to-be-part-time tourist, I got excited. The apartment was only about a block from St. Peter's.

All six of us, the girls and the guys, started having meals together while we got to know each other. As pleasant as that was, it forced me to look once again at my financial predicament. Rome was even more expensive than I'd anticipated, and I had to decide what my next step was going to be. For about ten days now I'd felt like the proverbial "Man in the Middle" going back and forth between risking adventure or being sanely conservative, to make sure I had enough money to get home. I had to make a decision. I hadn't totally bought into the conversations I'd had in Greece suggesting that the travel gods would protect me on my journey and ensure my passage home.

It was a godsend to me that the girls sharing their apartment weren't charging us. This enabled me to live frugally while waiting for a miracle. Unfortunately, that ended suddenly when their landlord announced that he did not approve of so many people in the apartment and we had to get out by that night.

Doug began to search for a hotel. Liam packed his bag to begin hitching north. I went back to panicking while I counted and recounted my money. Maria, Penny and Karen had come to like me; of the three guys, I was the only one they spoke to more than briefly. Maria and I got along best. They all wanted me to stay in Rome and thought I could give private English lessons to rich Italians. The idea was intriguing; they had connections through their newspaper and thought I could make up to 5000 lire an hour. (At that time, 625 lire were worth $1.00.)

We spent hours discussing what it would be like to teach English. I could not picture myself trying to teach someone English when I couldn't speak their language. Karen said not to worry; she had heard it was like teaching a baby how to talk.

"You don't know baby language, do you? Well, we all get it done eventually, and the baby starts to speak in English," she said.

Maria said that when the teacher doesn't know the host language he or she forces all the students to speak English; it was called the direct method. During these conversations, I kept thinking that if my Father or my high school English teacher knew I was considering teaching English to unsuspecting innocent people they would have thrown up their hands in disbelief. They had both been witness to my English papers and grades. Karen said she could put a small free ad in her paper tomorrow, but we passed on the ad for the time being while she checked on a couple of things back at her office that might give me some leads.

I did think I could try the English teacher route. I didn't know how to get clients, though, and I would have to get an apartment and make a deposit, which was a real commitment, a scary one. I'd be betting everything I had on this one idea.

After saying goodbye to Liam, and thanking him for his help, I went to find a quiet place to think and stretch my legs. While walking I stopped at the American Express office, hoping to find mail from home, but nothing was waiting for me. I kept on walking until I found my quiet place in the chaos of St. Peter's Square, the plaza in front of the Basilica and Vatican grounds. I took a seat on a bench and began to draw.

On that day, at that hour, I was the only artist in the square attempting to draw, centuries later, what Michelangelo had created. A little group started to form, watching me. They looked over my shoulder to see what I was drawing and tried to talk, but we were all speaking different languages and conversation was difficult. No grandmothers pulled out chairs to sit beside me and chat like they did in Istanbul, but many shook their heads with approval at my approach as I drew—with an ink pen now instead of pencil, which I had left in Istanbul. I am sure most days there were many real and aspiring artists attempting to reproduce on paper the divine feeling of looking at St. Peter's for the first time. The square was just breathtaking; seeing it on television did not do it justice. As I sketched, I anticipated the awe I would experience when I entered the Basilica tomorrow. I planned to spend all day at the Vatican church, museum and grounds and was looking forward to being overwhelmed by being in the presence of the history there.

I began to lose interest in drawing the structural aspect of St. Peters and needed to try my hand at something more freeform. As I looked at the art surrounding me, I was drawn to one of the numerous statues everywhere in Rome. This one was of a riderless horse and appeared to be part of a narrative connected to a sculpture across the street. Wondering what that story was, I stared, and began to remember another muscular horse in my life.

I was twelve years old in 1959 and a sixth-grader in Mrs. Andrew's second-floor homeroom class. Although we changed classes during the day, Mrs. Andrews was also my history teacher. We had been studying ancient Rome, and one day, so she could grade papers, she instructed us to draw something about the Roman Empire that had made an impression. She handed out oversized sheets of paper for us to draw on and we all jumped in quickly. In short order, there were drawings of awkward-looking coliseums, rickety bridges flying flags over the Tiber River, and suspicious renderings of the Sistine Chapel ceiling.

I watched my classmates for a while, not wanting to draw what everyone else was drawing. I caught Mrs. Andrews giving me the evil eye because I wasn't doing anything, so I put my head down and pretended to sketch. Suddenly I envisioned a bold horse, a significant horse. I thought a moment and added a Roman soldier. I quickly sketched the boundaries of the drawing and decided I wouldn't show the entire horse or the full figure of the soldier. The horse would be fierce and maybe a little mad, with flaring nostrils and mane flowing. The soldier would have a strong hold on the leather reins and look ready for battle. As I started to draw the horse, I exaggerated the entire scene, creating an unusual close-up with extreme angles portraying power and movement.

My drawing was progressing nicely when I noticed Mrs. Andrews walking around the room and looking over shoulders to see the different drawings. She made her way over to me and stopped. She didn't say anything, which unnerved me. I kept on drawing until she sat down in an empty chair and moved it closer to me, looking over my right shoulder. She still had not said a word. I remember I was afraid to even look at her—was I really off-course with my subject? As I continued, she still didn't say anything, which worried me even more. Had I had done something so wrong she was speechless? Intrigued, several other kids wandered over and started watching me too.

Suddenly Billy Cuttingham cried out, "Hey, that's not a

building or church. Casper is cheating! Mrs. Andrews, you should give him an F." My pal Billy, always looking out for me. Mrs. Andrews turned toward him and gave him her *Quiet, Billy* look.

She looked at the class and said, "I have to say, everyone, all your drawings look very good, but I had to stop at Paul's. I know some think he's not doing what he's supposed to do by drawing something out of the box. Something so different. I know Billy especially thinks this."

Again, she turned to him, giving him the evil eye. "But I have to say, Paul has stopped me in my tracks. I just never expected anything like this."

Just then Chrissy Johnston informed those who didn't know, "Yea, he's a good artist. Mrs. Hart in art class is always talking about his work and hanging it up."

Mrs. Andrews watched me for a long while but said no more before she got up to continue with the class. As I walked out, she called me over to her desk. She said she hadn't wanted to say too much about one person's work over the others, but now in person, she could. She said I had a special talent. Not only could I draw what I saw; I could see things differently, as an artist would. She was going to hang up some of the drawings in the room, but mine would be hung in the hallway with a sign telling kids they could look at the others when the room was empty. Taking out a box of notepaper, she wrote a quick note to my Mother, saying she believed I had a special talent and hoped that my mother knew this and would nurture it going forward. She put the note in an envelope and said, "Please give that to her tonight."

I smiled to myself; I hadn't thought about that moment for quite a while. It gave me confidence at a time when I sorely needed some. *Thank you, Mrs. Andrews.* I began to sketch again, no horse this time, but a quick study of St. Peter's in the fading Roman afternoon light.

As the sun set, I remembered yesterday, before we went to the Spanish Steps. I had spent some time on a bridge overlooking the Tiber, the third largest river in Italy that flows through the middle of Rome, on my way to the Coliseum. Once there, I sat for hours imagining the goings-on of over 2000 years ago. I was so moved by being in the actual place and structure where the events I had read about or seen in movies had occurred. These became real in the in the Coliseum, a place alive with the vivid and mysterious spirits of the past.

I finished my sketch and thought that my Mother would love to see it. Suddenly I realized I hadn't sent any postcards home recently about what I was doing or what my plans were. When I was in Paris, I knew I was going to Istanbul and dropped a postcard to my Mother, Father and younger sister Joyce to let them know. When I decided to go to Athens, I sent another postcard urging everyone to contact me in care of the American Express office in that city. But it had been a month and no word from home. Strange, but I hoped it was par for the course for mail going back and forth at that distance.

When I got back to the apartment, Doug was packing. He had found a hotel, and casually mentioned what it would cost. There was no way; it was too expensive for me and I couldn't join him. We had been together since we had arrived in Paris, but he understood my situation, wished me luck and walked out the door. Not how I would have liked us to part, but it was inevitable, and I had bigger problems. I needed to out of the girls' apartment by dark. It looked like I'd be sleeping at the railroad station.

I was ready to say goodbye to the girls when they surrounded me and said, "You're not going anywhere. We're going to make it okay for you to stay a while longer. You can believe us or not what we told you guys about the landlord. But what mattered to us was that they needed to go; the vibe wasn't right. On the other hand, your vibe is wanted around here."

They took me out to dinner that night and gave me a great briefing on what to see at St. Peter's the next day. The girls really were angels, smart ones at that. I wondered, were they living Jake Barnes' life in 1970, expatriates looking for...? Good question; what were they looking for?

Monday morning, I got up early, ready to start my day at St. Peter's. I was glad I got the lay of the land the other day when I sketched in the square. The exterior was magnificent, and I couldn't wait to see all the art and history inside. Thirty minutes later I finally entered St. Peter's Basilica in Vatican City.

I was not disappointed. My first thought was that this glorious structure could have only been conceived and built with the help of God. I was so awestruck, I had to sit down in one of the pews.

A baby was being christened at one of the fonts and across a row of pews, a small choir was rehearsing. The Basilica began to fill with music that made the beauty all around me even more overwhelming. The choir sang in Latin, and I didn't understand a word, but it remains one of the more perfect experiences of my life. It was literally heavenly.

I sat in my pew and listened until they finished, all the while gazing at every detail of the main portico. The altar was such a surprise, so different than anything I had ever seen in the States. Of course, I reminded myself—Michelangelo designed and managed the construction of this stunning structure.

It is no exaggeration to say I felt the presence of God while

I was in St. Peter's. If God can be found in art and music, I was right. The entire time I sat there, I had goosebumps. Eventually, I rose to walk around the free-standing altar. There were easily 200 other visitors and I wasn't alone, but the enormity of St. Peter's made their presence slip away while I walked the exquisite marble floors.

I knew when I began my day that I would not have enough time to see all I wanted to see. The Vatican Museum is attached to St. Peter's and contains history upon history and some of the greatest art in the world, but I could not go there next. From my discussions with Maria, Penny and Karen, I knew I had to leave enough time for the Sistine Chapel.

To get there I had to leave the Vatican hallways, make my way out to the street and walk around the entire city-state of the Vatican. When I reached the entrance to the Chapel I had to wait in line with the rest of the tourists. The line was slow and long, and I worried I wouldn't get in and began to question my plan.

Once inside the Chapel, so small compared to St. Peter's, I saw immediately why the girls had insisted that I visit. The Chapel ceiling was breathtaking; Michelangelo's images were so powerful. I could almost hear Rex Harrison yelling at Charlton Heston in that great movie, *The Agony and the Ecstasy*, "When will it be finished?!" As I squinted my eyes, I could see the swaying scaffolding and hear the nervous movements of Michelangelo's assistants working feverishly on the Chapel while Pope Julius II paced below. It was all worth it: however long it took for Michelangelo to finish his masterpiece, it was the perfect amount of time.

As they had when I visited the Acropolis, the guards had to literally escort me out when the Chapel closed. While the sun set, I walked back to the entrance of the Basilica in front of St. Peter's.

I stopped not far away, at a little hole-in-the-wall café, and had pasta and a couple of beers. Almost overcome with emotion after spending the day immersed in beauty and history, I struggled to find the words to describe in poetry all I had experienced.

My day ended with a large pale moon rising behind Vatican Square. I had decided: the next phase of my adventure was about to begin. Tomorrow I would begin to hitchhike by myself through Europe. The teaching English plan? I didn't see myself as a teacher. It was obvious I would have to leave Europe soon, no matter what, and I wanted to see as much of it as possible before that time came. I was nervous. I was going to be totally on my own, with very limited resources, making my way through foreign lands. Anything could happen, and if it did, I would be on my own. Yes, I was nervous, but I was also ready—I'd gotten my feet wet traveling this first month. I knew there was more waiting for me out there; first *Beyond Paris* and now *Beyond Rome*. My first solo destination: the Cannes Film Festival.

As confident as I was in my decision, I still worried constantly about how to get more money. After Cannes, I had no idea what I would do. The recent information I had received about cheap airline tickets home in London might work, or if all failed—I was very dubious about this—I could go to the American Embassy and ask them to send me home. That slim hope of that gave me the impetus to start the next leg of my adventure. Tomorrow could be very good or very bad—or even something else?

The Road

I had no idea what he was singing, but this song always got to me whenever I had heard it during my time in Rome.

Lia seemed to sense this and tried to explain the words to me.

"Paolo, lascia che ti spieghi."

She put her hand above her eyes and turned her head as if searching.

"Looking for?" I guessed

"Sì, alla ricercar," she nodded. Then she pointed to me, took my hand and placed it on my chest.

"Me, myself," I said, after hesitating. "Ah, sì, looking for myself!"

7.

Open Road
(Becoming a Road Knight)

Tuesday 1:00 PM, May 5, 1970

I had tried to get up early, but it was already one in the afternoon. The time had come to make critical decisions on clothes. Now that I was going to start hitchhiking, I needed to travel light, really light. The girls were great; they said leave what you don't want to carry, and sometime in the future we will send them to you wherever you are in the world. They also gave me an old sleeping bag to carry the few clothes I decided to keep, and if I ever had to sleep outdoors, I'd be very happy I had one. I told them if I needed a sleeping bag to sleep, I would be in big trouble—I was a hotel kind of guy. I never saw (in the movie) Jake Barnes with a sleeping bag, but I could imagine Larry Darrell carrying one, especially in the

Himalayas. I wound a rope twice around the rolled-up bag and tested carrying it over my shoulder. It worked, it was light enough and it didn't look too bad.

And this is what I carried:

- *1 beat-up dark-greenish sleeping bag*
- *1 pair of desert boots*
- *1 pair not-so-used John Wayne Calvary boots*
- *3 pairs blue jeans*
- *1 belt*
- *1 wallet*
- *3 pairs of underwear*
- *1 blue work shirt*
- *1 white dress shirt*
- *3 pairs socks*
- *1 Henley shirt*
- *1 towel*
- *1 washcloth*
- *1 small thin Dopp kit*
- *1 brown corduroy sports coat*
- *1 sweater*
- *1 sketchbook*
- *1 trip journal and a few pencils and pens*

It all fit in the sleeping bag. I'd left clothes in Paris, on the Orient Express, in Istanbul, in Athens, and now in Rome. I didn't think I'd be leaving any more behind—I was down to the essentials.

The girls, Maria, Penny and Karen, prepared a hearty brunch and surprised me with a bag of food packed for the journey. They had two last warnings. The first: beware of dog packs. Believe it or not, they said, there had been reports on TV of dogs attacking people in groups north of Rome, and the results weren't pretty. The other warning—and I wish they had mentioned this earlier— was that there were laws in parts of Italy prohibiting hitchhiking. They weren't sure which areas, but the farther I got away from Rome, the more problems I might have. Great! Not only would I wonder if the person offering me a ride was an ax murderer or worse, now I had to worry that the *Polizia,* whom I hoped would save me from the ax murderer, would throw me in jail after they had done their job.

After many hugs and kisses, I promised someday we would meet again, and when that happened I would treat them to them the biggest dinner they'd ever had. They were angels when angels were needed; I'll never forget them.

Farewells made, and warnings digested, I was ready to start the next phase of my new adventure. I walked to the bus station, note from the girls written in Italian in hand, to get a ticket on the bus that would drop me off at the entrance to Via Flaminia, the major highway leading north out of Rome and then to Cannes. As I sat on the sparsely populated bus on my way to the highway entrance, I felt overwhelmed with competing emotions. I was exhilarated anticipating the start of a new adventure, now that I was truly on my own, but I was not unaware of what could also lie ahead—failure, problems, disaster! It wasn't the hitchhiking; I'd done it before. I had hitchhiked as a kid in Cincinnati and had confidence earned from experience. As a freshman at Drake, a fellow freshman, Bill Cason, and I hitchhiked from Des Moines, Iowa, to the University of Missouri in Columbia. Bill just had to see his hometown girlfriend and asked me to keep him company. The trip should have taken no longer than four hours, but because of the crazy detours on the rides with the weird people who picked us up, the trip ended up taking eight. It had been a while since I hitchhiked, and I worried that hitchhiking could be very different in Italy. Should I do something special, something more Italian? The bus stopped, and the driver nodded to me as he looked at the note I had given him. I would find out about Italian hitchhiking soon enough; time to get off the bus.

The doors closed behind me, and the bus rumbled off, leaving me standing alone on a busy highway as a variety of foreign cars whizzed by. It was the perfect time for a small red Italian sports car to pull up beside me, driven by a movie-star-beautiful Italian woman who would open the door and pat the seat beside her. "Ciao, darling," she would purr in heavily-accented English. "Where would you like to go? I will take you anywhere."

The weather had been generally warm and sunny in Rome, but this day was spectacular. My spirits rose as I stood by the side of the road with my thumb out, slouched a little in what I imagined was sophisticated Italian style. After about an hour I was picked up by a young Italian guy who spoke minimal English and drove me a few kilometers before he had to turn off the main highway.

My plan was to reach Genoa that night, and if I fell short, Pisa. But with my late start and not getting very far on my first ride, I looked at my map and wondered if not Pisa, where? I didn't have to wonder too long, because within a few minutes a Renault Dauphine with barely any room for me stopped a few feet away. A very attractive young woman got out of the passenger side, laughing, and asked, "Buongiorno, siete inglesi?" I wasn't English but close enough. From the driver's side I heard "Salve!" from a second young woman. Both appeared to be Italian, and in their twenties.

"Buon giorno, ladies," I replied. Before I could ask them

about heading north to Pisa, the first girl grabbed her long, flowing ponytail with one hand and pulled up her seat with the other, nodding at me to get in. This was even better than my dream of an hour ago: not one Italian babe, but two. Apparently, this was my lucky day; little did I know how lucky. We were off.

I could barely fit myself and the sleeping bag in the back without putting my legs over the front seat. I've always hated small foreign cars. As happy as I was to be in the company of these lovely women I thought, *Damned if I do and damned if I don't*. If the ride was short, I'd be off-schedule and in trouble. But, if this was a long ride, I would be a pretzel for days to come.

We started driving, and I introduced myself: "My name is Paul."

"Ciao, Paolo—Mi chiamo Allegra, E questo e Lia."

Both Allegra and Lia were gorgeous; Allegra looked like she had walked off the pages of a fashion magazine.

"I'm from Chicago."

"Si, Chicago, molto buona," Allegra laughed, as she turned to Lia and nudged her on the arm.

As they continued to giggle and talk in Italian, I wanted in on the conversation: "Do you speak any English? Habla English?"

They laughed, and it immediately became obvious that there was a language barrier here. This could be a quiet and boring trip.

I pulled out a pack of Marlboros and offered them a cigarette. Still laughing, they each took one. From time to time I could see Lia glance at me in the rearview mirror, sort of checking me out. I tried to comment on the Italian song playing on the radio. Even though Maria, Penny and Karen had attempted to teach me some useful Italian phrases, I was less than so-so at speaking it. It was much harder than French. But I liked the variety of Italian rock music I'd been hearing in Rome, including the song playing in the car. I thought, *Just say something to break the silence*: "Buona musica italiana, I like."

"Sì, buona musica. Anche a me piace."

I guessed she liked it, too, a good guess; she started bouncing up and down to the beat of the song and singing along.

Suddenly Lia stopped, had a quick animated conversation with Allegra, and turned to me: "Paolo, you like, come diresti ... the eating, pasta?"

She tried to illustrate her question by mimicking eating, still driving ninety miles an hour.

Pasta, *why not*? "Sì, bene!"

About 20 minutes later we turned off the highway onto quieter, smaller roads until I saw the sea. Before I knew it, we pulled into a huge driveway which lead to an impressively large contemporary house covered entirely in white marble with a large sculpture of Neptune in the front yard.

I didn't expect all of this, but hey, if they had pasta, okay with me. They bounded out of the front seat, talking and giggling, ignoring me. Wondering if I should wait or get out of the car, I saw Allegra turn at the front door and wave me in. I wrenched my sleeping bag out of the back seat and followed her inside.

The house was beautiful, minimalist design, with large contemporary paintings on many walls. I took my time looking around, then followed the laughter into a huge kitchen with large bay windows looking out on the rolling blue-green waves of the Mediterranean. It was still late morning, but Lia had poured us glasses of red wine, lifting hers to make a toast: "Alla tua salute!"

So, this is what good wine should taste like, I thought. The quality of the wine was, no doubt, enhanced by the loveliness of my companions, a fact that remained true the rest of my life. A fine wine was always better drunk in the company of a beautiful woman, and in this case, I was lucky enough to have two.

Lia and Allegra pulled out some dry pasta, dumped it in boiling water, added a sauce, and piled some on a plate for me. It was delicious; these girls knew how to live. I wondered what was going on here. Did these girls own this house? Were they rich? Did they know someone who was very rich? Should I be concerned? Was this a good situation that could turn very bad?

I continued to eat and drink while wondering about the girls, the house, the car. Lia turned on a stereo in the living room and started blasting the Italian rock song I had liked earlier. A minute later, she came back into the kitchen with the album. The singer's name was Riccardo Cocciante, and she pointed to the song, "Cervo a Primavera," on the back of the album cover. I had no idea what he was singing, but this song always got to me whenever I had heard it during my time in Rome. Lia seemed to sense this and tried to explain the words to me.

"Paolo, lascia che ti spieghi ." She put her hand above her eyes and turned her head as if searching.

"Looking for?" I guessed.

"Si, alla ricercar," she nodded. Then she pointed to me, took my hand and placed it on my chest. "Me, myself," I said, after hesitating. "Ah, si, looking for myself!"

Lia didn't understand, but I liked the sound of it. That *was* me then, *looking for myself.* She gave me a funny look and smiled, which made me smile. I think she was proud of her successful translation effort. Me, well, I was in love, hook line and sinker.

It was hard to tell how old they Allegra and Lia were. They were about my age, I guessed, maybe a little younger. Both had beautiful brown eyes, enhanced by dramatic eye makeup. Lia wore a faded blue work shirt with shorts; Allegra wore shorts, too, and a half-unbuttoned, loose-fitting men's white shirt. They were both lively attractive Italian women, with accents that made them even more alluring—and they knew it.

Allegra poured me another huge glass of wine and pushed me into the living room where Lia was yelling for me. I carried my glass into a beautiful space decorated in hues of white and cream, thinking only, *Do not spill this wine!*

"Paolo, fantastica musica, si?" murmured Allegra as she started moving to the heavy bass beat filling the room.

"Bella casa, sei d'accordo?" she asked, waving her arms at the walls around her while swaying and spinning, inviting me to admire both the beautiful room and her nice equally lovely ass. I forced myself to look away from Allegra and appreciate yet another great view of the Mediterranean. The rolling waves changed colors as I watched: further out, the sea was dark blue, but as the waves tumbled to shore, they turned lighter shades of green and blue.

I guessed Allegra not only liked the music but really loved this house, whether it was hers or not. She danced over to me and nudged my arm, nodding at the stairs. Lia had disappeared.

Upstairs were three or four bedrooms, all sparsely decorated in a contemporary style, with big, beautiful beds and windows with views of the sea.

By the time Allegra and I got to the master bedroom, Lia was already there, lying on the bed. Unbelievable as it may seem, she had unbuttoned her blouse and was softly saying something in Italian I could barely hear over the continuing beat of the stereo that was booming all through the house. I assumed it was something like this: "Paolo, now that you've had some wine and some food, it's time for us to…" I stood there for a moment in disbelief and almost uncontrollable joy. Allegra elbowed me again as she walked past me to the bed as if to say, *What are you waiting for?* She also started to take off her top.

An hour or so later, all three of us were dozing on the bed when Lia suddenly jumped up, rubbed her eyes and frantically searched for her clothes. She mumbled to herself, something about "Roberto" and the "aeroporto." Allegra began to rush around now, too, grabbing clothes and straightening the room. They both appeared to have realized that they had a problem.

It didn't take too long to figure that at least one of them was late picking up some guy named Roberto at the airport. Worse, he had already landed and could show up here any minute. They hurried me downstairs and grabbed my sleeping bag roll. We left the house and jumped in the car, taking off in a cloud of dust. As we drove they continued to wave their hands and yell at each other in that animated Italian way, totally serious but very funny. I tried to get their attention, pleading to let me stay the night.

"Allegra…Lia, we should go back to the casa," I begged, pointing out the back window toward the house that was now out of sight.

They stopped arguing, turned to me, and said in unison, "Roberto." You could see the fear in their eyes as Lia pounded on the dashboard, yelling at Allegra to drive faster. So, Roberto. *How big was Roberto?* I wondered. *How mean was Roberto or, perhaps, how understanding and forgiving might Roberto be?* I did know Roberto was a very lucky guy.

When we got to the highway all three of us jumped out of the car. Allegra started talking to herself, arguing really, eventually pausing to look at me. The sun was setting behind her as she gazed at me with her beautiful brown eyes and shook her head: Thinking I'm sure: *Good luck, fucker, you'll never make Genoa by nightfall.* Lia had never stopped ranting, waving her arms and blaming Allegra for falling asleep. It was Allegra's fault their beloved new friend, Paolo, was in deep shit.

The mystery of Roberto unresolved, we hugged and kissed and said goodbye. Lia leaned out the car window, shouting in Italian what I hoped was, "Paolo, you now have a memory you will treasure for the rest of your life. You will remember Lia and Allegra forever." The last thing I heard her say was, "Ciao, innamorato!"

"Ciao, Lia! Ciao, Allegra!" I yelled over traffic as they vanished out of sight. I wondered briefly what might have evolved with these lovely Italian women if there were no Roberto? Oh well.

Okay, now what? I wondered. The sun was almost below the horizon and darkness would come much too quickly. As dire as my present situation was, nothing could get me down. This was still my lucky day—so far, it had been one of my luckiest days ever. You never know; I could still get a ride that could take me all the way to Genoa.

I stood there for half an hour, cars and trucks whizzing by. The sun had finished its descent for the day and soon it would be hard for passing cars to see me. This was a problem, soon to be a big problem. But as I extended my thumb to the passing cars, I could only smile as I relived today's events. It had been a very nice afternoon.

Are you kidding! The afternoon was a fucking Grand Slam, a 99-yard run for a touchdown, a half-court swish to sink the final basket for a win. It was the afternoon of my life, of my dreams, it was the jackpot of all jackpots. And it had happened because of my first good ride hitchhiking alone. Well, I loved hitchhiking now! I couldn't wait to see who picked me up next.

I'm sure a lot of motorists going by probably thought, *what a stupid hitchhiker, he's not getting a ride and he's smiling like he just won the Italian lottery. What a dick; what can he possibly be thinking? They can't see you in the dark!*

All that said, reality was setting in. I knew from hitchhiking in the States that there was no chance of getting a ride in the dark, but a hundred-percent chance of getting hit by a car flying by. I didn't have much time.

A couple of short rides later, some guy left me off in the middle of some factories. I had dozed off and not noticed he had gotten off the main highway. Wishing he had alerted me, I started walking. It was dark now, with no prospect of finding a hotel or even a ride. I began to look for a safe spot where I could sleep, remembering what Maria said in Rome about being careful around stray dogs, or worse, packs of wild dogs. There had been too many news reports, she had warned. People had been very badly hurt by attacking dogs. As I prowled around looking for a place to lay my sleeping bag, I began to hear howling—a lot of howling, many dogs howling—and it sounded like it was getting closer. That did it. I was tired, frustrated over my predicament and in no man's land, and now wild dogs. My heart was beating wildly at the prospect of waking up to big dogs gnawing on different parts of my body.

A huge truck passed, almost hitting me, and as I yelled some choice offensive words at it, and as its light swept the area along the road, I saw a high wire fence with what looked like a fair-sized hole in the ground by the fence. I walked over to a fenced-in cornfield that looked like an agricultural laboratory with controlled experiments going on. I could also see a building on stilts with lights on in the office looking out over the cornfield. Yes, there was a hole that some animal had dug to get in, which the owners hadn't noticed yet. It was big enough for me to get through, pushing my bedroll ahead of me. This at least would get me off the road, give me protection against any dog packs and finally allow me to get off my feet and lie down. As I made my way into the rows of corn to where I felt was a safe place to lay out my sleeping bag, I was uneasy and somewhat suspicious, but my mouth was watering at the thought of lying down. I had to get off my feet.

Suddenly spotlights started flashing around the field, and three different alarm sirens went off. What had I climbed into? Was this corn crop made from gold? Was this a secure site for government testing? I peeked at the guardhouse and saw two men pointing at the area where I had settled. A guard dog began to bark furiously and I saw a man come down the guardhouse stairs with the dog, barely able to restrain it.

I may have been exhausted, but I made like a jackrabbit on fire and fled to the hole I had climbed through. Flashing searchlights and screaming alarm sirens can shake you out of a stupor, fast.

Safely outside the fence, I started walking back the way I had come, fading into the darkness. An hour later, I was still walking, ready to sleep in the road, on the road, above the road, anywhere. I saw a roadside berm, climbed up and collapsed. After eating some of the leftover food the girls had given me, I fell asleep, regardless of the whizzing trucks beneath me and the howling dogs in the distance.

The sun was rising as I awoke, itching from head to foot. Little insects and critters were inside the sleeping bag and crawling all over me. I jumped up, stamping my feet and shaking out the sleeping bag, trying to rid my body and bag of as many bugs as possible. After wiping dew off my bag, I packed up and I slid down the embankment to the road.

So began my second day of hitchhiking. What would it bring? My first had brought the best of times and the worst of times. Sorry, Charles Dickens, for taking your line, but it seemed to fit me as perfectly in 1970 as it did your novel in 1859.

The morning was chilly. I wasn't sure what time it was, what day it was, or where I was, but as I walked backward on the road north with my thumb out, I still had to smile thinking about the best of yesterday. One "best" was a kiss Lia had given me when I climbed into their bed. She held my head with one hand, and after for a second or two of looking into each other's eyes she lightly dragged her tongue horizontally across my lips. So unexpected. So perfect. Lost in this thought, my reverie was ended abruptly by the squealing sound of heavy gears grinding to a halt behind me.

A truck had stopped for me. I grabbed the door handle and hoisted myself up. The cab door was high, and it was like climbing a two-story building to get into the seat. I was surprised to see two guys in the cab. One climbed back into the sleeping area, and I settled into the passenger seat. Both were in their fifties, I would guess, and both had jovial smiles on their friendly faces. It was soon obvious that neither spoke any English, but I tried to strike up a conversation.

"Buongiorno, my name is Paul, from USA, from Chicago," I smiled, pointing to myself.

"Ah, Americano. Il mio nome e Dario e il suo nome Pepe." We shook hands, Dario muttering, *You look like shit, where did you sleep? In the woods?* I was just guessing, but we all laughed heartily at his joke. Smiling, I offered a Marlboro to each of my new friends and we all lit up.

The area we were driving through seemed an unlikely place for this huge truck. We were on a two-lane road, and it felt like we were driving into some place beyond no-man's land. We traveled over endless small hills, up and down, requiring Dario to downshift constantly to keep the big semi moving without stalling.

As we finished our cigarettes, Dario asked me, "Americano, tu, tu dici Chicago, torrefattore? Hmm, sei tu, vieni dadi, ah, il gangster!" Dario looked at Pepe, who looked at me, and both laughed uproariously.

I understood enough, and smiled back, "Si, Chicago gangster. Sure, all of us in Chicago are gangsters!" I stuck out my chest and flexed my biceps to emphasize my Chicago "gangster-ness."

We pulled up in front of a group of adobe buildings; the area looked like a beat-up Western town from the 1800s. A perpendicular road crossing was across the road, with a major highway on the other side. To get there, you had to cross a small wooden bridge over a dry streambed. As we got out of the cab, Dario pointed to that small bridge. He held up his thumb and smiled; they were going the opposite way and it was time for me to start hitchhiking again. Dario and Pepe motioned to me to come into the little grocery store for something to drink, but I declined with a smile and lots of "Grazies," deciding that I needed to quickly find out where I was and what my options were.

It was a beautiful morning, and the sun felt good on my shoulders as I walked to the bridge. I took off my coat and lit a cigarette, feeling very "Zen" and in-the-moment. *This isn't bad*, I thought, *it would be okay to wait here for a while.* I brushed my hand through my hair, feeling for grass strands or dirt left from last night's sleeping arrangement. Rubbing my chin with its now month-old stubble, I noticed a small tumbleweed bouncing over my dusty, palomino-colored cavalry boots. I lit a cigarette in that barren Italian landscape and smiled, feeling a kinship to the Man with No Name, Clint Eastwood, in Sergio Leone's Spaghetti Western, *For a Few Dollars More*. I could almost hear the film's haunting theme music, the eerie whistling accompanied by the twanging electric guitar. I could imagine a cowboy with whom I had a history waiting for me across the road; we stared each other down as I took a long drag on my cigarette, exhaling slowly, a camera panning around us as we waited for the other to move. In the crisp, dry Italian desert that morning I could have been in 1970 or 1870.

That movie really did make an impression on me. I saw it in college with my best friend Jim Wells, and afterward we almost ran out of gas going to over ten different stores looking for those small cigars Clint smoked in the movie

This hitchhiking was going to be okay. It had only been two days, and already I'd had two experiences I would remember for the rest of my life.

I was jolted out of my Spaghetti Western moment when I saw the two truck drivers, Dario and Pepe, sitting on chairs outside the store, waving to me. Before I could wave back, I saw an Italian police car pull up in front of them.

Trying to make myself invisible, I turned and started to walk slowly in the other direction. Hard as I tried, I was not fading into the landscape. I peeked over my shoulder: Dario and Pepi were having a very animated conversation with that policeman.

How bad can this be? I thought. First, it was against the law to hitchhike in most of Italy. *How can I explain what I am doing here?* I didn't have paints or an easel as I stood by the side of the road.

Of course, I'm hitchhiking! Not only can the cop see this, by now my truck-driver friends have told him that they picked me up a couple of hours ago. And by now they may have mentioned that I am a gangster from Chicago! I'm dead, not only dead; I'm fucked!

The entire time they talked, the policeman stared at me. He eventually went inside the store, giving me a moment to think. I wanted to run, but I was in a desert: nowhere to run, nowhere to hide.

Accepting my fate, I decided to look good for my arrest. I put on my sports coat, made sure my shirt was tucked in, smoothed my hair a bit, and lit another cigarette. While I was doing this, I saw the policeman leave the store and heard some faint goodbyes and a car door slam shut.

I was leaning on the railing of the bridge trying to look as innocent as possible when the officer pulled up beside me. He rolled down the passenger side window, looked me over head-to-toe for a minute and asked, in pretty good English, "They tell me you're hitchhiking; is that correct?"

I replied, hesitantly, "Well, yes sir, I guess so. Is there a problem?"

"They also say you're a gangster from Chicago."

I immediately straightened up and looked over at the building. *Thanks a million, guys, thanks a lot.*

"No, no, officer, I'm just a student trying to see parts of my most favorite country on earth." I was pretty proud of myself, coming up with that out of nowhere.

He stared at me, expressionless, then smiled, "I'm just joking with you, son, come on, get in. I'm headed up to Pisa; I'll give you a ride."

What luck! I had really enjoyed my "Man-with-No-Name"

moments there at the Dry Gulch Bridge, but I could have stood there all day trying to get picked up.

It was a nice ride. We talked about different things, where I'd been and where I planned to go. He was a great guy; when we got to Pisa, he bought me some ice cream and walked with me to the Leaning Tower. He had a camera and asked some tourists to take a picture of us under the Tower. Before we parted we exchanged addresses, and I promised that he ever got to Chicago I'd buy dinner and show him some real gangsters. He left me off at what he said was a good road to hitch north.

The rest of the day included seven rides with the last one a nice older couple, a Russian diplomat and his French wife, who went out of their way to drop me off at a youth hostel just outside of Genoa.

The hostel guests, interesting, like-minded travelers, provided me with a wealth of information. Many were coming from Spain, and all agreed they loved the country. They all also warned me about the LaGuardia Seville, the hard-nosed police, and the precarious political situation; Franco, the strong-arm dictator, was still president then. Several of the people I met were going north, but would return to Pamplona, Spain, at the beginning of July, for the running of the bulls.

I liked that idea. Jake from *The Sun Also Rises* ran with the bulls, so should I, I thought. If I could jump on and off a train, I could probably dodge a 1500-pound bull. You only live once— who knows? I hadn't thought much about Spain much before meeting my fellow hostel guest. I was still unsure of my travel plans, but the last two days—starting to hitch, the experiences I'd had, the people I'd met—encouraged me to venture onward. But where? Until now north was my only destination, to be closer to

To the Shores of Babylon

The first voice was faint, then strong, then here,
It seemed to be searching for some hidden holy place,

This voice says...

"Set sail it's time to search out there,
Come with me, let's go beyond time,
Beyond ancient sin to a place of holy grace."

The other voice said...

"Come! Come travel into dreams,
Far out beyond the possible, beyond the known."

That voice was like the wind along the shore,
That seems a music out of nowhere, into nowhere blown.

And still another voice comes,
This one different, this one mystic,
It seems to be pulling me, pushing me, pointing me East,
Could my ship be hungry, wanting—is it time to ocean?

And then this voice said...

"Go to Babylon, to the past,
Set sail to where the music comes from,
First to Ceylon, then to Pompeii & Atlantis,
Then and only then,
To the Shores of Babylon."

Written May 7, while on the train to Monte Carlo

Luxembourg and the airport, to get back to the States.

I still wanted to go to the Cannes Film Festival, but had heard that the Monte Carlo Grand Prix would run on Sunday, May 10, just four days away. The newspapers were full of stories about Jackie Stewart, the world's hottest Formula One driver, and 1969 Grand Prix winner. This intrigued me, maybe my next destination should be Monaco.

My fellow bunkmates warned me that I should be careful trying to get out of Genoa. The highways and roads I would need to navigate were more like Italian spaghetti than sensible paved thoroughfares. Getting a ride west to the south of France might be very hard. I finally decided just to get out of Genoa quickly, taking a short train ride to Monte Carlo.

Monte Carlo

I walked up and found a young guy,
more than half in the bag,
holding up a bottle of wine.

"I need a corkscrew. Do you have a
corkscrew?"

"Sorry, no corkscrew."

"Can you get me one fast? Can you find one?
I really need this second bottle of wine."

8.

The Grand Prix of Monte Carlo

Monday, 4:00 PM, May 7, 1970

I walked from the Monte Carlo train station into an entirely new world. Officially the administrative area of Monaco that is home to the Monte Carlo casino, Monte Carlo is an experience unto itself, oozing wealth and cosmopolitan upper-class excess. The world's most famous Formula One race, the Grand Prix of Monte Carlo, was running; I had come to a celestial circus for the very elite.

As usual, I needed to exchange money, Italian lire to French francs. And, as usual, once again I had arrived on a holiday; no banks were open. What was I doing there? Monaco is one of the richest countries in Europe, thus one of the most expensive.

Second, I arrived during the biggest event of the year, along with tons of other people from all over the world. And, I didn't have a hotel reservation. I didn't look forward to looking for one, either; one look at me and the desk clerk would be sure the hotel was full. All of this was sinking in and starting to concern me. It was one thing being on the road and being able to sleep in a pasture or woods, but Monaco had no pastures or woods, just five-star hotels.

I hadn't eaten since the morning; it was now after six. And I was worried, as all Road Knights worry in the late afternoon, about when the sun would go down and where I would sleep. The Grand Prix runs through the city streets in Monte Carlo, so many roads were blocked off, with no access for hitchhiking. I walked aimlessly through the streets, occasionally watching the cars doing their trial runs, hoping to have an angel fall out of the sky to tell me what to do next. Eventually, my wandering brought me to one of the beaches bordering the city. It was absolutely beautiful and almost empty.

I walked a while on the beach, the light beginning to fade, continuing to mull over my worsening predicament. My agonizing was suddenly interrupted by a voice behind me:

"Hey, hey you, come over here."

I looked around, didn't see anyone, then heard the call again. Finally, I saw someone sitting alone near the water. I walked up and found a young guy, more than half in the bag, holding up a bottle of wine.

"I need a corkscrew. Do you have a corkscrew?"

This guy looked different from most of the young people I had met. He had short hair, not common in those days of hippie-long hair, with a two-or-three-day stubble and a painful-looking sunburn on his face. He was dressed in blue-jean cut-offs and a light brown shirt, worn and military-looking.

"Sorry, no corkscrew."

"Can you get me one fast? Can you find one? I really need this second bottle of wine."

Given his slurred speech and half-closed eyes, I didn't think he "really" needed the second bottle at all. But he was American and had asked for my help, so I said, "Listen, I'm leaving my bedroll here with you. Watch it; don't go anywhere. Do you have a couple of francs? I just got in from Italy."

An hour later, after talking a bartender in a café into giving me a corkscrew, I was back on the beach, talking with my new friend as we drank that second bottle.

"I'm Paul, from Chicago. What's your name? What are you doing in Monte Carlo?"

Slowly, he said, "Captain, I'm Jacks. I'm with two other GIs down here to see the race."

It didn't take us long to finish the bottle, and I was increasingly aware that the afternoon was fast becoming evening. I told Jacks I needed to be going; I was in trouble because I didn't have a room for the night.

"Don't worry. Follow me; I've got your back," he mumbled, and motioned to me to follow him off the beach.

We seemed to walk in circles through the city streets, all the while serenaded by the roar of the Formula One engines making their practice runs. Jacks stopped along the way to buy two more bottles of wine and gave one to me. At any other time, two guys like us walking around the city drinking openly out of wine bottles would probably stop traffic. In Monaco before the Grand Prix, this apparently was the norm: we weren't the only ones drinking in public.

Monaco is one of the most glamorous places on earth, perfectly positioned between the Alps and the shimmering Mediterranean Sea, and it was in party mode. It is about half the size of New York's Central Park and one of the world's most densely populated countries, as well as the richest per capita. As we climbed up the small streets, we could see one of the city's yacht-laden harbors illuminated by the setting sun glowing overhead.

Suddenly, my guide took two quick turns, and we arrived at one of the race's gated pit areas. As we approached the guarded gate, Jacks pulled out a plastic pass, tied around his neck, from under his shirt. The guard waved us in, and within a minute we were walking amid Formula One race cars, mechanics and their drivers. I stopped to eavesdrop on a conversation between an Italian driver and a newspaper reporter when I lost track of Jacks.

I turned and found him talking to one of the drivers, who was trying to decline, in German, a drink from Jack's bottle of wine. As I took his arm to guide him away from the situation, I turned to my opposite side and recognized Jackie Stewart, the "Flying Scot," with his trademark long hair and impressive sideburns.

Stewart had won the Formula One World Championship the previous year and was a big-time European celebrity. I watched, with Jacks, while Stewart was interviewed and filmed by a local news station, amazed it was happening and that I was there. I don't know if Jacks and I made the 11 o'clock news that night in Monaco, but there was a good chance we were and I refuse to believe otherwise. We had to be in the picture.

It was getting dark as we left the pit area, and the lights of the city were beginning to glow in the night sky. I continued to follow the weaving Jacks, increasingly worried about my lack of a bed for the night. Like we had earlier, we walked in circles but, like earlier, we took a sudden turn and arrived at a big gravel-paved parking lot by the sea. It was filled to overflowing with cars, vans and trucks. We snaked through parked cars, row after row, until a six-foot-plus guy stood up from his folding chair and yelled for Jacks. He handed him a half-filled Coke, into which he poured a large amount of Seagram's.

"It's about time, Jacks. We were about to send out a search party," said a guy from behind a VW beetle. Then he spoke to me.

"Hi, I'm Reno, and that over there is The Greek . I see you already know Jacks."

Jacks explained, collapsing into another folding chair, "He saved my life. I was on the beach by the sidewalk without a corkscrew, and the fucker just pulled one out of thin air."

"Well, no, I didn't have one on me, but somehow I found one," I clarified unnecessarily. "I'm Paul."

"Where you from, Paul? Looks like you've been doing a good amount of traveling."

"The Chicago area. Yes, I've been around: Paris, Istanbul, Athens and Rome. I came over to work in Paris, but that didn't work out. I'm running out of money but will try and get to Spain before I get into some serious money problems."

"I don't know if Jacks told you or even, for that matter, could tell you, but we're G.I.s stationed in Stuttgart, Germany, down here for the race."

At that point, Jacks chimed in: "He's like us. I think he should stay with us; he's got no hotel."

"Sure, no problem. We just have a little space here laid out for our sleeping bags next to our VW; you're more than welcome to bunk here too," came from The Greek. With that, he handed me a sandwich with a big glass of Seagram's and Coke.

Our little spot in the parking lot was a magnet for other young guys and gals in the lot to congregate that night. The loud and infectious generosity and good humor of Jacks, Reno and The Greek drew our neighbors to the little campsite. The Coke and Seagram's probably helped, too.

We talked into the night, and in every conversation I learned something. People were eager to share their stories and ideas on how to be a successful traveler. Many hours and many drinks later, the group began to break up and stumble to their cars. I think I fell asleep sitting against a car tire. I remember staring at my sleeping bag, freezing, but too inebriated to attempt getting in.

Thunder woke me, and the rains came. It began to pour around 3:30 a.m. The guys frantically started to pick up their sleeping bags and get inside the car. I was trying to scrunch down inside my soaking wet bag when Jacks yelled, "Hey, Chicago, you coming in here also or what? You're one of the F Troop now, aren't you?"

He didn't have to ask twice. It was a VW bug, and two of the GIs had to be 6'4" or so, but we all squeezed in, soaking wet but glad to be protected from the rain and the lightning.

Friday morning started with more rain that eventually stopped, finally letting us escape the car. I mingled a little bit with our parking-lot neighbors, always ready to hear travel stories and tips. My wandering led to a fortuitous encounter with a couple of Swedish guys who had just come from Spain. They offered me some food and some interesting information that would change the course of my journey—and life.

I had heard about a Spanish island called Ibiza before, in conversations here and in Athens. It was supposed to be a wild place, with travelers coming from all over Europe to party; there was a rumor you could go to restaurants and choose various drugs from the menus. That kind of talk did nothing for me. My life had been chaotic and I was feeling miserable. Since the cold rain last night I couldn't seem to stop shivering. The thought of an island with a beach and sun was very appealing, but not a twenty-four-hour party island like Ibiza.

The guys saw my reluctance to get excited about Ibiza, so one of them mentioned Formentera, a small island below Ibiza in the southern Mediterranean. As they described it, Formentera sounded like exactly what I needed. The weather was the best in Europe, they said, sunny every day and in the 80s. The Mediterranean was warm, and if you ever wanted to escape from life, a sparsely populated island is where you could reinvent yourself.

They continued to talk, saying the island used to be a prison for witches in the Middle Ages. Even today there were weird things happening on that island, things that couldn't be explained. They weren't on Formentera very long, they said, but travelers were few and Americans did not travel there. It was a Spanish farming and fishing island, very quiet compared to Ibiza. Everyone traveled to Ibiza and drank or drugged themselves into stupors before going back to the mainland. Formentera was left to itself.

I decided to go island hopping. I would go to Ibiza first and take a look, knowing that if it didn't feel right I would be on to Formentera.

The next couple of days were spent dodging raindrops, watching practice runs from various locations overlooking the Grand Prix course, eventually drinking at night.

On Sunday, Jacks, Reno, The Greek and I tried to sneak onto race grounds for a better look but ended up watching from a hill overlooking one of the famous Grand Prix hairpin turns. Until almost the last lap it looked like Jack Brabham would win, but Jochen Rindt beat him in the end. Brabham had a problem on a late turn. I was, of course, rooting for Jackie Stewart, whom I considered to be a good friend by now. I should have offered a good luck handshake to the Formula One legend—he had needed either good luck or divine intervention. Jackie led for almost half the race, but ran into trouble and finished fifth or sixth.

As the race ended I lost contact with my GI buddies. We had gotten separated in the huge crowds moving up and down the narrow streets of Monaco. After searching for a couple of hours, I met two English guys who mentioned they were considering going to Spain from Monte Carlo. While we stopped for lunch, one of them suggested going to the Monte Carlo Casino. I suspected we had no chance to get in the way we were dressed, but decided *why not?* If a ride to Spain was on offer, I would stick with them.

While waiting for our check, I noticed a copy of the *International Herald Tribune* discarded on a chair. It had been too long since I had seen if Rip Kirby had found the Elysian Fields. Now that I was traveling alone, having a connection to someone, even a fictional someone, made me feel I had a traveling companion. I was with him, he was with me. Sort of child-like I suppose, but there was a reality to it, and I remembered, as always, two heads are better than one. Rip was still looking for those elusive fields, continuing to have as many twists and turns in his travels as I was having in mine. There were only about three panels in each strip, but once you got hooked, there was no going back, and it was hard to wait for the next day's reveal. "Go get 'em, Rip!"

Later that night, after a number of beers and swapped travel stories, we decided we were ready for the Monte Carlo Casino. I had read a newspaper article about the casino's architect, Charles

Garnier, who was also the architect of the Paris Opera House. The Paris Opera House was completed in 1875; five years later, Garnier put the finishing touches on the Monte Carlo Casino. I was hoping I would get to see Garnier's work inside the building.

As we approached the front door of the casino, there was a commotion to the left, not far from the Hotel de Paris, and a couple of the doormen moved over to help the hotel guards. We made our way stealthily into the casino, trying to look like we belonged there. As we entered the huge, ornately-decorated foyer with its large, brightly-lit chandeliers, I almost ran into a beautiful young woman—model or actress or princess? She turned and as our eyes met for a long split-second, I started to imagine a meaningful romantic connection. Unfortunately, she was imagining trouble and yelled something in my direction. It sounded Spanish, but her wide eyes were doing most of the talking.

By then my friends had seen some guards coming and taken off, but I had been distracted by my imagined romantic liaison. The guards came at me and I was grabbed with no questions asked; I guess my wardrobe said it all in a room full of men in tuxes and women in long gowns and expensive jewels. Two larger-than-normal gentlemen in tuxes escorted me, each holding one of my arms, mumbling in very unpleasant French, to the exit's double doors. With impressive ease, they picked me up, sliding and sidestepping through the casino doors, and threw me down the front steps. I landed in a heap next to the shiny red and white sports cars parked in front of the casino.

The fancy couples continued to enter the casino, scarcely looking at me; apparently intruders were thrown out of the casino on a regular basis. I looked back at the door, where a stern-looking doorman, dressed in a black and red uniform, stood at the top of the stairs. With a flick of his head, he made it clear: *move on, this place is not for you.*

Rick and Jim, my soon-to-be riding mates, came out from between some cars and helped me up. As we made our way down the casino's circular drive to a main street, I felt for broken bones as they laughed, reliving over and over again my graceful tumble down the casino stairs.

I spent that night in my sleeping bag in the parking lot with the GIs. On Monday morning Jacks, Reno and The Greek said goodbye and headed back to Germany and the real world. We made plans to meet again; they would come to Formentera next month and find me. They had traveled a lot while stationed in Germany but had not been to the Spanish islands, and what I had described made them interested in checking them out.

How lucky was I to meet those guys? We had such a great time in Monte Carlo watching the race, and rain aside, our night in the parking lot was one to remember. Without a doubt, this was a friendship that could last as long time. I hoped I'd see them next month in Spain, but if not I hoped our paths would cross again someday.

The parking lot was buzzing as people who had come for the race left for home. As the cars and vans drove off I sat down on the cement base of a light pole in the middle of the parking area. My future two riding partners had said they were parked somewhere in that area and I waited for them to spot me. But as I watched more and more cars leave, they were nowhere to be found. They had either forgotten about me overnight—not out of the realm of possibility considering the amount of liquor we had consumed—or had decided not to go to Spain after all.

I did not want to be left in Monaco with no ride out. As I

pondered my next move, a car stopped and a couple of Dutch guys asked if I wanted to go north. Unfortunately, no; I was going west. I told them I was going to Spain and an island off the coast called Formentera. Oddly enough, these guys had been there several years ago. They didn't like it, too quiet, but they did enjoy Ibiza. After talking a couple of minutes, one of the guys reached in the back seat and grabbed a beat-up paperback called *The Devil's Guard* and asked if I wanted a book to read. He had just finished it. He didn't wait for an answer, just tossed it to me, and yelled as the driver put the car in drive, "Remember, to find your island, go to Barcelona and turn left. Eventually, you'll find Formentera."

As I watched car after car going every direction except west, I opened the book. It was, at first glance, an adventure book. The narrator talked about a guy named Jimgrim: adventure was in his blood. I looked up from the page, hoping for some car headed west, and wished adventure would embrace me. My adventure had stalled. It appeared this trip would end before anything more happened to me.

A little about Jimgrim: he was born James Schuyler Grim, but was known as Jimgrim all over the Near East, Arabia, parts of Africa, and from Dera Isfail Khan to Sikkim. He had served in the Intelligence Departments of at least five nations, always reserving United States citizenship. He spoke a dozen languages so fluently that he could pass as a native; and since he was old enough to build a fire and skin a rabbit, a life of danger was his goal, just as most folks spend their lives looking for safety and comfort. When he was what other men would reckon to be safe, the sheer discomfort of it bored him. Copyright 1926.

Jimgrim became a traveling companion. As the day became hotter by the minute, so was my interest in Jimgrim heating up.

Four Months

Four months,
of feeling like a stray dog,

Four months,
of running out of money,
would this be my epilogue?

Four months,
of doing without,

Four months,
of no treasure to count,

Four months,
of a thousand days,

Four months,
of living in a million countless ways,

Four months,
of my life passed,

Four months,
of a dye that has been cast,

Four months,
of lonely dark deserted streets,

Four months,
of never ever finding that Golden Fleece.

Written May 10, while watching the tide ebb & flow during the Grand Prix of Monaco

What would he encounter in the coming pages, what would I?

Midafternoon, I struck gold. Wandering around the parking area, I found a couple of guys from Atlanta with a VW van. They were leaving Tuesday morning, going all the way to Barcelona. Jackpot! All I had to do was help pay for gas along the way.

Barcelona

It was then that I noticed the package James had left with me. I started to wonder what was inside.

Hmm!

Well, it didn't take me long to come to the conclusion...

Oh shit! Great! It's probably drugs!

That's all I need, getting caught with drugs in Franco's backyard.

And just then I see some Spanish policia walking in my direction.

9.

Setting Sail

Tuesday 11:50 PM, May 12, 1970

It was not that far from Monte Carlo to Barcelona, but Sam and Chuck, the two guys who picked me up, wanted to stop everywhere, get out of the car, and look at everything. I liked to explore new places, too, but every small town we passed through didn't have the allure that these two tourists imagined it might. We traveled only 504 kilometers, about 313 miles, and averaging 60 mph, we should have arrived around mid-afternoon, in daylight. Instead, we got in about 12 midnight to a quiet, dark, and tightly shut-down area of Barcelona.

Our prospects of finding a pension or hotel room looked bleak. We didn't have any Spanish pesetas; all of us were still carrying French francs. Spaniards did not like French francs, a fact that had been made clear to us on our drive from Monte Carlo.

We roamed the dark streets of Barcelona for an hour, looking for a hotel that had been recommended to Sam and Chuck. Sam had been following some sketchy directions, and we finally paused on a quiet, dimly lit street. We started walking again, and after three or four more turns, we arrived at a large hotel.

"Here we are, guys," announced Chuck.

The hotel looked expensive and unfortunately, it was. After talking with the half-asleep desk clerk, I confirmed it was too pricey for me, so I thanked Sam and Chuck for the ride and returned to wandering the lonely Barcelona streets.

It was now about 2 a.m., and as I walked alone down the dark, quiet streets, a choking mist began to envelop me. It was harder and harder to navigate the unfamiliar city, and my exhaustion, hunger, and lack of even basic sleeping quarters made me want to scream with despair.

I turned a corner, and as I looked over my shoulder at a real or imagined someone following me, I stumbled over a guy sitting on the curb. A fast pirouette saved both of us from a crash and burn, and before I could berate him for his seating choice, he introduced himself. He was an American, from Pittsburgh. The building behind us was a pension, but he did not have enough money to get a bed for the night. He anxiously asked how much money I had and begged to share a room. Ordinarily, if someone I'd nearly tripped over on a dark street in the middle of the night asked me how much money I had, I'd keep on moving. But it was late, this guy had done the research, and this pension had a bed waiting for me. I told him I didn't have any pesetas, but he thought they would take francs.

Twenty minutes later I was in a small room on the third floor of a way-past-its-prime pension, exhausted and trying to ignore my roommate as he told me the sad history of his day. The poor guy had no money because he had lost his wallet and was going tomorrow to the American Embassy to get help. He was still muttering to himself as I drifted off.

Up and showered by 9 a.m., I began to walk down the Ramblas, a main pedestrian boulevard that runs through central Barcelona from the harbor north to different parts of the city. The busy street was lined with shops, cafés, bars, restaurants, hotels, art galleries, and fruit and flower stands. There were street performers of every kind, and even at that hour it was noisy and full of people. I found a bank and exchanged my money, and grabbed a pastry and a coffee at a bakery close by.

The lyrics of the old Otis Redding song echoed through my head as I made my way down to the Port of Barcelona to sit and contemplate my options. "I'm sittin' on the dock of the bay..." Barcelona was a huge, bustling city with people filling every sidewalk. Cars were bumper to bumper, and the noise was like a three-ring circus. I searched in vain for anything that looked like a ticket office or any kind of place to ask for help. So, I sat down on the edge of the water, my feet hanging down over a retaining wall above some splashing waves, and watched "the tide roll away... wastin' time..."

Behind me, towering over the port area, was the huge, historic Christopher Columbus statue; in front of me, the Mediterranean was endlessly waving in and out—mostly out as the tide headed east to where I had recently come from. I must admit, even though it was a sunny morning and the gulls seemed to be mid-air dancing to some hidden beat, I had no idea what to do next, where to go, or even whom to ask for advice. I had lucked out last night and found an affordable and safe place to sleep, and I had no idea what would happen today or tonight. My destination was Formentera, but I didn't know where to find a boat, when that boat might leave, or if I could even afford a ticket.

As I looked in every direction from my perch on the seawall with my legs dangling over the swirling sea, no direction seemed logical... no small or large passenger ships of any kind were in sight. And as despair and concern started to invade my mind, it appeared it was time, as per my predicament, to pull out a Marlboro and light up. That first inhale usually made me pause and step back from sinking too far and too fast into worry.

From behind me came a voice: "Hey, mon, you have some more of those?" Before I could turn to see who had spoken, two big, tall guys, both with hair to the middle of their backs, sat down on either side of me, bookending me fairly tightly as their outstretched hands demanded the cigarettes. Uncomfortable, to say the least, I didn't feel I had much choice. I took my pack out and flicked my wrist to advance two Marlboros. They were snapped up quickly and lit as quickly, and all three of us simultaneously took large drags, holding the smoke in our lungs a little longer than usual and then letting it out with a rush in concert with each other.

It seemed longer than a couple of minutes that we all sat there in silence, but I had a million thoughts racing through my mind. I was wary of these two characters and unsure of their intentions. Each of them was bigger than I was; fighting didn't seem to be an option. They were blocking my escape to the right and left, but I considered that I could backflip out of my sitting position, land on my feet, and get away... yeah, that would be easy, sure. That left pushing off the stone ledge and falling twenty feet to the pulsating Mediterranean Sea, leaving them my bedroll and all my clothes. While that would undoubtedly make a memorable and dramatic exit, it just didn't seem it was my time to swim with the fishes. Just as that thought passed through my mind, one of the guys put his arm around my shoulder and grabbed hold with an unusually strong grip.

The other asked, "Mon, what's your name? Are you American or English?"

Hesitantly, I responded, "I'm Paul, and I'm from Chicago."

The one with his arm around my shoulder responded in a slight German or Scandinavian accent, "I'm James, and this other guy is Gregory." At that point, Gregory asked, "Wow, Chicago, a long way from home. Why are you here in Barcelona? You look like you've really been traveling."

His friendly tone relaxed me. "Yeah, I have been traveling—Paris, Istanbul, Athens, Rome. Now I would like to find a way to the islands, ultimately Formentera."

"Ah, yes, Formentera, very out there, mon, the wild island. Very rough, very isolated. We know Formentera; we live on Ibiza. We are going home tonight on the boat. Do you go tonight also?"

"Yes, I want to. I don't have a ticket yet though."

"We go to get our tickets now. Do you want us to buy you a ticket?"

"Oh no, I can come with you. I can buy my own ticket."

"Mon, actually, we have this package," and motioned to a notebook-sized parcel wrapped in brown paper lying behind him. "James is too tired to keep carrying it around, and besides, he wants to buy some food to eat as he's walking. Can we leave it with you, and we'll get your ticket? We are going to get a second-class cabin; you can buck with us." I was puzzled for a moment, then realized they were inviting me to *bunk* with them.

"Really, are you sure? Isn't that a hassle for you?" I said, dubiously considering the prospect of handing my money over to them.

"Nein, no problem. The boat leaves tonight at 11:00 p.m., and we heard about this party later near the beach. We can all go and get something to eat. Just give us a hundred pesetas, and if there is any left, we'll give some back to you. I think the boat lands in Ibiza later tomorrow afternoon sometime."

I hardly knew these guys, but somehow, the vibe had changed, and anyway, I needed to think positively. Hadn't I just been wondering how to get a ticket? I gave them the money. They took off and said they'd be back soon.

Now the Spanish sun was starting to climb, and I could tell that it was not a regular European sun. This sun was the real deal; it was lasting, and it was hot. The waterfront presented nowhere to move to; the nearest shady spots were a football field or two away, and all of them were crowded. Anyway, I couldn't move until the guys returned. I had no choice but to stick it out and bake.

The heat soon became sweltering. I tried to take cover under my corduroy sports coat, but that made it even worse. I stretched and flung my arms up in the air just to get some blood moving when my eyes fell on the package James had left with me. My mind started to race. It didn't help that I'd caught a news clip on TV the previous night about Spain's ruthless dictator, Franco, and his current crackdown on the riffraff from other parts of Europe. While I couldn't understand the voiceover, I was sure that the Spanish commentary included a message of drugs being brought into Spain by these wicked undesirables. *Oh shit! It's probably drugs! Am I babysitting a box of hashish, marijuana, cocaine, worse? That's all*

I need, getting caught with drugs in Franco's backyard. And just then I saw a trio of Spanish *policia* in their green uniforms walking in my direction. Yeah, they were definitely headed for me. They'd surround me. Question me. "What's in the package, hippie?"

"I don't know; it's not mine," I'd say—like they'd believe that. Fortunately, they stopped and turned back to the Ramblas and headed away.

Even so, I scooted away from the package. I looked around to see if there were any more *policia* close by and if they were watching me. The next hour or two passed quickly as the package and I stared at each other. The sun continued to cook me.

James and Gregory finally returned with baguette sandwiches and some drinks.

"Paul, let's go over and sit at that café. It's still siesta time and no one will bother us."

As we made our way to some seating near the Columbus statue, James said, "We would look over at you from time to time, Paul, and it seemed like you were talking to the package, and don't laugh at me, but Gregory thought you looked mad at the package after talking with it."

"No, no—no problem, I'm just not used to the sun here in Spain. I was just fidgety."

"Well, I'm glad you watched it so well; there's very important merchandise inside."

That comment only increased my suspicion that the package contained substances that we did not want to get caught with, and I continued to keep an eye out for any Guardia Seville. Still, all told, I was feeling much more comfortable with James and Gregory and how my situation in Barcelona had apparently changed for the better.

Though both spoke only a little English with heavy German accents, we talked and told each other about our lives and why we were there. They said they'd been living on Ibiza for ten years, so long that I could tell they spoke Spanish almost as well as they spoke German. They had their own company on Ibiza, though I never found out what they did. We mostly talked about our taste in popular music. They had met several artists, and they had even once had drinks with Bob Dylan in a bar in Santa Eulalia, a town north of the city of Ibiza. Matter of fact, they said he lived on Formentera for a while—in a deserted windmill! They even looked like rock stars, only better. Actually, these guys could be models on any runway in Paris. Most of the women passing by were tripping over themselves staring at these two.

After an hour or so, a couple of the café waiters shooed us out since we weren't buying anything. James suggested we look at some shops on the Ramblas while Gregory found out where the party was going to be that night.

James recommended that I buy some Spanish peasant work shirts to get ready for the heat. Holding one or two of them, sort of thinking out loud while looking at me, he said, "Ja, das sollten Sie Schon—how do you say—buy today, ya, I think," shaking his head up and down. I had packed for my trip during a Chicago winter with a destination of Paris, so my wardrobe wasn't at all suitable for Spain. The shirts were a little pricey, but I took his advice.

As we continued to walk around, he mused about his feeling that life was changing. He and Gregory had moved to the islands for a certain type of life, a life that was calm and peaceful. And it still was, but he continued to mumble something about the future. These islands would change. People, many people, new people, would pressure the islands to change, and it sounded like that change would be not what they were looking for.

As best as I could understand, he and Gregory had traveled to most of the seven continents. I think he said they were in a foreign movie or two in the last three to five years. They had an air of mystery. Who were they? What kind of company did they have, and why were they taking me into their little group?

As I continued to wonder about their intent, I couldn't help but think about—and please indulge me for a second—the story of Pinocchio. Were these guys doppelgangers of Honest John, the fox, and Gideon, the cat? And more importantly, was I the innocent 1970 version of Pinocchio? It didn't take them long to part me from some of my gold as the fox and cat did with Pinocchio. Pinocchio was hustled into thinking if he gave the fox and cat some of his gold coins, they would plant them in a place they knew where trees would grow not with ordinary leaves but with leaves made of gold coins. To do that they had to dissuade Pinocchio from going to school and convince him instead follow them. Well, Gregory and James had earlier convinced me to give them money for boat tickets. They said they had bought me a ticket, but I wouldn't find out until later tonight when I would —or would not —board the ship. And with all this talk of going to Ibiza and staying on Ibiza with them instead of going to Formentera, I wondered if Ibiza was the theater in the story of Pinocchio—the easy road to success as they positioned it, compared to Formentera, which was the school for Pinocchio and me? Was there a con going on with me, or were they truly nice guys going out of their way to help a guy along the side of the road? Either way, I would find out shortly.

As the sun was setting, we made our way to the party. The

entire scene looked surreal, as it was being held on the construction site of a half-built condo. I'd say there were fifty to seventy-five young men and women from almost as many countries eating, drinking, laughing, telling stories, and smoking many different types of cigarettes. Not that I would pretend to be an expert on hazy, free-floating, nostril-stimulating smoke, but as we walked around, I could identify marijuana, hashish, and maybe even opium. This new world I'd gotten myself into was starting to feel like some of the Jefferson Airplane's song "White Rabbit." Was I entering Alice's Wonderland… was Alice here, and was she big or small?

The food was great. It was a hodgepodge of many different things. People just brought what they could get their hands on. Others brought beer, liquor or juice, and soft drinks. Some other very popular men and women brought drugs. I saw a lot being given away for free, but I also saw a good amount of selling—different pills and other things wrapped in small packages.

We stopped by a group of people sitting on some paint and oil buckets and grabbed some sandwiches and beers.

"Enchantè, je m'appelle Julien. Your name and from where guys are you from?" came the broken English from a young-looking Frenchman with long frizzy hair, dressed in a beat-up vest of indeterminate colors and torn blue jeans, lying next to a long-haired girl wearing the same vest with a long skirt.

Gregory responded quickly, "I'm Gregory, and this is my friend James. We are from Munich. We now live in Ibiza. This is Chicago, and he's from the States. He's been a traveler. I think he's looking for something; he just doesn't know what it is yet. We want to show him Ibiza, but I think he wants to be more lost, so lost that then, and only then, he is thinking, he will find his mysterious something."

"Ah, Ibiza, the island of pleasure; I want to go there someday myself. This beautiful, wild woman is Michelle, who is going to be the world's great new singer. We are on our way to Morocco and then maybe to…to…ah, merde, to do a bar…so I can run a bar…you know…ah."

I chimed in, "Do you mean Casablanca? You want to have a café like Rick's?"

"Oui, ah merci, bon, merci, Chicago. Yes, like Rick's… and Michelle will sing in our bar. I like you, Chicago, we think the same way," he said as he pulled out a large hashish joint, lit it, took a big drag, and handed it to me.

As the night went on, the loudness and rowdiness increased, so much so that the Guardia Seville came screeching in and started walking through the crowds of the various multi-European and Near Eastern young men and women. It was like magic the way any indication of drugs vanished immediately on their arrival. At the same time, I lost sight of James and Gregory. Again, my mind started to wonder. Did they need to hide from *la policia?* Were they wanted? Even though I had only met them that morning, they were my friends. If they needed to hide, so be it, though it would be nice if I could find out more about them before I was maybe tabbed as an accomplice—or worse, part of their gang.

About an hour later, *la policia* had left—but not empty-handed. I saw all four officers with their arms full of food and even some wine. The revelers now seemed relaxed and mellow, especially the ones carrying bottles of wine or those who were full of one narcotic or another. I spotted a Swede who was sitting on a woodpile and talking with a skinny brown and white cat. I wasn't sure what they were conferring about, but it appeared to be a two-way conversation. He was obviously on a drug trip of some kind, and the cat pretended to understand his rambling gestures—and was more than likely biding its time until the contents of his woozy companion's plate of food wound up on the ground.

Eventually, Gregory and James appeared. "Paul, there you are. We thought we lost you." After a night of partying, we made our way to the boat. They informed me that they couldn't get a second-class cabin for us; we had to settle for fourth-class accommodations, whatever that was. They didn't seem to care. James said we'd be OK; he'd take care of it.

As we were making our way around the boat to where we were to sleep, the guys seemed to be unusually interested in everything we passed, especially what looked like top-of-the-line cabins on one of the first-class decks. I had the feeling that they were up to something. I'm not saying it was bad; they just generated that feeling as I watched them.

I left my bedroll tucked under one of the bunk beds in the fourth-class section, and we made our way topside. There were about thirty-five young people crowded together on deck. A couple had guitars and were singing as the ship made its way into the dark of the Mediterranean towards the next part of my adventure, the mysterious islands of Spain, the Balearic Islands.

An hour or two passed easily sitting and listening to the music and envisioning what the future might bring. Again James and Gregory had disappeared, but it didn't matter. It also didn't matter that I was almost out of cigarettes, because Marlboros were available at duty-free prices. Things were looking up.

The ship was much bigger than the one I took from Patras to Brindisi—maybe two to three times bigger with at least two to three more decks. There were many regular Europeans onboard, and it was apparent that the powers that be wanted to keep me and any of the other "travelers" away from the regular passengers. Our fourth-class area was in the bowels of the ship. I don't even remember if there was a window down there. The group of travelers I had been watching was cordoned off away from the regular walkways on the ship. It didn't matter; we had the wind in our faces, and everyone was just ignoring us.

James appeared from behind and said, "Let's turn in; we've got your bed roll."

"My bed roll?" I said. "Why did you take it—was someone looking through it?"

"Nein, nein, we have a surprise for you. Come, let's go."

We walked for a ways until we reached a set of stairs that led up this time rather than down.

"Here we are Chicago, our new home," Gregory said as he pulled out a key to open the door to a beautiful suite with floor-to-ceiling windows looking out onto the water. Not only did we have new accommodations, but we had some food and drinks in a minibar.

I turned to them and started to ask, "But how—how did you guys get us in here?" Before I could finish my thought, James said it was time to turn in; I was going to have a big new day tomorrow.

"Es ist OK. Don't worry, Chicago, let's sleep," he said.

I was too tired to dig for whatever shenanigans lay behind the securing of these much-improved quarters. Tomorrow would be a new day and hold another adventure, I thought, as I drifted off looking at the millions of stars above as we glided over the Mediterranean.

Ibiza

As we pulled closer to the dock,
I was starting to get a curious feeling.

I have to say that my first impression was
it looked like a circus, the circus of Ibiza.

It was something that looked like
it could only have sprung from the mind
of a writer on an acid trip.

10.

The Dragons
Have Been Blessed

Thursday, 3:30 PM, May 14, 1970

The sun on my face seemed even hotter than it had in Barcelona. I stood leaning on the railing on an upper deck as our ship turned towards the dock and entered Ibiza Harbor. Soon, I would step foot on my second foreign island. And as I had heard multiple times on this voyage, it was an island like no other, an island with quite a history. As a matter of fact, in the year 1500, Nostradamus predicted only Ibiza would survive the apocalypse.

Gregory disagreed with that observation. He said, "The way life on this island is going, Ibiza is the apocalypse, or at least it will grow to be that in the future." Even though my companions would be classified as hippies, they didn't feel a connection to the many longhairs and travelers coming to Ibiza or to those using Ibiza as a pit stop on the way to India and beyond. It's true that we had a significant language barrier, but even beyond that our conversations were odd sometimes, and their look was unusual, and they seemed, the more I knew of them, oddly sophisticated. They were young but several years older than I was, and more experienced. They had been models and had even acted in a film or two. They had an air of confidence and worldliness that transcended the typical aimless, drug-addled hippie of the 1970s.

Ibiza, as the crow flies, is fifty-seven miles from the coast of Spain. Ibiza was first occupied in 654 B.C and for years was ruled by the Carthaginians. For centuries, it was a quiet trading post connecting parts of Europe. In 123 B.C., the Romans conquered all the Balearic Islands. Then the Arabs conquered Ibiza in the 9th century A.D. After that, in 1235, the Catalans controlled it, and their language became the dominant one in the islands. When Franco seized power in 1939, he abolished the Catalan language. Although Ibiza was a bohemian destination throughout the 1940s and '50s, the true counterculture movement started in the late '60s, with many artists and writers relocating to the island. The '60s and '70s saw numerous conflicts between Franco and the hippies who continued to aggressively colonize and establish significant creative roots there. From time to time over the years, Franco had tried to rid the islands of any and all hippies, especially those who weren't Spanish.

As we pulled closer to the dock, my first impression was that it looked like a circus, the Circus of Ibiza. It was something that could only have sprung from the mind of a writer on an acid trip—and that was the feeling I had just from taking in the port area.

We had sailed a little north at first, stopping earlier in the day to let some travelers disembark at the port of Palma on Mallorca. That was a normal, everyday port, with normal people scurrying around in a normal manner. Ibiza looked far from normal.

"Paul, it's time to make our way to where we leave the ship. James and I are finally home," Gregory related as he put his arm around my shoulders and guided us to the disembarkation area.

The bird's eye view from the hulking ship was startling, but it could not compare to the sensations that visited me on the ground: Experiencing the port area on foot with its sounds, smells, the many foreign tongues and accents, and the pounding music of a distant rock beat all put a more definitive exclamation mark on this new world of mine. It seemed somehow more foreign than any of the other countries and cities I'd recently traveled through. It appeared to be a land comprised only of young people. The vibe was exotic, strange, like another planet altogether. I wondered if I knew the language.

As we proceeded into the city, we met Peter, a friend to James and Gregory. Peter was also German and unfortunately for me knew less English than his friends. Coincidently, Peter said he had to go to Formentera that day. We all sat down at an outdoor café table, ordered four beers, and sat back to watch the colorful, noisy, otherworldly procession of life pass in front of us. Eventually, Gregory and James got up to bid goodbye to Peter. James had not let go of that package for the last two days, and for the last two days, I had been wondering what in the world could be inside.

As they turned to me, James said, "Paul, Gregory and I have decided we want you to come with us, to where we live on the other side of the island. We have grown fond of you. There will be some good surprises for you there. We have very nice haus; you could help us. Come… we must go now."

Well, that hit me like a ton of bricks. I liked these guys, and they certainly seemed to cause a stir wherever they went, but I wasn't looking for adventure right now. I needed to lie on the beach and just soak up the sun. There were too many mysteries around them, too many unknowns, and with this journey I was at capacity on that front.

"James, Gregory: I have to go to Formentera. I need to escape the world and disappear. I would like to see your home, but not now. Please understand, and thank you for the offer." They wrote down their address in San Antonio, directly northwest from this port through the middle of Ibiza to the other coast. I told them that after I rested, I would find them. I still wonder to this day what would have happened if I had gone with them.

They were disappointed; they really wanted me to join them. James' parting words to me raised more questions than they answered: "Paul, be, how you say… watchful, maybe, on Formentera. It is very different than Ibiza or most anywhere else. There are things… things that happen there. There are people there and well yes, I think so… there be dragons there. Stay alert, *mon*, they want things and sometimes the witches…geben…how you say…geben und nehmen…I think you say…give and take."

"Adios, Paul. Until later, Chicago," they both yelled as their backs turned and they disappeared into the crowd.

Peter motioned for me to follow him. We walked to the next pier down from where the ship had docked where many smaller boats were tucked in for the night. The sun had begun to set. Peter approached one of the fishermen and was quite animated in his movements as they sparred with each other in Spanish about ferrying us over to Formentera. The elderly fisherman's exaggerated facial expressions were comical; it seemed like he had had a tougher day than normal, and the last thing he needed was two longhairs trying to talk him into an evening ride to Formentera. My two years of high-school Spanish, unfortunately did not stand me in good stead on this visit; the accents and different dialects and the speed with which the people spoke were way beyond me. I realized I'd have to roll up my sleeves and learn as much of the language as I could in a short amount of time if I was going to survive by myself on an isolated Spanish island in the middle of the Mediterranean.

Eventually, Peter held out a 500-peseta bill and motioned for me also to hand one over. At about seventy pesetas to the dollar, Peter had negotiated a five-dollar trip on a fishing boat to Formentera for both of us. From what I could understand, the boat would take us in three hours or so, and it was our only choice; the twice-daily ferry was done for the day. So, we headed back to the café and ordered more beers.

As I sat there staring at the crowds ebbing and flowing, I was really starting to feel the absence of the English language. I was in it now, and Ibiza was a cake walk compared to what was coming. Formentera would be off the grid and a real test of how to exist on an isolated island where English speakers would be few and far between.

As we returned to the fishing boat at the allotted time, we encountered a number of other foreign travelers who weren't willing to wait for tomorrow's ferry. We all boarded, and I soon discovered that a commercial fishing boat is not designed to be a passenger vessel. There was no normal seating at all—it was every man for himself. As best as I could understand, it was going to be an hour to an hour and a half journeying to the distant island of Formentera. I had heard the sun in this part of the world sets very late in the day, and we'd need all the daylight we could get. I located a wooden box to use as a makeshift seat.

The sea was more than a little agitated that evening. The waves were choppy, and as we made our way into the open water, they grew and splashed onto the deck. The boat rolled left and right, so much so that I and everyone else was wide-eyed and trying to hold on to something for fear of being thrown over the side. It was clear that our captain was no hero; he was going to be home for dinner regardless of who did or didn't make it to our destination. After half an hour, my death grip on the side of the boat was starting to numb parts of my wrists and fingers, and the rocking was so severe that the back of my neck skimmed the water.

When we spotted land, the island looked for all the world like a rock, and I worried that the alleged isolated hideaway was, in fact, a barren wasteland in the middle of the sea. As I was killing time at the café in Ibiza, I found a short blurb in an English paper about a couple of European movie stars who were recently seen on Formentera. At this moment, I found that hard to believe. I hoped that there would prove more to this rugged, windswept, hostile-looking rock than there appeared to be. What I'd seen so far was a rugged, windswept, hostile-looking rock with what appeared to be hundred to two-hundred-foot cliffs on the eastern side of the island leading up to the island's mountainous point. The newspaper article said that Formentera was about a hundred miles square and eleven miles long.

At last, we landed at a completely uninhabited, isolated dock. We thought it logical to ask our captain where the city and the people were. He said something in Spanish that I imagined would roughly translate to, "You stupid, far-out-looking, long-haired gringos, the town is north of here, and I hope you all fall into a big hole with vicious alligators while walking to the town tonight," topped off with what sounded like a number of colorful Spanish swear words.

After finally collapsing on firm dirt, we pulled out cigarettes while trying to get our stomachs and our sea legs back to normal. Through a cloud of smoke, we watched the huge orange ball of a distant sun sink on the horizon before us. After a rest, we decided to walk in the direction that Peter thought would lead us to the town of San Francisco. We walked and walked as the darkness got darker, surrounding us. There was no moon, no lights from any houses or towns in our vicinity, and we could barely see three feet in front of us. To add insult to injury, flying, screeching creatures whizzed by us at intervals. There was nothing to do but press on.

Stefan, who appeared to be Dutch, was the first to say, "That's it. I can't carry this backpack another step while walking blindly in the dark." Lukas, the German, agreed and pointed to a hill to our left that seemed a likely place to lay out our sleeping bags for the night.

We collapsed. A couple of guys had some leftover chocolate they had carried with them on the ship from Barcelona the day before that ended up being our late-night supper.

Stefan, twenty to twenty-five years old, made us laugh as we tried to forget our tired legs and sore feet. His English was very good as he had already traveled extensively, hitchhiking throughout much of the world including through a large part of the United States. He loved traveling and was also looking for a rest spot to regroup before his next plan to head south to Morocco. There was an instant and positive connection between us. I think the other two guys were from Switzerland; it appeared their native language was French. I remember one of them trying to tell me he had come here looking for a friend of theirs, some guy from Paris who lived in a famous windmill on Formentera. I don't know why a windmill would be famous, but who's to say? At each turn, this island was proving to be a surprise.

It appeared I was the last to fall asleep, as the snoring from the others sounded like terrible instruments in a concert that would not end. At least the noise should keep those mysterious flying things or even dragons away, I hoped.

As I lay there watching a couple of shooting stars dart across the sky, I wondered what tomorrow would bring. What was the island like? How would living here be different from the mainland? Was rest and recharging to be found here? Who would I meet, and would I like the people here? Would I be able to communicate with them?

As of that day, I had been on the road for about five and a half weeks. It seemed like five and a half months. I'd traveled halfway around the world; Spain was the twelfth or thirteenth country I'd been to. I had no idea of how many miles I'd traveled, but this I was sure of: I would be on Formentera for a while. I hoped the island would accept me and that we'd be compatible.

Those were the last thoughts I can remember before finally drifting off to sleep and into dreams. Sometimes, not often, but sometimes, dreams can seem very real. Sometimes you can almost smell different odors in a dream; you can feel actual touches in a dream, and sometimes you can even hear so clearly that you would think you're actually hearing sounds. Still half asleep and trying to understand the dream I was in, I had an urge to scratch my face. In the dream, something was creating this itch. With my eyes still closed, as I scratched the back of my head, I felt something more.

Then it was my nostrils being stimulated—and not in a good way. The odor was strong, almost not of this world. Then I remember, I was warned—watch out for the dragons. I did not want to be dinner tonight for any dragons. I was hesitant to even open my eyes. What does a dragon, a real dragon, look like? I remembered an intaglio print drawing I did my senior year in college, at the eleventh hour before my grade, that I titled "The Dragons Have Been Blessed." Was that an omen? No, it couldn't be. This thought process was all happening faster than the speed of light, but my mind was flashing red now and saying open your eyes immediately. It was now or never... what the fuck was happening?

I quickly sat up, startled, to find an animal almost on top of me. Again: "What the fuck?" It was dark, very dark, but the strange sounds that were coming from next to me and behind me and to the left of me baffled me. I finally realized we were being attacked by goats or sheep or both.

Almost as soon as I sat up, so did Stefan some five feet away, and then one by one, the others. I guess we weren't being attacked. This herd of goats and sheep were just grazing and slowly moving within their pasture. Though it was hard to make out all of them, I guess we were engulfed by twenty or thirty as they walked and grazed between us and hardly seemed to care if we were there or not. I believe we all slept with one eye open for the rest of the night.

Formentera

There were things I knew I'd never be able to talk about...because no one would believe me. And if they did, they wouldn't be able to understand.

"I knew my life would never ever be the same again..."

11.

Formentera

Friday, 7:00 AM, May 15, 1970

At first light, we exited our cocoons, trying to collect ourselves as we wiped the moist dew from our sleeping bags. We rolled them up and continued walking toward one of Formentera's largest towns, San Fernando, where Stefan said we would find one of the world's most renowned hippie travel oases, Fonda Pepes.

That this island could contain anything at all that was world renowned seemed unlikely to me. After walking for untold hours, we had passed nothing but rock-strewn fields and forests with unfamiliar vegetation. The more I saw of Formentera, the more I wondered why anyone would choose to be here; imprisonment seemed the only legitimate reason to stay.

As we walked over a hill, a town appeared, and the sun finally came out, torching and blazing aggressively and replacing the morning's cloudy coolness. San Fernando looked small and lonely as we cautiously approached from the west. The others, needing immediate sustenance, raced into Fonda Pepes, which looked like any other place you might pass on your travels when driving through a small, unknown town, a place you would never want to stop at if it weren't an emergency.

I stopped outside on the deserted, rocky dirt road to consider what I was doing here. Every street of this small town I had thus far encountered looked exactly the same, and the town appeared uninhabited. The buildings were whitewashed, plain, nondescript. Again, I felt the presence of Clint Eastwood in *A Fistful of Dollars* as "The Man With No Name," riding into that epitome of a small, poor Mexican town. I swear I could also faintly hear that movie's haunting music, the driving staccato beat and that whistling sound and rhythmic accompaniment. I could almost feel an invisible cowboy hat on top of my head; I subconsciously pushed it back a little to scratch my head as I wondered what was next.

Fonda Pepes had some tables and chairs inside, a bar, a billiard table, and a glass case or two offering a variety of food items. Many pictures, framed and unframed, hung from the walls with no rhyme or reason regarding content that I could discern. As I sat down, an older-looking Australian hippie who seemed to talk in his own cobbled-together language told me this place, this bar, this restaurant was the best Formentera had to offer. A little Aussie, a little Spanish, and I think a little Thai got mixed together as he talked. Obviously, this was the result of having visited too many countries, having met too many people, and, for sure, having taken too many drugs. While my travel mates from the night before were eating plates of steaming, odd-looking food, I finished a soft drink and a large cookie with dates and nuts interspersed throughout.

"My Girl" by the Temptations mysteriously started to waft from somewhere behind the bar, but I wasn't feeling the vibe, so I abandoned Fonda Pepes and started down one of the streets. As I turned a corner, I ran into Lukas carrying a couple of bottles of beer.

"Come on, Chicago, let's do some exploring." We walked a ways and climbed a hill, leaving the town behind us and looked out over the edge of a cliff to the rolling sea below. Lukas handed me one of the beers, and we sat in silence for a long while. Finally he asked me, "What's your story, man? Where have you been and what are you doing here?"

Before I could answer, he took a pack of German cigarettes out of his shirt pocket and offered me one. The taste was different. I seem to remember it was a pack of German Kim's. He said it was his last pack and indicated we'd both have to start smoking some wicked-looking Spanish cigarettes if we were going to stay on the island.

As I took a couple of quick drags, I thought how funny it was that someone on my travels was again asking, "What is your story?"

After an hour or two of good conversation, we headed back into town and decided along with a few others to seek out the town of El Pilar in the hopes that something interesting might be happening there. El Pilar was on the mountain of La Mola, to the southeast, a little town on the highest point of the island. We caught the 5:00 p.m. bus—the island apparently had one bus and one driver who started at one end of the island, stopped a few times, and then turned back the other way at the end of the day.

A French guy seated behind me on the bus was telling a Norwegian traveler about the mysteries of Formentera, specifically the witches of the island. They continued discussing the history of Formentera and the fact that during the Dark Ages, the island was established as a prison for witches from all over Europe. The French guy said he remembered reading about it in school when he studied the Middle Ages. It still seemed to me outlandish—like talking seriously about the Loch Ness Monster and UFOs—but I was beginning to wonder if it might be more than just folklore.

The bus seemed to need as many gears as it could find to make it up the mountain at the end of the island. Thankfully, the road zigzagged back and forth on the way up. I'm not sure it would have made it all the way if the road had been straight. As we progressed higher and higher, the scenery out of the window never changed: pine trees and normal forest vegetation, nothing very interesting.

Finally, we reached a plateau with some small farms and a few small adobe homes here and there dotting the landscape. We stopped in a small-town square that boasted a couple of buildings and a small church. So, this was El Pilar. On first impression, this was even more uninhabited and bleak than San Fernando and Fonda Pepe's bar.

As I jumped from the stairs of the bus, I noticed the bus driver mumbling to himself, agitated that he had to climb up to get some boxes and other things that were positioned on a rack on top of the bus. I made a mental note: travel light on this bus; the bus driver doesn't like to be climbing around and moving things up and down. Just as I thought that, he turned his head and looked at me. I imagined what was in his mind: don't even think about giving me anything to transport unless you can carry it yourself.

I descended the bus's stairs and found myself standing in front of what appeared to be a restaurant café. The structure had a covered roof but was open on all sides and had outdoor seating that was bordered by a three-or four-foot stone wall. I felt that I had come to the end of the earth. I couldn't tell if this was exactly what I was searching for, but as the sun set behind me, I began to feel that something might happen here, that this might be my place to be lost, to find who I really was, to discover my story.

As I was trying to get my bearings, turning little by little in a circle, Lukas appeared. He said that he and the guys had found out there was no place to stay on La Mola that offered a roof over our heads, so they had decided to make their way to the forest to find a place to camp.

Just as I was about to follow them, a flash of light caught my eye. A door opened on the second floor of a building across the square, and a woman emerged and stopped for a moment at the top of the outer stairway that led down to a small courtyard. The light from inside the doorway caught her figure in such a way as to stop me in my tracks.

There are moments in life when there is an electricity in the air. Time stops, and it feels as though the universe has singled you out for something big. This was unmistakably one of those moments.

Lukas turned and asked if I was coming with them.

"No, I think I better stay and maybe get something to eat at the café," I said. As they continued to walk down the road, I turned to look across the street, up the stairs to the doorway. Now there was no light, no open door, just darkness. And I started to wonder. *Was that previous sighting of that woman a mirage? Had she really been there?*

I walked over to a crumbling roadside wall to sit down and have a cigarette and try and understand what had just happened. As I watched the setting sun behind the town square, I realized that I was alone. The town of El Pilar was smaller and quieter than San Fernando, but similar in that there were only white sandstone buildings. If this place was inhabited, it sure didn't seem like it: this place had a different vibe than the other part of the island, a strange atmosphere. I couldn't knock this feeling I had, something was going to happen. Did that something have to do with that woman?

Part I

"The Dog Might Not Be a Dog"

Just as I was lighting up another cigarette, the mystery woman appeared in front of me as if from out of thin air.

"Are you lost? You seem lost somehow. My name is Olivia. I've been watching you and, by the way, you shouldn't smoke so much," she said in what I heard as a Nordic accent.

She startled me, even though I had felt earlier I'd see her again—just not like this, mysteriously popping up out of nowhere in the dark, almost like, well, a witch or something.

"Yes," I said.

"Yes, what?" she threw back quickly.

"Yes, I'm starting to think maybe I've really done what I was hoping to do. And that was just to find a way to get lost, to disappear somehow and start over. And as I look around me right now, I'm not exactly sure of where I am and what I'm doing here."

"I don't know what you're doing here, but have you heard of a writer called Jules Verne? In one of his novels, he declared El Pilar as a place at the end of the world. When the sun is shining, you can look to the north and see a windmill. That windmill was built in the eighteenth century, I think around 1778. That windmill is strange and just one of many things on this island that somehow sidestep reality. This is a small island, but there are a lot of strange things that happen here. By the way, you are an American, right? It's easy to tell. Like all or most Americans, you appear to be something of a crybaby. You have more than anyone in any country, and you complain the most. You don't know what you want."

"Yes, I am American, but just because I decided to try some traveling and searching for a direction or some answers doesn't mean, well, you know what you said. And by the way, my name is Paul; I'm from the Chicago area… and before you ask, no, I'm not a gangster. And I guess I'm somewhat in trouble because I have no place to stay, and I'm hungry." As I said that, I was hoping she'd give me some relief and say I could stay with her in that house across the way, but she said nothing.

I continued, "Well, before I freeze tonight on this stupid island, I might as well get something to eat. When the sun goes down, I'm sure it gets cold on this mountain."

"Get up," she said. "Behind you is the café. Everyone calls it the Fat Ladies Café. It's Spanish, of course, and no one speaks any English there. Come on, you'll probably need some help ordering, so you don't starve to death."

As we sat down, she immediately ordered in Spanish. "Dos café con leche con Cognac." The hot coffee mixed with sweet milk and the intense liquor was a surprise pick, very exotic compared to what I had been consuming lately and absolutely warming and perfect for the moment.

The nickname for the café derived from the clientele of this establishment. Two of the tables were occupied by elderly, heavyset Spanish ladies in the typical long, black dresses of this Iberian farming community. Then there was the proprietor, dressed the same, but with a different air; you could immediately tell she ruled inside these walls. The ladies dominated the inside visually and aurally even though there was a Spanish soccer game playing fairly loudly on a TV from somewhere in the back. A few dark-skinned Spanish men, each with a beer in front of him, were seated at a few of the remaining eight tables. There was a small bar area, and the kitchen was behind the wall at the end of the room. The decor was sparse; a couple of nondescript pictures hung on plain white walls. Even though we were aliens in a foreign land and especially in this isolated mountain town, nobody even looked up as we entered and sat down. The feeling of destiny I experienced outside persisted.

We shared a rice and fish plate, though Olivia just picked at the rice and vegetables as she was a vegetarian. She was in her early twenties, from Gothenburg, Sweden. She revealed that she was here on the islands with a special dispensation to study for a certain amount of time before she had to go back to the University. She talked about the need for the world to be less aggressive and selfish. She said she was somewhere between a socialist and a communist.

Personally, I thought all Swedish women automatically came with long blonde hair, but I guess not. She was dark from the sun, and her face was framed by long hair as black as the night. Even though her looks were striking, reminding me of several actresses I'd seen in foreign movies, she had chosen to wear what appeared to be a typical European peasant ensemble with a loose, dark-blue top and a long black skirt to her sandaled feet. It didn't do her looks justice.

It was now about 9:30 at night, and I was nursing my second Spanish beer as I watched Olivia leave the café. She'd had it for the day and I think had enough of me. The dinner started cordially enough, but then we started arguing. We disagreed about world politics, about the color of the café's walls. About my smoking. About whether men or women were smarter. We even argued who was the smarter of the two of us. She classified herself as a tried-and-true socialist and me as a typical uninformed and naïve capitalist from the USA. It seemed that we had a disagreement about everything. I swear, anyone watching us would have guessed we'd been married for years the way we went at each other.

But as I finished my beer and paid the bill, I came to a disturbing realization. I think she was the smarter one of the two of us right now as she was nice and warm indoors while I was about to go out into the cool mountain air to find a place to sleep on the hard ground.

I wandered around for a while, trying to imagine where I could go or if I could find a place to sleep that made any sense. As I was cursing myself for getting into this predicament, I noticed a dog watching me talk to myself. Then he moved closer, out into the moonlight. He was medium-sized, of undetermined breed, mostly black and brown with one eye surrounded by a white patch. He was quietly following me. We both stopped pacing at almost the same moment, and as I looked at him, he cocked his head a bit and stared back. He then trotted over to a nearby bakery, paused, and gave me a look suggesting I come over and sit also. I joined him and proceeded to have a one-sided conversation with the dog, telling him of my predicament.

After some time passed, a warm feeling started to come over me, a premonition that all was going to be okay. It was hard to explain, but it was real. A minute later, Olivia opened her second-story door, walked down a couple of steps and said, "Do I have to do everything for you? What are you waiting for; it's getting late. Are you coming up or not?" In a flash, I threw my sleeping bag over my shoulder and was halfway up the stairs when I remembered the dog. When I turned around, he was already gone.

The room inside was lit with an isolated candle on a small table flanked by two simple matching wooden chairs. A small bed with some metal bars as a headboard and framed by a couple of open windows was the only other furnishing. It was certainly sparse but heaven sent for me at that moment.

After some minutes of bossing me around, telling me where to lay out my sleeping bag and where and how to wash up, Olivia blew out the candle and instructed me to cover my eyes as she undressed and changed. We didn't say much as I got myself settled and finally stretched out inside my sleeping bag, lighting up one last cigarette for the day. She spoke then. "So, are you okay now; how is the floor?"

"The floor is hard, harder than any hard floor I've ever felt, but…"

"But what?"

"But I owe you. I could still be wandering around on the top of this mountain looking for someplace to sleep, and with my luck, I'd probably have run into some bear or something."

"You idiot, there are no bears here, just… well, you know, the witches."

I couldn't see her face when she said that to be able to tell if she was laughing, but then she followed up with, "In a couple of days, you'll be able to see them and talk to them yourself. Wednesday is the full moon celebration. They will be there with their magic, their spells, and their mystery. This is a strange island. You will see this island has history. There are many strange things that happen here, more so than other places on earth."

"Well, if you say so, but I find that hard to believe," I responded. She didn't seem to be the kind of person who would be prone to be saying such things, but there is no doubt she was serious. There was also no doubt this island had some odd vibe. Last night I slept in the field with goats, and tonight I was sleeping with someone who believed in witches. It occurred to me that Olivia herself may be a witch, although given the love-hate nature of the relationship thus far, I knew better than to broach that subject.

At some point in the night, a shuffling sound began to emanate from the ceiling or the roof and disturbed the half-sleep that I had achieved. I lay there still as could be to try and figure out what it was.

Olivia whispered, "Are you awake? Do you hear that? I think it's maybe some type of big wild animal."

"What... what kind of wild animal?" I whispered back.

"I don't know, but I'm scared. I can't see anything. I don't want it to get me."

We heard more scraping and rustling above, and then we became transfixed on a pair of yellow eyes that were motionlessly trained on us from the inner hallway. Our minds were reeling. After another round of screeching sounds, I turned quickly toward the window to watch in horror as another animal flung itself in and landed on the table, knocking some bowls onto the floor. As I was desperately trying to see what it was, I felt Olivia's hand grasp my shoulder and her nails dig into me as she let out a yell.

If that wasn't enough to facilitate two heart attacks, we heard a soft growl coming from the other side of the room where the two yellow eyes were, and then all hell broke loose. The growling intensified, and Olivia now was grabbing me from behind with both hands, fingers, and ten sharp nails as she yelled out again. The thing on the table gave a blood-curdling cry and jumped straight up in the air a foot or two, knocking more plates off the table. Upon landing, it jumped towards me. I tried to evade it, but Olivia's death grip held me back.

But because of that, I was able to see the animal as it bounded onto my lap and quickly jumped up over me. It was a big, scrawny, brown and yellow cat, still yowling as it pounced. As I lurched to try and avoid it, I saw out of the corner of my eye the thing with the yellow eyes flying by my head. It landed on the table, too late to bite the cat. As the clouds parted for a second to let an almost full moon shine down through the window, I saw it was the dog I had talked to earlier, yelping. The dog regained its feet and lept off the table onto me and up onto the bed, just missing the cat. The cat ran towards the hall and into the dark, followed by the yapping dog until both were out of sight. Apparently, there was a door to another set of stairs leading who knows where.

The room suddenly was totally silent except for our heavy breathing. Our breathing was starting to relax when, in the dark of the room, I felt her hand stretching to find me. I met her hand with mine, and we touched—no words, just two hands intertwining in the dark. What was my socialist adversary doing? Was she giving me a sign?

Just then we heard a racket by the stable in the back of the pension. It was the dog still chasing the cat and apparently still knocking into things as they tried to wake up the mountaintop's inhabitants way before dawn. With that, and at the same time, we both broke out laughing.

The divide between us had changed. We both knew and because of that became quiet again. She broke the silence by saying, "I don't even smoke, but after that, I need one. It's time for you to light up."

I did and took a big drag before pressing the glowing cigarette in her direction. She accepted it and, though I knew she didn't smoke, took a big drag. She held the smoke in and then let it out quickly as she took another one. A couple of minutes later, the clouds dispersed a little to again let the moonshine in just as I was blowing a couple of perfectly-formed smoke rings straight up from where I was lying. I could see her clearly for a moment or two as she leaned over and speared each smoke ring with her finger.

"Why do you do that... why with the rings? I'm trying to understand you, why you do the things you do; we are so different," she whispered in her accented Swedish English. The accent was starting to get to me.

"I have no idea why I blow smoke rings. I started doing it as a kid. I don't know why I do most of the things I do. Do you?"

"Yes, I do, and I have for a long time. You in America are just interested in money. Not the more important things of life."

"Well, that might be true; I'm still trying to figure out life. Maybe you are much more accomplished in that area; maybe you could help me look at life differently. I think you and I should..." Before I could continue, I was interrupted.

Although it was still dark, and as I was looking up at her from the floor, I saw her lift the blanket covering her and say, "I might regret this later, but again, do I have to do everything for you?

Come up here."

***

The last couple of days had been the best of times and the worst of times. After the first night, I was in love with Olivia, hook, line and sinker, but we continue to spar. One of those days, she had to go to one of the port cities on the island, and as the night grew late and the weather threatened, I couldn't take the chance she wasn't coming, and I walked to one of the cliff areas. I had been told that there was a path that led to one of the caves that could be used as a shelter in an emergency. I would have never found the path if it wasn't for the soon-to-be-full moon lighting up the mountaintop.

As I filed down the path to the edge of the cliff, I stood and looked at the sea, asking myself, why am I looking for a cave? I'm not a cave guy; I don't even like motels, let alone caves. Do these caves have animals? How dark will it be? Will I even see the animals, or would it be better if I didn't?

I assumed, as the path ended, that this was either the place to start climbing down or maybe, 200 years ago, it was a jump-off-the-cliff spot for the witches or those fleeing witches. I slowly felt my way down the side of the cliff, not believing I was doing it. One false move and it's a hundred-feet-or-more fall either onto the huge boulders below or into the rough, crashing sea. This part was closer to the sea than where the lighthouse was. It was not as steep, and there were more bushes to hold onto. The lighthouse appeared maybe a quarter mile away.

The cave I found may not have been the cave I was told about, but I had had enough. The opening wasn't very inviting, but it did give me cover for the evening and was big enough to lay out my sleeping bag. I could see lightning in the distance, and the temperature had dropped maybe 10° since I started my cave search. Beyond where I lay, it was totally dark, and even though there appeared to be a hint of a much smaller opening, possibly leading deeper into the cave, I had decided this was it for me tonight. It was a quiet cave, and I didn't hear any animals although I listened for them.

Almost as soon as I got inside my sleeping bag, the rain started. My view became eerie, with a foggy mist playing just outside the cave lit by a humungous moon. I was unable to decide if it wanted to enter or was just lazily positioning itself to keep me in—or the witches out.

I lay awake for some time as I pondered the moment. Maybe not everyone would consider it a moment of life, but I was feeling it. This was my first cave—the first, anyway, that I was going to sleep in. Sleeping in a cave was an archetypal experience that had been shared by many before me, animals and men, whether primitive cave dwellers eons ago or my contemporaries. I was becoming a member of another type of fraternity, a fraternity of travelers. I realized I was changing. This wasn't happening overnight. But I was different.

Just as I was feeling proud of myself and enjoying a new and important confidence in my abilities, I heard an ominous screech from the back of the cave. I could hardly even turn to see what it was, I was so afraid. I slid down into my sleeping bag to cover up to just below my eyes and was frozen like that till I don't know when, just as anyone would who had been telling himself he was a step above, confident, strong, and capable of adventure.

Olivia and I had spent time both together and apart during

the last couple of days. I had come here to rest, to… as they say… "Get my act together." That was not happening. The island had this vibe, a restless vibe that was affecting me.

One place where I did find a little surprising solace, a couple of times, was the small church on the top of the mountain. Though my father was Catholic and put my two sisters through religious education at night at the Catholic school outside of the public school when they were in grade school, he didn't pursue that with my brother or me. Growing up, I would go every Sunday with my father to church and now, older and on my own, I had often thought about going through confirmation and taking communion. But the time I spent in La Mola's little church was not about whether to become a true Catholic; it was just about me finding a little quiet and maybe comfort sitting alone in that place. I had never done that before, but I believed that it would not be my last time doing so.

Recently Stefan had invited me to stay overnight in an abandoned VW bus that had mysteriously found its way a few years ago some 200 to 300 yards off the road and into the forest. Although beaten and battered, it was a roof over your head in an emergency. The night I spent there was uneventful besides the fact that there were two girls from New Zealand who had brought a lot of food to cook for all—about six of us—who were there. My stomach was finally full for the first time days.

Early the next day I made my way to Fonda Pepe's. Along my walk back up the mountain road to El Pilar, I stopped to adjust the rope on my bedroll. As I turned around, there looking at me was the dog. He laid down, sort of saying, *Let's rest a bit. This uphill winding road is tiring…why don't you have a cigarette?* I understood, and sat down and lit up. We talked for a while even though it was mostly a one-sided conversation. He argued with me about this Swedish chick. She was a curiosity, and she was starting to be on both of our minds, day and night.

Our conversation was interrupted by a tractor pulling a small flatbed trailer with several Spanish women chatting loudly—and laughing even louder as they looked at us as they passed, heading to the top of the mountain. The dog and I decided that our rest stop was over and it was time to start walking up to El Pilar again. After walking a while, one of the island's green and black lizards jumped out onto the road right in front of us, and we both froze. The lizard looked up at us, realizing his mistake, after seeing the dog's eyes popping out of its head. The dog had a look in its eye: *Thank you, thank you, big dog in the sky, I'd love to chase this lizard.* The lizard looked left, then right, and decided left was his best bet. Just as he jumped up, spinning his legs in midair, the dog jumped and snapped but missed. The last I saw of them, they were tearing through the brush and into the forest. I walked alone the rest of the way up the mountain and eventually to the Fat Ladies Café for a much-needed beer. I checked at the bar to see if there was any mail for me but was disappointed. Any mail this soon would have been witchcraft anyway, as I had only written home a couple of days ago to alert friends and family as to how I could be reached on my new island abode.

It was now early evening on May 20th, the night of the full moon party. Olivia met me at the Fat Ladies at my table on the outside patio. Following behind her were three guys and a woman, all with painted faces and wearing long black robes. As they passed by me to another table, I thought I heard them speaking in a different language. I also could smell an exceptionally strong odor of hashish. At about the same time, I saw the woman taking a long drag of the biggest, rolled-up hashish cigar I'd ever seen in my life. As they sat down at the table next to ours, a huge cloud of twirling smoke floated toward and encircled us as Olivia ordered a coffee. While one part of me was trying not to inhale and another part wanted to join the action, we saw other groups obviously making their way to the place of tonight's full moon party. We knew the party was taking place in a secret hideaway, so we'd need an invitation.

As the group of painted people left their table next to us, one of them nodded to me in an accepting way as he walked past. Though I didn't recognize him, he had obviously seen or met me and felt I was OK to go to the party. I threw out some pesetas on the table to pay for our drinks and indicated to Olivia that we should follow them.

The sky had an unusual mixture of colors as we walked to a part of the mountaintop that was unfamiliar to me. Just as it looked like we couldn't walk any farther, the painted people ahead of us pushed the heavy branches of some pine trees aside and held them back for us. We followed a very narrow walking path down along the cliffs of the mountain. The path started to get scarier along the cliff, especially as the moonlight was intermittently blocked by the clouds. I started to become somewhat unnerved by the situation. I reminded myself that I was on a strange island in the middle of nowhere, following a group of strangers in the dark to an unknown destination, all to take part in some kind of ancient ritual that was sure to be at the very least a bit bizarre.

After some time, the painted people indicated that their group should take a rest break and without talking sat down. They indicated, using hand gestures, that we should do the same.

Suddenly, the dog emerged from behind a big rock just ahead

of us on the path and came right to me and lay down. Everyone did a double take and looked at me with curiosity. What was that all about? The dog was known to be strange. And what was the dog doing appearing on the side of the mountain just now? I shrugged my shoulders in some attempt to answer the numerous unspoken questions. I had by now accepted my unusual relationship with this strange dog.

Olivia whispered to me, "That dog might not be a dog."

That got me for a second, and I froze. I immediately looked over to the painted-face people to see if they had heard that. Apparently, they hadn't.

"What... why would you say that?" I whispered back. "He's a dog. Dogs are dogs."

"Look at the way he looks at us, especially at you. He's even sort of squinting his eyes like a human as he stares at you. Almost like he's trying to read your mind or maybe manipulate your mind. Just think about it, why is this dog here now? Do you see any other dogs? And why you? Why has this dog adopted you? Nothing against you, but you are nothing on this island. You don't have a house. You don't have a roof. You don't even feed him. Why you? Why is this dog here with you now? And why does he keep looking at you in that strange way?"

"I don't know; I don't know. But, really, you think he might be a witch? What have you been drinking? He's a dog, a stupid, cat-chasing dog." As I softly said that, he sat up and stared at me in an even more curious way.

Then Olivia wispered, "And I think the cat might be a witch also."

Before I could respond, the painted faces got up, and then a very odd thing happened. They looked at the dog, and as they did so, the dog got up and looked over his shoulder back at me as he passed the others who now, it seemed, were waiting for the dog to go ahead down the trail and lead the way. They started to follow him.

Wide-eyed and now maybe rethinking my position on the dog, I looked at Olivia. She tilted her head a little as she also raised her hands in a gesture, as if to say, "See, there's something going on with that dog."

We eventually made our way down to a secluded beach lit up by one very large bonfire and two or three other smaller fires some distance away from each other. There were about fifty to seventy people, mostly around the campfires with others splashing in the Mediterranean. As we walked on the beach, music started out of nowhere. I looked left and right but could not locate its origin. It felt like a chorus from a church choir, but more, different, something dark but somehow appropriate tonight.

Olivia pulled me to one of the blankets laid out on the sand covered with different foods and containers of drinks. She immediately knelt to score some food and drink before it was all gone. As she grabbed things and cradled them in her arms like a professional juggler, I noticed the dog lying on an overhang watching us. A couple of other painted faces walked by us and nodded. As hard as I tried, I couldn't identify any of these people as ones I might have met. Everyone seemed to be very friendly, whether they were dressed in costume or attending out of curiosity. There was an overriding feeling that something was about to happen.

We moved closer to one of the smaller fires. The dark had come and the temperature was much cooler. Both of us were wide-eyed as we ate and watched. People started moving around more as they finished eating. Neither she nor I accepted any drugs although they were offered to us repeatedly as we sat there—as we thought, abstaining. As the night went on, however, there was no doubt that we were being affected by the clouds of pulsating, smoky, drugged air hovering around us and each of the bonfires.

As Olivia attended to a stray dog that was whimpering near one of the other bonfires, a woman in a black mask and long black robe sat down next to me and took out a deck of large Tarot cards. Without asking me whether I even wanted my fortune read, she jumped in and immediately started explaining some of the cards laid out on the sand in front of her. She had four cards across and the lonely left-side one face up. Looking at that card, she said softly in a French accent, "Monsieur, your first card is the Two of Wands. Très intéressant. You have a decision to make, stay the course or change. Also, quel est votre signe?"

"Libra."

She looked at me for a long second as she turned the next card over, hesitated oddly, and then looked at me again as if she were trying to peer inside of me. The next card appeared to be a Knight—if I remember correctly, the Knight of Swords.

She seemed to indicate that there was trouble in my future and that the next card she would turn over would give her a glimpse into what that would be. As she reached for the card, Olivia and the dog approached us. The dog headed straight for me, sliding on the sand and into the cards. The woman in black raised her hands in frustration and yelled "Merde!" She picked up the cards that had been scattered and walked off. I looked after her and was left wondering, *What about my fortune, my future?* She was just about to say something. I looked for the dog to yell at it, but it had disappeared.

As the night went on, the volume was turned up on the festivities. It seemed each new song had a louder and more driving bass beat. Some started dancing, not necessarily with partners but quite possibly with people or things that couldn't be seen. Some were off to the side near the rolling waves ebbing and flowing— endlessly lit by the moon, as they created ribbons of many-colored sparks by waving strange-looking wands that seemed to float along the crests of the waves. Either by accident or on purpose, though it seemed to happen spontaneously, the dog was lit on fire. It was hard to see clearly that far across the beach, but some type of cloth attached to the dog shot a flame two or three feet in the air as the dog raced around frantically, not knowing what to do. Finally, I think through some ghostly intervention, the dog raced into the ocean, thus putting out the flame. I couldn't tell if the dog made it out of the water or just decided that at that point it was better to take its chances paddling out into the Mediterranean.

Just then a young guy with his face painted green and white approached us with more to drink, and we gratefully lifted the glass fruit jars we'd been sipping from. Almost on cue, as he left to pour for someone else, a woman screamed and started running around behind us. As she passed closer to us, I could finally make out her words. "Run, run everyone! I just saw a werewolf. He will collect his friends, and they will come get us!"

Now, in regular life, you wouldn't hear something like that, and in regular life, if you did, you would probably pass it off as nonsense. But I'll tell you, being there in a hidden cove, in the dark of night on a mysterious island in the middle of a large group of people, in the midst of a full moon party, I started twisting my head left and right and back again as my psyche was telling me not to take any chances… because there really could be werewolves.

As I was contemplating the potential existence of werewolves, a girl with a lightning bolt painted in red across her face, and with hair, it seemed, down to her waist, told us to watch out for the guy filling up everyone's glass with more spirits. Apparently, he had mixed some mescaline with the alcoholic drink he was giving out. I immediately looked down to my drink and found that it was empty. I saw that Olivia's jar was full and tossed its contents into the sand. I had never used mescaline before but heard it was one of the most hallucinogenic drugs besides LSD, which I had never had either.

As Olivia punched my upper arm in retaliation for pouring out her drink, I tried to indicate to her there was a bug, but at the same time I realized I was, for some reason, feeling different parts of my head for things that might be sticking out. I was feeling heat rising in my body toward my head. My body was relaxed but my mind was anxious. I couldn't decide if that was positive as I kept feeling my head with my hands and finding nothing good or bad.

After most people had departed for the night, a few of us decided to sleep on the beach. It was cold, but people talked about how this was a great location to see the sunrise. I tossed and turned while everyone else seemed to sleep quickly and easily. I eventually stopped feeling my head for protrusions, but I was agitated and couldn't get settled. It was so cold even though all of us were squeezing together on a little rocky ledge facing the ebbing sea about a hundred feet away. Matter of fact, it was the same ledge the dog had positioned himself on earlier in the evening, looking at everyone but especially me. The dog was nowhere to be found. After realizing my head was feeling more normal, I finally fell asleep.

The next morning, I awoke first, lit a cigarette and just lay there, watching some seagulls dancing in the sky back and forth overhead. I was trying to remember a dream I had had about the dog. One part seemed so real that I did wonder if it was it a dream or if it had really happened last night. In any case, in my dream, the dog could talk. The language was not one I could readily identify, but the dog carried on quiet conversations with a couple of painted-face people for a long time. Everyone was quite animated in movement and gesture as they talked, even the dog as he made human gestures with his paws. Eventually, they all shook hands and paused to look around and then walked in different directions until they disappeared.

Olivia, who was sleeping next to me, woke up and told me something that surprised me. Although I had spent a good amount of time with her day and night during my time on the island, there were times when she was away. As she lay there, sliding closer to me, she divulged that she was living part-time with an owner of a bar-restaurant on Ibiza, an older guy named Jack.

I was dumbfounded; I didn't know what to think about this mystery man. Again, I found myself trying to think straight, but again the island interfered. I couldn't think logically. I decided I'd have to wait and see what came next. Without much conversation, we all started walking out of the cove, up the cliff, and eventually back to La Mola and a hot café con leche at the Fat Ladies Café.

The café was full of foreigners, inside and out—none, mind you, with painted faces. The full moon had come and gone. The party was interesting, both for the things that certainly happened and the ones I'm not sure about. It's funny, what I'm most curious about from that night is the reality or not of the dreams that I still remember very clearly.

After almost a week of walking all over the island, I decided that I needed a better mode of transportation, and I rented a bicycle. It was old and a little rusty, and the brakes made a little creaking sound as I pushed hard on the pedals to test their efficacy. But it worked, and it was time for me to up my game here as I tried to decide what my next moves were going to be. I guess I did what a lot of 1800s cowboys would have done: I packed my bag and got on my horse (bike) and rode off into the rising sun and down the mountain.

Since the full moon party, three or four days had come and gone with no new developments. Except one. I did go to Ibiza for a day, and when I had just gotten back to Formentera, I ran into Stefan kicking a soccer ball around with some young Spanish kids by the church on La Mola. He motioned me to join them, which I had no interest in doing, but he was persistent, so I came over in my John Wayne boots to try to play soccer. Just as I got in my first kick, an elderly priest—I would have to guess that he was in his late 70s—came out and said, "Espana versus The World." So, the four kids and the priest against Stefan and me. We were up 4-1 and fairly dominant when the priest said he was too old and had to quit. Almost on cue, a young priest came out of the church, and the kids bade him join their team. He looked Stefan and me up and down, smiled a little devilish smile, and joined the game. Within minutes, the score was tied, and more than that, Stefan and I were panting for air. One of the kids was a real loudmouth. I didn't know enough Spanish to understand him very well, but it did piss me off to hear him yelling, "Stupido English" repeatedly.

The kid was laughing and wouldn't stop. Stefan moved over closer to him at one point and gave the kid a little bump. And though it was just a little bump, the young priest, who had already proved he was a very good athlete, evidently took it as an attack on the kid and him and the whole Catholic Church. The game changed immediately. The priest was everywhere, a one-man show. Quickly the score went from 4-4 to 8-4, and we were running in circles. Not only were we running in circles, but we spent a good amount of time in the dirt. This guy could have been a professional soccer star; he was like the guys on TV. At one point, after a timeout, Stefan, the more experienced with soccer, came up with a play for us. We moved in tandem down the part of the street that was our field, and then Stefan made a sharp cut toward the make-believe soccer goal of two large flowerpots with the intention that I quickly kick to him as he faked a move to the goal. He hoped the priest would follow him and get himself out of position, then Stefan would rebound the ball to me instead for an easy goal. It was a good plan except that the priest read our minds and instead of following Stefan out of position, he stopped and followed the ball back to me. Unfortunately, Stefan's pass was off-center, and I started to lose my balance while reaching behind for it. The priest saw that and immediately jumped for the ball before I could touch it, catching it in midair between his feet. Before turning, he made sure he smashed into me, hitting me as I was flailing for stability into the two large flowerpots. I knocked them over, and the flowers spewed in multiple directions. I landed in a heap with a scrape on my forehead, though it felt more like a big hole in my head. And the priest still wasn't done; after knocking into me, and before his feet touched the ground, he flipped the ball up in front of him. Though I only saw his feet as I was flying headfirst, he proceeded to do a semi-over-the-head-behind-him kick, and the ball sailed all the way down our abstract field and bounced once as it made its way to a goal. Both Stefan and I were lying on the ground watching as the priest put his arm around the kids and walked off, waving to us as they entered the church.

Stefan and I lay there a minute or two, but then Stefan said he needed a beer badly. I said I'd join him shortly. I was aching and needed to just lie there for a few minutes. As I was almost back to feeling most of my body, the young priest came out holding two glasses of water and sat down next to me after giving me one of them.

"Gracias, Padre," I said with a little smile.

He surprised me when he asked in almost perfect English, "Are you OK, Americano?"

"Si, I think OK, but sore and feeling Espana fooled us. You are amazing. When you're not a priest, are you a professional soccer player on the mainland?"

He laughed and then said, "¿Dónde está, ah... your home? You look liked you've traveled far."

"Chicago. A very long way away from here."

"Were you in the army? I see that..."

I interrupted him. "No, Padre... just... well, just something between me and my amigo way up above, I guess." Just then the soccer ball came bouncing by, and as we both looked up, the cocky little Spanish kid mischievously smiled at us.

"You know, this isn't the first time I've seen you. I've seen you in the church alone, I think, a couple of times. Are you religious?"

"No, I don't think so. I was born and baptized Roman Catholic, but my parents didn't follow through with any formal training, and I didn't go to a Catholic school. And you wonder why I was in the church... well, I'm not sure. It's not the first time I've done that on my travels.

"I guess you could say I'm searching for something, Padre, on this sojourn of mine. And sometimes I'm pulled somehow to enter and sit. And if you asked me what am I searching for, I'm not sure I could tell you. I started on this trip hoping to get a job in Paris. That didn't work out, and then I just started traveling. I don't suppose you ever saw the movie *The Razor's Edge?* It's not important. But as I go along, there seems to be some connection between that movie and me. Life is funny, isn't it? I'm not sure I'll ever figure it out. And to be honest with you, the more I travel, the more I started to wonder about things. All kinds of things. Things big and small. I've never done that before. For me, this is very strange. So, like many people, I guess, Father, I call it searching. But in all honesty, the way this is all going, I'm not sure I'd know even if I found it. That is, if there really is anything to find. Sorry... I guess I'm rambling and somewhat talking in circles."

"No, I hear you. Some take it upon themselves to search more than others. You appear to be one of those. I wish I could help you. But what you are looking for, I think, you must find yourself. The door here is always open, day or night. None of your friends ever seem to want to come in, but we are open to all. By the way, my name is Antonio. I'm not sure we'll see each other again. I hope we do, but if not, go with God wherever that might be and keep finding churches and never be afraid to come in and just sit. Sometimes it just might be very quiet and restful. And other times, while feeling that restful feeling, you might also feel something else. God very rarely speaks to me, but often I feel him, and that means so very much to me." As he finished talking, he stood and shook my hand and asked my name.

"My name is Paul—Pablo—Father. And thank you for the drink. And I just want to remind you that you never answered me earlier when I said it looked like to me that besides being a priest that you were also a soccer star. I'll make sure to watch for you in any future Spanish soccer games on TV." We both laughed as he walked away.

***

It seemed more new people were coming to Formentera each day. I'd moved from the pension to Stefan's VW bus and was sleeping out by the beach mostly because some days Olivia was on the island and some not. I'd stay with her, but when she went to Ibiza, I'd be on my own. I missed her but felt I had no claim on her. This thing between us was not like any relationship I'd had with a girl before; rather, it was what you would expect on an island of witches, on an adventure. I was just feeling my way through the experience, hoping to find some type of answer.

I met Olivia in the square one morning as she was heading to Ibiza for a few days. She was leading the dog with a piece of rope, and behind her was the lady from the pension mumbling something to Olivia in Spanish.

Olivia told me the lady said the dog was mine. She'd seen him with me more than with anyone else. The Guardia Seville were looking for me, as a stray dog had created some trouble chasing farm animals in the area. Olivia was worried for me and urged me to stay away from any of the towns on the island for a while in order to avoid them. She had really liked reading some of my poems and said it was a perfect time to find an out-of-the-way place, even a cave, where I could just write for a while. As I was leaving she called, "Take the dog!" and he soon appeared behind the bike without a word from me.

So, for the next three to four days, I took up residence in a new cave (new to me, anyway) that was hard to get to and therefore had my name on it. The entrance was in what I thought was a prominent limestone outcrop at an elevation of about three or four stories above the sea. The passage sloped downward gently— to what I wasn't sure. To get down to the cave, I had to walk along the cliff after hiding my bike under some shrubs.

Upon entering the cave there were signs of animal nests. I didn't know if they belonged to rats, squirrels, chipmunks, or worse. For the sake of my sanity, I decided to make my peace with a chipmunk that I called Chip, from the Chip & Dale cartoons. The thick, small candle I had brought with me only illuminated a small circle around where I laid my sleeping bag. Though there were some wet spots, the cave was basically dry. The only food I had was bread, peanut butter, some oranges, and some chocolate I had bought as I left the outskirts of El Pilar.

Though bigger than my first cave, it still was an eerie cave. You wouldn't want to be a claustrophobic here, as regardless of how big it was, the walls always seemed to be closing in on you, especially at night. I decided to stay close to the entrance so I could make a quick escape if need be.

I'd never spent so much time alone. I hadn't been bored, and I'd written quite a lot and filled pages and pages in my sketchbook. I'd also had a lot of time to think. I debated whether to depart the island after July 1 to Pamplona for the world-famous Running of the Bulls. That event takes place every year on the seventh hour of the seventh day of the seventh month. If you recall, Jake Barnes in the 1926 novel *The Sun Also Rises* had that on his bucket list and spent his holiday week there. When I broached that possibility in conversations on Formentera, I got comments like, "Are you crazy? Those bulls in Spain are like small elephants, and they are mean." Many said you couldn't pay them to do it—it was way too dangerous. Apparently, more people get badly hurt by other people running wildly to try and escape the bulls than by the bulls themselves. On top of that, each year there are tens and tens who got stomped on, trampled, nicked by horns, or gored, suffering major injuries that require emergency surgery just to survive. There was even an occasional fatality.

During my cave sojourn, I took the opportunity to wash some clothes. It had been a while, and my only current option was to sneak into a washroom of one of the beach restaurants and wash as much as I could in the sink, hopefully escape undetected, then find an uninhabited area to stretch them out to dry in the sun. While having a beer early one afternoon, I also took the time to count my remaining funds—something I avoided doing as there was never going to be any good news there. The current count registered only $360 left. A plane ticket to New York on an Icelandic flight would be around $275 unless I could find that rumored, sought-after cheap ticket out of London.

Here are some costs of things on the island of Formentera (again, in 1970 there were about seventy pesetas to $1). One pack of unfiltered Celtas Spanish cigarettes, five pesetas; one pack of Dueadas filtered cigarettes, fourteen pesetas; rent for a small house for one month, one to two thousand pesetas; a freshly baked loaf of bread, seven pesetas; a liter of beer, twenty pesetas; one orange, two pesetas; a chocolate bar, twelve to twenty pesetas; an egg and potato omelet, eighteen pesetas; green salad, seventeen pesetas; juice, twelve pesetas; a ride on the Formentera bus, ten pesetas; a boat to Ibiza, twenty-five pesetas.

While my finances were always lurking in my thoughts, I stayed surprisingly calm. This was a new mindset for me, but as I thought about my trip so far, I realized I'd had many experiences that had brought about significant changes in me. I'd pursued a half-baked idea to take a train to India and start a clothing business; traveled to or through fifteen different European and Near Eastern countries; negotiated through different languages and money changing; eluded police in Italy, Bulgaria, Yugoslavia, and now in Spain; experienced a wide new variety of sleeping accommodations and unusual places; and last, but not least, jumped off of trains. I'd had more experiences and adventures by far in the last two months than totaled cumulatively in my previous twenty-one years of life. How could I not be different? It's not that I was a hermit who was afraid of life or oblivious to the living universe, but as I sat under one of the awnings of the beach bar, I imagined looking at myself as another person might. Even as that other person, I could sense a calm within me. I believe most would be more than worried in my shoes, but I was at peace, a peace that experience brings. In only a couple of months, I was much older, and maybe even to the tune of years more confident. I didn't know how much longer this trip would continue; I just hoped I could have one or two more experiences of a lifetime before it ended.

Part II

"...I was leaving the earth, traversing invisible dimensions."

"Are you all right? Are you okay?" came from behind me in a thick British or Irish accent. As I turned, I saw an older man with a white beard and white hair, dressed in bleached linen casual clothes, wearing a black T-shirt and tipping his head as he looked closely at me.

"Yeah, I'm okay. Maybe I was just daydreaming. Did you asked me something?" I replied.

"No, I didn't ask you anything, but now that I see you—you look like a gambling man. How about a game of chess for a big glass of Bushmills?"

I wasn't sure what Bushmills was, but regardless, I didn't have any money to bet on anything let alone on a chess game. But as I started to decline, he raised his arm and ordered two large whiskeys with ice from the bartender across the patio.

"Really, I'm not in a position to bet, thank you but no, I…"

"Okay, okay, mate, just relax." He held up his finger to keep me from interrupting him further, but instead of finishing his thought, he changed the subject. "My name's Emilio. What's yours?"

"Paul, from Chicago. And no, I don't know any gangsters," I responded with a little smile, at the same time not believing this Irish guy was named Emilio.

He continued as the bartender brought over the drinks, "You look like a traveler, Paul. What's your story? Where have you been?"

I discovered that this bartender knew Emilio and knew he liked his whiskey with soda. The drink was still strong, but at least it wouldn't put me on my ass right away. I did worry about the combination of the whiskey and the huge joint he was lighting and passing over to me.

"You play white. First move," he said. My mind wasn't there. I moved my king's pawn up two spaces haphazardly. He answered by moving his right knight up and over the row in front and to the left, immediately giving more protection to his king.

He smiled a sly smile, obviously happy with his opening move and probably anticipating his next five moves as he continued to prod me. "Again, Paul, what's your story? How did you get here?"

I hadn't played chess in years, and by the time I had made my second move, my left Castle's pawn out two spaces, I was feeling the effects in my body of those two long drags I took off his joint.

As I sipped the whiskey, I knew it wouldn't be long before my ability even to play let alone win this chess game would be in doubt. My mind was racing. Had I really bet on this match? If so, how much were whiskeys? It occurred to me that the reason I was here in the first place was to try to sneak into the washroom to clean some of my clothes.

"Hey, amigo, I've moved again. What's your move? Are you daydreaming again?"

Without thinking, I moved my bishop out diagonally three squares.

He would not let up. As he moved his other knight up two and over one to the far left side of the board, he said, "Mate, as you can see, I like my knights in play and I'm getting ready to attack you—are you ever gonna tell me why you are on this island in the middle of nowhere? And mate, it's your turn again."

This guy was really getting on my nerves. If he called me "mate" one more time, I'd, I'd… wait a minute, that just reminded me. I looked down at the board. It was available; I needed just a little distraction…something was there if I could do it. What he had unintentionally reminded me about was a play in chess called The Scholar's Mate.

Distraction came to me. I immediately shifted my weight in the chair, took a big gulp of whiskey, and asked him if he knew any witches here on the island. Well, that got his attention.

"What do you mean?" he said.

"You know, the ones who put spells on people here on the island," I replied.

And as he took a big drag on his joint and thought for a second about what I had just said, I moved my queen out diagonally four squares to butt up against his knight.

Before he could think, I muttered, "You better put that knight back home, or you won't have him to fight later. And you didn't answer me about the witches." I wouldn't let up; I kept on firing at him. "The one I heard about was absolutely beautiful, and I know where she lives."

"Give me another drag on that joint," I said. "And again, you should probably move that knight back."

I had him a little confused. He didn't know what to do—take another drag himself as I gave it back to him or take a big gulp of his drink or ask me more about that witch or make his next board move. He decided to ask about the witch as he moved his knight back home.

I didn't wait a second before I move my bishop in to take his left bishop's pawn and throw out the loveliest chess term ever created: "Checkmate!"

I had gotten him. Mate in four moves. If he took my bishop with his king, my queen was diagonal on the same color to take his king and lay it down in the victory. He was dead, and I had won.

He sat back, dejected. "How did you do that? I have never lost so fast. Merde!"

As I got up, I said, "Thanks for the drink and thanks for the game. It was fun." He didn't even look up as I headed to the washroom to wash my clothes, although I did hear some grumbling and his fist hitting the table pretty hard.

It was siesta time, a great opportunity for me to wash clothes in the bathroom sink as most of the island was relaxing and resting. It didn't take long. Within twenty minutes, I had hiked to a closed-off cove and had gathered some branches to act as a clothesline on which to dry my clothes in the exceedingly hot Formentera sun.

Time goes by slowly on a quiet island. Another group of days had passed as I mostly stayed in my hidden cove. In all honesty, I hadn't had much energy or motivation. I guess my decision was to stay on Formentera for the time being, but I also knew I could change my mind at any time.

Eventually, and inevitably, this traveler needed to eat, at least a little every day. I think yesterday I had only had an apple, some bread, and some orange soft drink. It was time to climb up and make my way to civilization. Besides, I was low on cigarettes.

I went to Fonda Pepe's. Of course, no mail, but there was news, and it wasn't good. Two girls I had met a couple of times on the island told me a story of two guys who had been arrested by the Guardia Seville at the abandoned Volkswagen bus, and I knew immediately that it was Christopher and Freddie. The word was they knew there was a third person, and they were looking for him. That third person was me. The girls said that Christopher and Freddie were fined a thousand pesetas each and had to leave the island. Neither of those eventualities was on my agenda; I couldn't afford any fines, and I wasn't ready to leave the island just yet.

I rushed to buy some food, drink, and smokes and made my way down the road as fast as I could, peddling my bike furiously, not sure of what to do or where to go. I stayed far away from the abandoned VW bus and made my way to La Mola in hopes of hiding out with someone for a while.

I met Michael, one of the French contingent on the island. We had seen each other a couple of times and shared food together. His ability to speak English was minimal, but we still managed to enjoy each other's company. Matter of fact, he had mentioned me to one of his French friends, Sebastian, whom I had met briefly earlier, and I had been invited to dinner this evening with Sebastian and Colette, who lived with him in a windmill on the mountain's plateau. I wondered if that was the windmill that Bob Dylan had lived in a few years ago.

After hanging out at the Fat Ladies Café for a while, I decided it was time to go to the windmill. It was an opportunity to get away; it was getting to be too nerve-racking looking over my shoulder for the Guardia Seville.

A big smile came over my face as I wheeled my bike closer to the windmill. I could hear music; it was the Jefferson Airplane singing "White Rabbit." Music? Out here, out in the middle of nowhere on the mountain? This was going to be a good, no, maybe even a great dinner. And little did I know as I walked over dirt and scrub grass from the paved road to the windmill that the song would be so very appropriate.

As I approached, I saw Sebastian kneeling by a small outdoor fire, stirring something in a pot hanging over the fire. He was a tall man with wavy dark hair to his shoulders, a gentle manner, and soft blue eyes.

"Buenas tardes, Sebastian," I put forth as I held out my hand to shake his.

"Enchanté, Paul. Welcome. C'est le moulin à vent."

Whatever was cooking outside had my mind reeling with delight. Most of my meals in the last ten days had been cold, and most included peanut butter and bread. I couldn't tell what was cooking, but the smells were orgasmic.

"Comment sur une bière, Pablo?" Sebastian enticed as he got up and jumped up the three steps leading into the windmill.

I went over and sat down on the steps, pulled out a pack of Celtas, and lit one just as Sebastian was coming out with a two-liter bottle of beer and two plastic glasses.

I didn't know how to say "Would you like a cigarette" in French, but I tried my own pidgin French. "Cas Ca say la Celtas?" He poured the beer and took out his own pack of filtered French Gauloises and offered me one of them. Immediately I threw away the unfiltered Spanish Celtas (made of tobacco, grass, and sticks, or so it seemed) and responded "Merci" as I took one.

He sat down next to me, and for a long time we were just quiet. At one point as the sun was starting to set and our top of the mountain was completely still, a lone, floating, high-flying hawk circling and looking for dinner above us, I unconsciously blew a perfect thick smoke ring just as Sebastian opened his mouth to say something.

He stopped himself and with a big smile said, "Wow, fantastique, comment avez-vous fait cela—J'aimerais pouvoir faire ces anneaux de fumée."

I was guessing, but I thought he wanted me to teach him how to blow smoke rings.

We lit two more of his cigarettes, and I started teaching him. He was a quick learner and before long he was getting it.

Just then Colette came to the doorway with a big smile and said, "Bonsoir, Paul, j'espère que vous avez faim. Nous ont beaucoup de nourriture et Patice a fait en sorte que nous ont également beaucoup de bière."

I heard and understood the word for beer. I wasn't sure of

anything else she said, but I was sure of this: she looked beautiful. Her hair was the color of wheat and rippled down her back. She was wearing a long, flowing, and flowering skirt to her ankles and a pale, completely sheer blouse. With the sun setting, the light hit her just right, creating a perfect vision of a vibrant European woman. The transparent top showed her small but plump breasts and perfectly shaped puffy nipples standing at attention almost as if from a movie director's cue.

At that moment in my life, I thought that with the beautiful evening air and the setting sun, the Airplane album still playing, the gourmet smells from the cooking food, the cold Spanish beer, the filtered French cigarettes, and now these beautiful breasts, there could be nothing better, nothing, but nothing in the world could add anything to this experience.

Despite the relative quiet due to the language barrier, it was a very comfortable and enjoyable evening. I had traveled enough to have encountered numerous situations where I was the only one speaking English or where I had to communicate with people whose English was poor. It didn't bother me. The meal turned out to be French crepes that we spread with a chicken curry with bright Spanish peppers, then folded and dipped in a spicy brown sauce accompanied by the baked beans that Sebastian had been cooking outside. I was discovering on this trip that new experiences would become great and lasting memories. This is a meal I will never forget, along with the hamburgers in Istanbul. I enjoyed every bite.

Even though my hosts' ability to speak English was minimal, they could understand much of what I said. As we ate, they urged me to tell my story. Where was I from, why was I traveling, and what stimulated me to come to a distant island in the Mediterranean called Formentera?

I told them everything. I'm not sure how much they got, but they were attentive throughout my dissertation. I wished I could have asked them the same questions and heard their answers, but that was just not in the cards.

The food, the company, and the music were a great distraction from my worries about the Guardia Seville boys. In fact, the music eliminated them from my mind altogether. We listened to the Jefferson Airplane album twice, then a Beatles album, and now, as all three of us lit up, Sebastian put on the album *Sssh* by Ten Years After, a band with which I wasn't familiar. One song, "Bad Scene," embedded itself in my mind. It was different. The acoustic approach just really got to me, especially propped up on a pair of air mattresses around the fire in front of the windmill just lazing out after a great full meal. As we lay there, I couldn't seem to put down the group's album cover. I mentioned to Sebastian, "The illustration on the cover is mesmerizing." The multi-exposure, multi-angled face on the cover seemed to be in motion. Holding it up and pointing to it, I said, "I can't stop looking at this. I wonder—was this drawing created by an artist on some drug? I wonder what the artist was feeling. Could a drug make that happen?"

As I put the album down, I felt that unlike other of my ramblings that evening, they understood this completely.

"Please one more time," I said to Colette and pointed to the record. Sebastian stretched, yawned, carried some of the dishes inside, and motioned for me to come in and look at the inside of the windmill. It was small. The ladder went to another level, which I couldn't really see, but what was visible was suggestive of what living in a covered wagon in the days of the Wild West might have been like. But it was their home; it was a roof over their heads, and they seemed very happy with the primitive setting. I offered to clean up more, but Sebastian pushed me outside to relax.

Sunset, it seemed, was lasting longer than usual. I didn't know if it had been affected by the recent full moon, but the sky was multicolored, magenta and plum and deep coral, some clouds lit up and some in shadow, all drifting in a hypnotic motion. Sebastian came out a minute or so later, and he and Colette came over to me and knelt down. They said, "Paul, c'est pour toi, c'est une bonne nuit pour cela, et nous voulons la partager avec toi. Avez-tu déjà pris un trip au LSD avant?"

Of course, I didn't understand really anything he had said until he got to LSD trip and held out a small purple pill between his thumb and forefinger.

Outwardly, I was proud of my cool persona, but inside I was yelling *What? LSD? Wow, wait—did he just say LSD?!* Then, suddenly, my mind was as calm as my outward appearance. *Why not? You'll never know unless you try it.* What better time, what better place, what better people to join you on an LSD trip? Sebastian pulled out two additional pills as I had taken the first one from him. And almost magically, he handed me a glass of wine as Colette said, "Bon appétit." I swallowed the pill with a big gulp of red wine, and they both.

Nothing earth-shattering happened right away. They put on a Dylan album, and whether the trip had begun to kick in or it was just the beautiful evening, I felt like I was really hearing him for the first time. The vibe was just about perfect.

Sebastian started talking about Bob Dylan, and what I could make out was that he had met Dylan, and Dylan had chosen him to take over the windmill. In any case, it was true that this had been Bob Dylan's hideout from civilization for a while not long ago.

Sebastian carried on his part of the conversation in French, and although I had no idea what he was talking about, I felt comfortable and actually felt I was learning something. My acid trip was flowing nicely from a feeling of earthly bliss to feeling more like I was leaving the earth, traversing invisible dimensions. I kept on looking at my hands, which felt light and tingling. I was a little worried that they might leave my body also.

Sebastian moved closer to me as he sensed a little confusion starting. He tried to distract me. "Paul, tu vas bien?"

At that point, I really wasn't sure what "okay" was. Time was not a reality for the most part. I would start to watch or do something, but then it all merged into Sebastian doing something. The earth was moving but I wasn't, and I couldn't get a grip on the minute-to-minute or hour-to-hour. The music was a familiar and comforting element, an anchor for an experience that I had no reference point for.

At one point Sebastian came over to where I was sort of leaning against my bedroll and handed me a cup of used crayons. He knew I was an artist and I understood that he wanted me to draw something to communicate what I was experiencing. I proceeded to open my sleeping bag and pull out my sketchbook. It was a curious but friendly gesture, but I had no idea what to begin to draw.

I could see Sebastian was somewhat interested in what I could come up with using crayon on paper in the middle of my acid trip, but I could also sense he and Colette had other plans. They stole away inside and shut the door to the windmill, not being rude in any way but just to give the two of them some privacy. They had plans for their acid trip to be a romantic one. As I set up to start to draw something, I wondered what it would be like to make love on LSD.

In any case, I was alone with my crayons and a small, almost unusable Spanish pencil inside the crayon box, stars aplenty, music muffled but still loud enough to feel the heavy bass beat of some rock band, a crackling fire sending flames up in embers floating directly, it seemed, toward the windmill but swerving to either side or moving high above it. With my sketchbook on my lap, I found a blank page and tried to decide what to draw. I was clearheaded, but it was hard to draw, as the world was moving, as if everything around me was part of a carnival ride. I was worried the fire wanted to talk to me, and as I was trying to plan the conversation, I couldn't decide which color crayons to pick up first.

The more I looked at the fire and the floating embers, the more my mind wandered to a million things. All positive, all soothing things, past and present, with some thoughts of the future. I became very relaxed as a new album started to play, some rock group singing, I believe, in French. As with other foreign music experiences recently, I didn't understand the words, but now on this acid trip, I felt I did understand. I didn't need words to know what was being said; the meaning took up residence in me in a place beyond language. In any case, it seemed the right time to start to draw. Without thinking about it too much, I started to draw the windmill, which now appeared to be pulsating. And though I'm sure the embers from the fire went straight up, I drew them circling the windmill, and because I loved the music even though I couldn't understand it, I put the music in my drawing also.

The next morning, I woke up with a blanket over me. A small but raging fire was glowing beside me as Colette came down the windmill's stairs with a hot cup of coffee, smiled at me, and said something softly in French. Eventually, my head became my own, and it was time for me to go.

The next few days were spent mostly trying to stay out of sight, moving from beach cove to some friends' little houses and then back to the beach.

It was now somewhere in the first week of June. Time had been going slowly and fast at once. Mostly I was floating and starting to feel at odds with myself. The rest and relaxation that was supposed to happen here on Formentera had not developed. Yes, there were restful days here and there on the beach, but this was more an island of activity. What I really felt the need for was direction; I needed something to attach to. As I walked my bike from one of the caves on the mountain, purposely skirting El Pilar and any Guardia Seville that might be there, I started to wonder if I should move on from Formentera. But my destination was unclear. Maybe I should have stayed the course, switched trains in Istanbul and continued to try to get to India or parts thereof. Anyway, I would never know. The question was what to do next.

If I stayed on the island, I'd have to quit running and hiding. There were a couple of girls living alone in houses here. Unless I totally misinterpreted their inferences, they approached me about coming to live with them. Now if one of them were Olivia, done deal. I wondered, was I in love with her? Did I really think I could find love like this, here, on an island of strange happenings? It seemed from day to day I changed my mind from yes to no from absolutely to maybe as I thought about her. I didn't know what to do. More importantly, was there anything I *could* do, or did I just have to sit back and let life play out? I was in a new world that might be beyond my pay grade.

Olivia had her own problems. We seemed to be missing each other from town to town, and besides, she was arguing with Jack on Ibiza. The other girls on the island were nice, but in both cases I saw problems. Monique was very attractive, French, but she was really hung up on dope of all kinds. When I thought of her, I thought of the movie *More* (Barbet Schroeder, 1969), and I just didn't see us with any of the same interests. Drugs were never an end, but more a social lubricant. Sarah was German and really kept to herself. I once went to her little house with an invite for dinner. I brought a large bottle of wine, and in the end I drank it all as I choked down the unidentifiable things she cooked that evening. I will have nightmares for years to come thinking about the tastes I experienced that night.

As I made my way to the road leading down from the top of the mountain, I ran into Stefan.

"Buenas tardes, Stefan," I yelled as he made his way out of the woods onto the road. "When did you return to the island? And what about the *policia?* Did you escape?"

"No, I didn't escape. They took me to Ibiza and said leave the islands, but after a few days, I snuck back here. I don't know; I needed to get back here. I left some things with Joyce, and I can't travel without them. I'm going to meet her now at Fonda Pepes. Can we ride together down the mountain?"

"Oh, I don't know, this bike is as old as we are and not in as good shape as we are. But I'm so glad to see you. Okay, yeah, let's try it. I've been dodging here and there, trying to stay away from the towns and the Guardia Seville myself. It's great having you back. Okay, climb up on the handlebars and put your feet here." The day was bright and sunny, the air crisp—all good and surprising as we glided down the mountain road effortlessly as one entity. Even on the curves, there was this combined sense of stability between Stefan sitting on the handlebars and guiding me to the left or right, as seeing over him was difficult.

Stefan started to tell me about a big bullfight that was going to happen on TV that night. He said we should watch it at the Fat Ladies Café. Evidently, he had been reading about this one bullfighter who was just spectacular. And just as he was going to say something else about the event, and as we were really trucking down the road gliding through a turn, he moaned, "Uh-oh." I tried to hike myself up to see over him, and as I did that, I shifted our previously perfect weight distribution, and just like a shot from a lightning bolt the bike started to shake. Stefan shifted his weight on the handlebars a little, and I then could clearly see around him and the scene we were speeding directly into.

I heard him yell in a guttural tone, "Merde!" As the bike now really started wobbling, my eyes almost popped out of my head. There was a small herd of cows passing across the road thirty to forty feet in front of us. Given that we were speeding down the mountain at thirty miles an hour, I was hesitant to brake quickly, but instincts pushed my thinking aside, and I stood up as hard as I could to brake with force. Stefan sensed that immediately and looked back at me just as my left foot slipped off the pedal. The shaking of the bike increased to a major earthquake. Stefan was clinging on for dear life as I attempted to relocate the brake. He screamed something and jumped off the handlebars. I didn't have time to look back and see if he was still alive because that jump put the bike in an irreversible death convulsion that I fruitlessly tried to prevent. I started to tip over to the right side. The bike crashed to the ground first as instinctively I tried to stretch to the opposite left side—to no avail. One second later, I was whipped to the highway also, and both the bike and I started to slide as our velocity hurled us down the mountain. My elbow and wrist seared with pain, then the side of my face slid along the road, some skin tearing excruciatingly from my cheek as the skidding pushed me this way and that toward the cows. I lifted my head just a little as I continued to slide—miraculously seeing that the bike and I might just miss the cows—and then it was over, a big puff of dust following us as the bike and I screeched to a halt.

"Oh no...desastre...esta bien, Senor?" I looked up to see an old Spaniard looking down at me. I guessed he was either saying, "You stupid, stupid hippie. You almost killed my cows and me," or, "Are you alright, mister?" I chose to believe the latter, as he was shaking his head and smiling as he looked back at me. Just then I remembered Stefan. I turned to look for him and saw him lying face down by the side of the road twenty to thirty feet behind me. He wasn't moving. Oh no, he looked dead. I thought, "Shit, I've killed Stefan." Just then he started to move, looked in our direction for a second, and then jumped up and ran into the woods. Either he had bumped his head and was now acting crazy or sensing that I couldn't stop in time had assumed I'd crashed into a cow or two and maybe killed them, and now the farmer was trying to make a citizen's arrest. In any case, it was better for him to leave the scene of the accident.

I sat up saying, "Si, si, Senor, I'm okay." He started to dust me off as we were serenaded by the cows, which had stopped as soon as they heard the commotion. Just then a couple of drops of blood splashed onto one of my hands. I immediately put my hand to my head to feel for a gash.

The old man put his arm around my shoulder to comfort me and reached into his back pocket to locate a handkerchief. I'm sure it had been white at some point, but it looked like it was many years old, and I doubted if it had ever been washed. Just as I was about to politely object, he pushed it into the side of my head—right smack into the wound. All I could do was say, "Gracias, mui gracias, Senor," but I was freaking out thinking that now besides a head wound I had alien elements of God-knows-what mixing with the blood coming out of my head.

After ten or so minutes, my triage doctor decided I would live, wished me luck, and continued driving his cows to a different pasture on the other side of the road.

I eventually picked myself up, checked the bike, which fared better than I did, and started walking back up the mountain to El Pilar, the Fat Ladies, and some type of liquor.

When I finally arrived in La Mola, the Fat Ladies Café was quiet both on the patio and inside. Usually, there were some of the mountain's Spanish grandmothers sitting around and chatting amongst themselves. Not today, it seemed. I walked inside and plopped down, half expecting to see Stefan there, but my company was only a couple of Spaniards, no longhairs.

The owner of the café—clothed in her typical long black dress, top, and black scarf headpiece covering the entire head except for her face—motioned in my direction to Miguel, her son and bar manager, as I sat down at one of the tables. He came over to her, looked at me and opened a drawer by the bar, then brought two clean napkins, one wet, one dry. Miguel was always cordial but never really talked to any of the longhairs, and as he laid down the cloth napkins, he didn't say anything to me either. I patted my forehead, and some dried blood came off. The damp cloth felt good and soothing.

As I understood it, longhairs had been calling this place the Fat Ladies long before Bob Dylan, for some reason I'll never know, but the name was just for identification; in no way was it meant to be derogatory. I'd never talked to the fat lady personally. She looked to be in her eighties. I'm sure she didn't speak English, but we had nodded to each other more than a few times over the last month, and there had been an acceptance of me. That had not been the case, quite frankly, with most travelers who came to the mountain of Formentera. The café certainly enjoyed the money from us, but there was no general approval of the variety of young people who passed through.

In any case, as I ordered a half-liter bottle of Spanish beer and some type of fish dish that was the special, I saw her come out from the back and give Miguel something to bring over to me. He handed me a couple of Band-Aids with a deadpan look. "Gracias," I said with a big smile, looking over at the proprietor, and she nodded back at me with a little smile. I guess I'd spent enough money here that it would be bad for business on her part let me drop dead from a head wound. As my meal came, I saw her motion with some authority to another elderly woman dressed in black to come over to me. Without speaking, she took the Band-Aids and put them strategically on my wound, then smiled and nodded as she went back to her table on the other side of the restaurant. The beer was much appreciated and savored as I started in on my fish.

Not long after, I saw my friend the cattleman—Johnny on the Spot, the ambulance man—come through the door with some other Spanish men and women. He yelled something like, "Hombre de accidente," which I took to mean "Crash Man."

"Gracias!" The entire café looked at me as he laughed and in an animated way proceeded to describe the earlier accident to his friends. His explanation seemed to be a lot longer than the actual event; I think he was expanding his role in the mishap so everyone would leave thinking he was the hero. I smiled and lifted my beer glass to salute him, in a way supporting his story with my gesture as many nodded their heads up and down—it must be a real story, then!

After finishing my meal, still keeping an eye out for Stefan and wondering where he was, I lit up one of my Celta's cigarettes. Miguel, almost on cue, turned on the TV hanging precariously from the wall. The bullfight was starting.

As the night went on, the room grew quiet. It was obvious that watching a bullfight was different in Spain than in any other country. I felt this was almost a religious event, as everyone except for one elderly Spaniard sitting close to me wanted to see the art of a great bullfighter and his magic with his cape and the eventual traditional killing of the bull. The old man, close by, kept saying, "No es bueno"—he had seen too many beautiful animals in his life being put to death. He didn't want any harm to the matador, but he wished the bulls could escape somehow.

As the café was closing, Stefan walked through the door. All evening he had been wandering on the side of the mountain and had gotten lost a couple of times. Finally, he found the road and made it up to the café. He needed a beer more than anyone I'd ever seen; he was exhausted. He was a good friend, so I bought him one last beer before we were asked to leave and told him no humans or cows were killed in the earlier accident. The Spanish cow herder was here earlier, and all was good.

As we walked out of the closing café, he invited me to spend the night with him and some other travelers in the pension. It was a beautiful night; a cooling breeze embraced us as we walked and gazed up at a clear sky with a billion stars. The urge to prolong the moment and take my time overtook me as I turned to him and told him that I would be up shortly but wanted to take a little walk first. What a day—what a first couple of months. Certainly not what I originally planned, but if I ever had felt at one with, really part of the earth, it was now. For the most part, I had never in my life thought of things like this—of the bond between man and earth, sky and sea, of the profound and wordless depths of living a simple, physical life. It was the island, the people, the caves, the solitude, Olivia, the dog, the music, the witches real or not. Hunger and being fed. I felt there was a change taking place in me whether I knew it or not, but at times like this, I absolutely knew it.

I slept soundly but woke up early as the snoring in the room drove me to escape. I wondered, as the sun was barely up, was the Fat Ladies Café open this early?

As I walked onto the covered patio area outside of the café and sat down, the door opened, and the fat lady, surprised to see me, nodded and went back inside. Too bad; it was obviously too early to order a coffee. But a couple of minutes later she came out with a big bubbling hot glass of café con leche and without saying a word put it down in front of me and walked back inside. It was a perfect way in the cool early morning, by myself with a coffee and the world, to just be me, whoever I was or was turning out to be. After a couple of gulps of my steaming hot coffee, I closed my eyes and leaned back, trying to just live and feel the moment and breathe deeply of that cool, crisp, fresh Spanish morning mountain air.

The sound of some pebbles moving made me open my eyes. Standing ten to twenty feet beyond the patio was a tall, good-looking, blond-haired surfer-type guy who seemed to want to approach me but was hesitating to do so. He continued to walk around in circles, every once in a while taking a sneak peek at me. As I ignored him and lit a cigarette, it hit me. I bet he's

American and can't figure out who or what nationality I am. If I'm a foreigner, will he be able to talk to me or not? And if not, would it be too embarrassing for him to try and start some going-nowhere conversation? That thought brought a little smile to my face. So, it looks like I'd done it: I'd traveled so much I'd become indistinguishable from anyone from any country on earth or at least in Europe. My appearance, my longish hair and full beard both bleached from the sun, my skin also dark from the Spanish sunlight, gaunt from lack of food, my dress that of a nondescript traveler. It was just coincidence that I was wearing my sunglasses, which also, I think, kept him somewhat unsure. He came a little closer as I took a sip of my tepid café con leche. I could see he wished someone else would come by, but I was the only one, and the fact that I hadn't said anything yet had created an aura of mystery. I was enjoying this. Finally, he advanced to the stone wall at the edge of the patio and asked me hesitantly, "Do—excuse me, do you. . . maybe speak any English?"

I was a table or two away from the wall. I looked up, hesitated, took a drag, and stared at him for a second or two and finally said with a pause, "A little," in a perfect sort of soft pitch, exactly like Paul Newman might have done in some scene from *Butch Cassidy and the Sundance Kid*. He started to turn away, half expecting my answer to be in some foreign language, and when he realized what I had just said, he turned abruptly around to me. The smile on my face made him smile, and we both started to laugh.

"So, you are American! Where are you from? What are you doing here? how long have…"

I interrupted him. "Whoa, slow down. One question at a time," I responded while motioning him over to my table. He sat down, and immediately the fat lady came to the door, looking at me to see if anything more needed to be ordered. He looked at my glass and asked what it was. I turned to the doorway and said, "Por favor, Senora, dos café con leche. Gracias!" Then I turned to him. "You'll see when she brings them—they are one of the joys of Spain. It appears you just got here."

"Yes, flew into Barcelona from San Francisco two days ago and my girlfriend immediately wanted to come to the islands. She had a friend who said we could live in a small house here for some weeks as she travels around Europe for a while. So here we are. I'm still jet-lagged, couldn't sleep, and thought I'd walk around a little."

I proceeded to tell him a little about the makeup of Formentera. He wouldn't or couldn't stop asking me questions about who I was and my travels. He was very jealous of all the places I'd seen, lamenting that he wouldn't have any chance to travel—not this trip anyway. His name was Steve, and he was about a month away from starting music school in Paris. His weapon of choice was the piano.

We talked for an hour before he said he'd better go back to his girlfriend before she worried about him. We shook hands, and a new good friendship was started.

The next week went by quickly with very little happening. Mostly I stayed by myself and wrote except for two interesting events. I'd seen Olivia here and there. We'd spent a day together, and she even tried to talk another girl into giving up her house so we could live in it. That didn't work out, and I wasn't sure that it would have been a solution to the ever-growing concern of fewer and fewer pesetas in my pocket each day. Not that I was spending a lot; if it weren't for the kindness of certain people on the island, I would have had to leave a long time ago. Many nights I'd been invited to dinner at various people's houses. Olivia was running out of money also, and because of that, she was spending more time, almost all the time, on Ibiza with Jack Waters. Their life didn't cost her anything. It seemed Olivia and I were in limbo; I wished I knew how to break the spell.

Part III

"I was right at the edge of a rogue storm"

While talking with several travelers on the patio of the Fat Ladies Café, I met another new arrival on the island. Bert had just been discharged from the Navy, and instead of going home to the States had made his way across Asia from Vietnam to Formentera. He was about twenty-five, an intense guy, with a full face and restless look, his scraggly long hair in a tight ponytail. We immediately hit it off, and as the group talked, it was obvious the two of us were in sync—we both needed money desperately.

As people left the café and the afternoon went on, Bert and I stayed. We mostly talked about how we could make money so we could travel longer in Europe. I liked Bert from the beginning; we not only thought alike, but he paid for my beers that first afternoon. He had no place to stay, and though I had planned to go back to the VW bus later that night, I told him it was already filled and he'd be better off finding something else. I told him about some caves at the end of the mountain, and he jumped at that. Just then one of the English girls living on Formentera walked by and said she was going to see a friend who lived not far from a cave. He left immediately with her but said he might have an idea on how to solve our money concerns. We made a date to meet the next morning at the Fat Ladies. He had asked me if I wanted to go to the cave with him, but I said I'd already taken that trip many times, and I wouldn't do it again. He couldn't wait to see it.

After buying a loaf of bread, a small jar of peanut butter, and a couple of cans of pop, I started down the mountain to the VW bus. Along the way, the dog came out of the woods. Who knows where he'd been, but he decided to follow me to the Volkswagen.

The next morning Bert was waiting for me at the café. He didn't much care for the cave either and said he had hardly slept.

As we ordered some coffee and a plate of eggs to share between us, we talked about different ideas to make money. Eventually, I said to him, "Hey, I thought you had one particular idea and it was a good one."

He responded, "Well, if you had any artistic experience or ability, I might have an idea, but I'm a dud when it comes to art or design."

"I do actually have a little art background. Why, what's your idea?" I responded quickly.

"Then this is a good idea, Paul; you and I are going to go into business together. We are going to make decorative candles and sell them here on Formentera and Ibiza."

"Candles!" I yelled. "I don't know how to make candles. Aren't they just simple things—long and thin and nothing else?"

He responded, "Not if they are sand candles!"

"Bert, I don't know anything about that kind of thing. I don't even understand candles in the sand. Makes no sense."

"Don't worry, with a little artistic eye from you, we've got it made. I've seen them being sold here and on Ibiza. If someone else can do it, so can we. Listen, all you do is go to the beach, dig a hole, pour in the melted wax, maybe with some color, put in a wick, maybe some shells and you've got a small little manufacturing company that will bring in money. Easy!"

"I'm sure there's more to it than that, but I guess we could do it. How much will this cost, and I assume we will split costs? And besides that, what kind of profit could we make?"

"I've seen candles in one shop selling for between 350 to 550 pesetas. That's about $5 to $7 dollars US. I bet we could buy what we need for half of that, and that would mean a 50 percent profit on each one we make and sell. And that's just based on one shop. Maybe other places, more touristy places, would sell them for more than that," he said as he rubbed his hands together and smiled, meaning there is money here.

"Okay," I said. "Let's go ahead. What do we need to do first?"

Bert took the bus to San Fernando to check out some shops and see some of the competition. We had pooled some money, and I took off on the same bus, but I was going all the way to the port and on the morning boat to Ibiza to buy our supplies. The bus driver smiled a little when he saw I had no bike this time. Usually, he had to lift my bike up to the roof to travel the island until I was ready to get off. He always mumbled many Spanish swearwords whenever he had to lift that bike up.

A full day of looking for supplies was very disappointing. I did buy some crayons for color and some stringy things that looked like wick, but there was no wax. As I was walking around in circles trying to mine some wax somehow, I ran into Olivia. I hadn't seen her in a week or more. She was just delighted to see me, hugs and kisses and an absolute demand to take the bus to

Escola and stay with her and Jack Waters and have dinner later that night. That was the best offer I'd had in a long time. Maybe I was a little jealous, but that was overshadowed by the idea of dinner—and of spending the evening with her.

The restaurant and bar Waters owned exceeded my expectations. It was very well done, interesting, quality all the way. I had the best meal I'd had in weeks and slept in a bed. I couldn't even remember last time I'd slept in a bed. Too bad he was the enemy, that third wheel between Olivia and me, because he was really a nice guy, and in every other way we could be great friends. I didn't know what he knew about Olivia and me, other than that we were good friends. Maybe he didn't care.

He thought the idea to go into business making sand candles was half-baked but said there were other things to do to make money. He said someday Ibiza was going to be like the Yukon years ago in the States—there was going to be a gold rush, not of minerals, but of tourism. He said he knew this Spanish contractor who wasn't getting much work; we could get him very cheaply. His idea was to build Roman Baths by the beach for the tourists. He said he had seen something like that in Morocco, and there was a two-week wait for reservations.

Sadly, I didn't have the capital to build Roman Baths or anything else for the tourists of the future.

Neither Jack nor Olivia had any ideas about where to buy wax. Maybe back in Barcelona, but that wasn't feasible. After another day and night, I returned to Formentera.

After a day of looking for Bert, I finally found him at one of the beach bars. He was heavily liquored up and so happy to see me; he thought I'd left for good. We got him ready for the world with a long shower and made plans for the next day. The hell with wax;

we decided to find and buy cheap candles and melt them down. That was his job. Mine was to find a candle-making place on the beach, someplace private and out of the way.

The next night we were having a simple dinner of a loaf of bread and some undetermined deli meats and sharing a liter bottle of beer. I had found a pretty good hidden cove. We had to climb down some rocks to get to it, so we'd have some privacy. We went to sleep early with visions of sand candles with dollar signs coming out of them as the waves serenaded us to sleep.

Morning always came early on the beach as the seagulls and other birds and animals started their lifelong morning search for nourishment, and we were up with the sun. Bert was our leader in the process of making our candles even though he had only been involved himself once before and that was as an observer. We built a fire to melt the candles into the liquid wax we needed to pour into our multiple sand-pit molds. Believe me, it did not go unnoticed that we were in the process of melting already made candles to produce wax to make and resurrect them again into their second life as new and different candles. Regardless, with Bert's Navy metal cooking kit and pots we were able to melt the wax and strip the paper covering from our crayons to produce colored candles. Unfortunately, I soon found out that the color was only visible on the flat top surface of the candles. Now, before we poured our wax in our holes in the sand, I needed to step up and create some designs on the outer edges to give them distinct personalities and make them more desirable.

The little cove I had found to make our candles was also a gold mine for tons of shells and glittery rocks and other beachy odds and ends. We picked up tons of them, and I spent an hour lying on my belly placing the shells and other pretty bits on the walls of our holes, always remembering to think in reverse, since when we took the formed candles out, we would see the better side of all the decoration.

The holes ready, the wax melted, we filled our seven holes to the top, carefully adjusting our wicks strategically. As we waited for them to harden, we lost some and had to remake others. Sometimes we misjudged the candles' ability to withstand the strength and effect of certain waves that flooded some of our holes. After hours of hardening, we excised the sand candles and carefully rubbed off the excess sand from the sides to make everything look smooth and finished. It had taken most of the day. We were exhausted but felt successful as we laid all seven out in front of us and admired our work. Maybe they weren't masterpieces, but I thought they were more attractive than lots of the tourist stuff I'd seen in shops.

The next day we took two to San Francisco and then another two to Escoloe. Unfortunately, neither place could buy them outright. That wasn't what we'd hoped for, but at least they took them on consignment. Bert went back to the beach, and I spent the day at Fonda Pepe's. I'd had it with sand for a while.

Bert and I met the next day in Escoloe, but nothing had sold. Granted, it had been less than 24 hours that the candles had been for sale, but Bert was anxious. He told me as we were walking down the street, "I'm broke, Paul, and I'm wiped out. I think I'm stuck on this island for the rest of my life. I could have some money waiting for me in the American Express office on Ibiza, but who knows."

Okay, now he was making me nervous. I'd gone into business with the guy who spent his last pesetas on our sand-candle-making supplies. "Listen, fucker," I said. "You won't have to live on

Formentera for the rest of your life. I've got your back."

He decided we shouldn't put all our eggs in one basket, that basket being Formentera. He grabbed two candles and borrowed some pesetas from me. He said he was going to Ibiza to check on his wire transfer and would either sell these sand candles or throw them through the window of the shop. He left to catch the boat.

The last day or two had seemed to be a hazy maze of chasing my tail and ending up where I began. I had spent part of a day trying to find Bert; this sand candle thing just wasn't coming to life very easily.

Later in the morning, I was walking back from the windmill. I had hoped to catch Sebastian relaxing and join him for a day of listening to music. The windmill was locked, however, and no one was around. As I walked back to the Fat Ladies, the dog came out of nowhere and started walking with me. He looked thirsty, so I told him to come with me and we'd get him some water as long as we could avoid the Guardia Seville. As we entered the town, I came across Steve and Annie. They said they were on their way to the beach to take an acid trip together. Steve asked if I had ever taken one and then proceeded to give me a tab before they walked off.

Entering the Fat Ladies, I asked for some water, but Miguel said the plumber was there and the water was turned off at the moment. I looked down at the dog, who seemed to have understood. He was looking even more upset than before. I don't know why but I felt some responsibility so I ordered two small beers and a bowl. I gave one beer to the dog and drank the other one. Halfway through it, I popped the LSD into my mouth and swallowed.

The dog either thought he was entirely beholden to me or that if I was such a fool as to buy him a beer in the first place, he should follow me; there might be more drink or food to come. We found a spot on the mountain under a small tree and settled in. After an hour of trying to write poems, I started to regret not having split the acid and given half to my partner the dog.

The rest of the day was spent in and out of reality. Out of reality, I was with the dog, who in that world could talk to me in English. We did talk a lot, but we also just looked out to the edge of the cliffs, each of us thinking and dreaming about different things. My second acid trip played out a lot easier than the first. Either I was mellower during the day or the dog was, but we played off of each other, and it was peaceful but uneventful. I continued to write poems until I couldn't write anymore. The trip produced too many colors, too many floating things, and too many distractions to even try to explain.

I eventually made my way back to my secret cove. I slept the night staring at the additional candle materials we still had. I couldn't take it. Even though these first candles hadn't sold right away, I still believed they would, and I decided I'd make more candles by myself. After a simple meal at the beach bar down the road, I started making candles late in the afternoon. One of the first things I did was I built a big dam. I wasn't prepared to lose any candles to the waves.

Everything was going well—until out of nowhere, it wasn't. As I was digging holes and kneeling in the sand, I started to feel something odd happening against my right leg. My first thought was that it was nothing, just my imagination. But it continued, and I finally thought it might be one of those beach dragonflies that had been flying around me on this part of the beach and for some reason hopping on and off my leg. As I brushed my right hand down my leg, still shoveling with my left hand and looking into the hole, I froze for a second. My hand came to rest against something—well, something I wasn't expecting. If this was a dragonfly, it was worthy of its own horror movie. This object was big, bigger than any Amazonian insect I'd ever heard of or seen or, for that matter, any I'd seen on the big screen at the movie theater. Slowly, I started to turn to my right and look down my leg, and then I saw it.

A large mass of spindly, odd-looking legs and tentacles and two big eyes met my glance. At that moment, the last thing I needed was a pissed-off crab disagreeing about where and how I was going to dig additional holes for the next portion of wax to set. It might have been the largest crab I had ever seen, at least in person. I yelled, "What the fuck!" and jumped to the left, falling into the sand head and body. Simultaneously, I swear, I heard a little crab-like guttural sound yelling in crab-speak "What the fuck!" It jumped at the same moment, and as I was scurrying on my knees towards a big boulder at the edge of the beach, I looked back. It appeared to have vanished in mid-air. I got up and peeked out behind the boulder but didn't see it. Still breathing heavily, I pulled out a pack of Celtas, lit one, and sucked in a big inhale. I was still wondering if it was some type of alien animal and how it managed to vanish instantaneously. In the middle of my second drag on the cigarette, I noticed motion in the area of my sand-candle hole. Then I saw those two big eyes.

From behind the boulder, it was spying on me from the hole. Was this the smartest crab on earth, really? It was spying on me, not taking any chances just the same as I, a human being, was doing with it. We continued to watch each other as I finished my smoke. Then it hit me. *What am I doing? I'm hiding from a crab.* What was I—a man or a mouse? I was at least ten times bigger than it was. It really was a big, mother-looking crab. I finally decided this beach was not big enough for both of us—it was either him or me, and I wasn't going anywhere. This was sand-candle central on Formentera. I looked around for a weapon before I moved out into the open, but there was nothing but sand. Forget it; I'd fight it body to body. I started to walk towards it hesitantly, not knowing exactly what I'd do when I got to it. As I walked, it climbed out of the hole and started walking on its six legs towards me. I imagined the scene from above. It looked like the two of us drawing down on each other, walking the main street of Old Dodge City in the 1830s, wondering who would draw first. We were just about five feet apart when it stopped and sort of stretched upward for a second, almost like it was trying to make itself as big as I was. And then it charged at me. I wasn't counting on that at all. I jumped up and over to the right, landing hard on the sand by the fire that was melting the wax. I was fully expecting it to have outflanked me and to find it about to attack me from behind, but when I quickly turned, all I saw was some sand flying up as it made its way to a hole in the boulder I had just left. Was that its hideout? Did he have a gang? Would I be outnumbered shortly? One minute, then another passed, and after about ten minutes of being frozen on the sand, I decided I had won. It had high-tailed it to another world, whether down under or on the other side of the boulder. I had won.

By the time I had formed eight candle holes and filled them with the last of our melted candle wax, it was dark. I was exhausted. I was also tired of looking over my shoulder every other minute for that unearthly crab. Fortunately, there still was no sign of it. I decided this time I'd let the wax harden all night. As

I lay on the flat rock overhang about four feet up from the sand watching the waves gently rolling under the remaining bright light of a recent full moon, I lit up one final cigarette and drank the last of some very warm and suspicious-tasting Spanish beer. Sand candle making by yourself is a lot harder than with a partner, but I did it, and if I do say so myself, every time I made one, it was better than the last. Those moments before falling asleep were golden. The scene was out of a motion picture with a big moon, puffy white clouds, the moonlight on the water, and the perfect sound of soft waves caressing my dam, continually trying to find a way over or around.

As I lay on my back looking up at one of the clearest, brightest, most star-filled night skies I've ever seen, I felt lonely for a second. The moment passed, but I started thinking about being alone and what happened sometimes when you are. Life is different from your normal life. I was starting to discover that repeatedly on this journey of mine. There are certain experiences you have alone that are more meaningful than they would be if you shared them with someone special. Those experiences often change people more than other types of experiences. As I watched a shooting star fly across the sky, I noticed in the horizon some far-off lightning flashes. Just then a large fish jumped in the water not far from my little cove, and I thought of an experience I'd had a long time ago, an experience that brought something out in me I hadn't known existed.

I was about nine years old. It was a hot summer, and as my mother, Inez, would often do to broaden her family's horizons, she had booked us into a resort with cabins and a main activity building in northern Minnesota by Leech Lake. The resort was called Merritt's Lodge. Of course, none of us wanted to go, neither

234

my brother Dave, seven years old, nor my sister Elaine, who was five-and-a-half years old at the time, but we did the long drive in our 1950s gray Packard anyway. When I first saw our isolated, musty-smelling log cabin, I panicked. This was going to be bad. I thought about telling the owner my father was a bank robber and we were on the run; lucky for him, I was the law-abiding one in our family, and he should call the police immediately. As you can see, I really felt concerned about this place. However, not knowing the ultimate consequences of that idea, I decided not to go through with it and to make the best of what was to come. My father, Alex, took Dave and me out in a small rowboat twice to fish, but we didn't catch anything. After some swimming one morning, I decided I had to catch something. My father would never let me go out in a rowboat by myself (smart move on his part), and it seemed no one else wanted to try fishing again for the rest of this trip.

So that afternoon, I took my rod and a small green tackle box and set off down a path not far from the shoreline to the north of the resort. After about a half hour, I came upon a little inlet harbor with some boats and people. I skirted them and after maybe another ten or fifteen minutes of walking, I wasn't getting very close to the water as the terrain was rocky with steep cliffs. But then I thought I saw an old path grown over, and I followed it to a little, overgrown, deserted beach surrounded by trees. This was it; I had found my place, no one around, all to myself.

As any nine-year-old would do, I took out my biggest lure first and immediately started casting. I was sure this gaudy lure would get me a big fish of some kind. Until then, the only fish I'd ever caught were some bluegills. I was sure I'd land a bass or a walleye at this spot. After about four or five casts, I snagged something.

Wow, this was a big one; I could hardly believe it. However, he was so big that I couldn't even reel him in. As fast as I thought I was the best fisherman at the resort, I soon discovered I had just snagged my lure—my best lure, unfortunately—on some stupid-ass log or something way out in the water. I had to cut my line and put on my second-best lure and started casting again. And again, after six or seven casts, I snagged my line on something under the water. After cutting my line and seeing I only had two lures left, I decided to put my pole down and go into the forest to look for some worms. The undergrowth was too thick. I barely even found any dirt to dig in, and when I did, all I came up with was more dirt. I had no watch and started to wonder how long I'd been gone. The more I thought about it, the more I imagined I was in store for a yelling when I got back. Of course, I didn't tell anyone where I was going, which was typical of me since I rarely considered the consequences of my actions. I surveyed the water in front of me, trying to be Superman with x-ray vision. I decided I needed to cast to the right side of my inlet, as I guessed there would be fewer logs under the water there. I put on another lure, this one green and brown all over, much smaller than the first couple, which didn't instill much optimism in me. I started to cast.

Okay, first casts, no snags. I was brilliant. I thought, I'm a true fisherman; I can adapt. More casts, no snags, but also no bites. I again wondered about the time as the sun moved closer to the horizon and peeked through the trees beyond my little cove.

Well, that was that, I thought. No fish and a good yelling waiting for me when I got back. I was kinda used to the yelling; I was that kind of kid. My father was as accommodating as any father, but I seemed to be always pushing the envelope. I decided one more cast and then I had to make tracks back to the cabin.

I hadn't paid much attention to my other casts, and remember, I was nine, barely responsible enough to be tying my shoes in the morning, but for some reason I remember watching that last cast gliding over my head as it appeared almost in slow motion floating to the surface of a tree-shadowed spot thirty to forty feet out in front of me. Not bad, I thought, and almost immediately as I started to reel it in, again, it was stuck. Great, snagged again. This really had turned out to be a shitty spot to fish. I pulled, walked to the left, and pulled again—stuck again. "Shit! Shit!" I laid my rod down and got my penknife, and as I turned around and then back again to reach for the pole, I saw it start to move. It was slowly being pulled into the water. I dove for it and got up, and no one at that point was more surprised than me to see the line moving in the water. I'd either hooked a submerged log that had come to life or I had some animal hooked, and it might even be a fish.

This was different. I knew all there was to know about hooking logs or branches underwater, but finally, I was standing there on the sandy shore like a real fisherman with a pole in hand feeling the significant pull of an animal on the line. For a minute I imagined it felt like a big animal, but I quickly came back to reality. What did I know about something big? It was probably another bluegill.

There are moments in life that are just one-of-a-kind amazing experiences you'll never forget. I was maybe having one. This was perfect: feeling the pull of the line, the sun setting, alone on a sandy shore, just me and the wild of nature. I thought it couldn't get any better as I put one good tug on the line and reeled quickly. That's when it happened. I've never forgotten that next sight. It lasted only for a second, but the image was burned into my brain forever.

Just as I finished setting the hook, the lake water broke out in front of me, and I was frozen for a second as a very large fish jumped all the way out of the water. "Whoa! Are you shitting me?" I yelled out as I grabbed the rod tighter. I thought to myself, *I've hooked a monster.*

I kept pulling it in; it kept fighting. Finally, after a good long while, I saw it close by the shore under the water. I was sure I had hooked a northern pike. Wow, I thought, wait until everyone sees this. The big fish was finally tired of fighting me. I pulled it out and laid it on the sand. It was as big as one of my legs, if not bigger. I immediately grabbed my tackle box and with the fish still dangling from my pole, I tore off running down the path.

As I was running, all I could think about was that I had caught a really big fish; I must be a professional fisherman. *Just wait till my brother Dave sees this!*

Bursting through some light branches from a bush, I jumped out on the path just by the dock I had circumvented earlier.

"Hey, kid, come here. Whatcha got there? Let me see that," rang out from one of three older guys sitting on the dock.

I sidestepped from running the path and jumped on the dock, out of breath. I cried out, "Look, I've caught a huge northern pike! Look at this whopper!"

As I stood there trying to catch my breath, my heart beating furiously, one of the guys, in a green plaid shirt, took my line and held the fish up close.

"Smitty, look at the markings. Whatta you think?"

"You know, I think I know what you're thinking, Frank. The dumb kid has actually hooked a Leopard Muskie. I'll be damned."

"I've got a tape measure in my pocket. Let's measure it."

"Kid, lay it down on the dock."

Then one of the guys, in a floppy hat with small lures stuck on the sides and wearing a tan shirt, measured and then looked at the other as the third guy threw a pail of water on the fish that looked like it was breathing its last.

"You see what I see, Frank? It's just short of a keeper; we'll have to throw it back in the water now."

"Let me have the fish, kid. I'll unhook it," he said as he grabbed the pole from me.

I could not believe my ears. Was this dipshit going to throw my trophy back in the water? Without thinking, overwhelmed with emotion, I tried to grab the pole back and yelled, "Fuck you! This is my fish. Give me my rod."

"Watch your language, kid. This fish is not a keeper. We measured and it's just under two and a half feet long. It's the law; we have to throw it back."

He grabbed my pole again and swung the line to the other guy, who unhooked it.

"No, no, you asshole, it's my fish," I screamed as the third guy grabbed my arm to make sure I didn't jump in the water after the fish. The other guy said, "Wow, haven't seen a Leopard Muskie like this in years," as he knelt and wiggled the fish, holding the tail back and forth as the fish was put in the water. Eventually, it swam away. "Sorry, kid. Go home. Go catch a real northern," I heard as they all sat down and reached for their beers.

I was dumbfounded; I couldn't believe what had happened. Suddenly, it was like I wasn't there; they were ignoring me. I was done. There wasn't anything I could do. I thought about putting my tackle box down beside them and starting to cast wildly right by them to piss them off, but then I looked at the dark water below the dock. I couldn't tell how deep it was, and there was the chance I would be playing with fire doing that. They just might pick me up and throw me in.

As I walked away, I turned to them periodically and gave them the finger. I was continually swearing under my breath as I eventually crested the hill overlooking our cabin. I was sure no one would believe me, as I had no evidence of my great feat. Dave especially would be skeptical. And to a certain degree, he had a right to be. My childhood was filled with wild imagination, though more than a few adventures that sounded like BS were real.

Now, lying on my rock outcropping, I did have one last thought. My fishing tale was a true tale. Many people joke about fish stories that are exaggerated or complete inventions. I've had to live all these years with my fishing story, and I've put up with both doubters and believers. Now, likewise, I've had experiences on this trip—some simple, but some extremely interesting. Years into the future, I would realize that most great interesting stories, told or written with passion, are true; at least the fundamentals are true. Mine was true. And that experience was a little change of life for me. That experience altered me in a number of ways, as do many experiences as we grow up. I obtained one more of those important inner-confidence builders some of us get as we move through our youth. They become part of the fabric of your adult life.

Sleep eventually came, that is, after continually leaning to my left still looking for that devil crab. Unfortunately, I was rudely awakened from a great dream with a bang and a clash. I jumped out of my skin, looking around for what had woken me up.

I could see nothing. The wind had picked up considerably; I felt that and had an uncomfortable chilled shudder as I stretched and sat up and looked around. I had no idea how long I had been asleep. Then I saw a lightning flash out in the water and heard thunder. The sky was still lit by the moon, but that perfect scene had disappeared, and now we had a little bit of eerie going on. I was awake now. Automatically, I reached for a cigarette. As I took a couple of drags, I watched the lightning in the distance. I had believed originally it was heading south toward the African coast. But the more I watched, I realized that the storm was growing, and the sound of the thunder was getting closer and louder. Then, out of nowhere, a flash came almost right over me, and then a huge clash of thunder boomed, almost knocking my socks off.

"Shit!" I yelled as all of a sudden, I was right at the edge of a rogue storm. Like clockwork, about thirteen seconds later, another flash. This time I saw the lightning strike out on the sea not that far from me. The wind jumped to a gale quickly, and as I looked at my candles, I saw a big wave come crashing over the dam, flooding the cove. I jumped down. I had to get those candles. I pushed away the sand surrounding the first hole and pulled out its candle, immediately placing it on the edge of my sleeping area. As I turned around to go for another one, the rain came in buckets. Now I was fighting water potentially deadly to my candles from both the sky and the sea. The next candle just wouldn't come free from the sand around it. I forced it, and the candle started to break apart as another crack of thunder above me jolted me. I froze for a second. Now the sea was three to four inches deep and covering the cove. I was having a hard time locating the candles; the intensity of the wind and rain was a major distraction. I worried that I was out in the open, a sitting target for the lightning. I dove with my hands for the next hole underwater in the dark, trying to free the sand candle. I started to feel the exercise was a losing one. I lifted it out, and it also started to fall apart. I sat back, the sea up to and above my hips, and just watched the waves crash in on me and around me. It was over, a complete loss, all that effort. I was soaking wet, and as I started to get up, as the waves continued to splash all around me, I looked to the rock ledge hoping my sleeping bag and everything that I owned inside of it was still there. It was, but as I reached it, I found it soaked through, some things inside wet or getting wetter. I grabbed it, rolling it into a ball, and started to climb out of Dead Candle Cove. Halfway up, I found another crevice in the rocks and stuffed my sleeping bag in. I turned around and sat dumbfounded and numb, staring at the lightning hitting the sea in front of me. As I looked down to the sand, I saw the crab walking through the small rippling ocean waves toward the Mediterranean. It was misty, and the rain was falling in my eyes, but I swear I saw it stop and turn to look at me and lift one of its claws. I know this would be impossible, but I swear it held the claw up at me like it was giving me the finger. It then turned and disappeared into the sea.

Lying there confused and demoralized, I started to wonder what other catastrophes had happened on this beach over the years or would happen in the years to come. Or was it just my catastrophes?

Of course, the next day was bright sunshine all day long. I spent the day not far from the beach bar, drying out everything that I owned. I was at wit's end. Physically and mentally, I felt the fates were against me; they were trying to tell me something. The end was coming. I was days away from having spent two months on Formentera, but every part of my body and mind was saying *leave the island now.*

The afternoon bus brought Bert and what else: more bad news. A couple of days before, someone had brought a hundred new sand candles to all the shops on Ibiza, and nobody wanted

Walking at Sunset on the Beach

I was walking alone on the sand.
The sky torch was fading,
The sea gulls were flying home,
I was standing calmly in the surf.
The wind was caressing me,
I was happy as I thought about tomorrow.

Then a figure in shadow appeared.
At the far end of the beach,
It came slowly towards me.
The wind stopped, the sea was silent,
I was face-to-face with death.

I stepped back.
He laughed and looked out to sea.
It was a glorious sunset,
I was glad for it was my last.
Then death and I walked to the end of the beach together.

Early the next morning,
An old couple stopped near the shore
Where I had also stopped the night before.
"What a beautiful spot, we should come
back this evening to watch the sunset
here on the beach,"
Said the old woman as they looked out to sea.

Written June 18, while spending time alone on the beach

ours. Bert had to sell two candles for $1 just to get a ticket back to our island.

That sealed it. We were done, and I was done with Formentera. Bert went to the cave to get his things, and I turned in my bike. By chance, I met Olivia in San Francisco. She was on the island two more days, staying with a girlfriend from Sweden. She told me to go to Ibiza. Jack would put us up until the boat left for Barcelona. She hated that I planned to leave. There was unfinished business. There was also something else, but I couldn't put my finger on it.

A couple of lazy days went by with many good conversations with Jack Waters. I felt he'd love us to start some business on Ibiza, and we talked about many ideas. At the same time, I was battling some illness. I was very lucky that I could rest there and lie around with free meals and lodgings.

Unfortunately, there was a lot of discussion about Olivia between Bert, Jack, and me. I was somewhat in the middle. Olivia had recently asked me to meet her in Switzerland; she was leaving the islands also, but Bert and Jack didn't know that.

A day later, the shit really hit the fan. Jack and Olivia had a big fight, and she stomped out. In addition, Bert and I had a big argument. He read something I wrote in my diary—I can't remember exactly what—that offended him. Something about Jack. He took Jack's side as I took Olivia's. He said, "I've had it with you—we're done. Stay away from me." So, though we had had tentative plans to travel to Switzerland together, Bert and I would go our separate ways when we got off the boat in Barcelona.

I spent the next day with Olivia. We rode bikes to the beach and talked about many things. One of the things we talked about was no more islands. The very next day I would get on a boat for Barcelona and for the first time in two months walk on land that was not surrounded by water on all sides. We also talked about the past, the present, and the future as we laughed and teared up together. We would try and meet up in the Alps; that would be great, but on the other hand, I also left her with the possibility that I might never see her again. I was in love with her still, but I didn't know what to do about it. Make plans? How could I make plans? I didn't know what I'd be doing tomorrow.

These islands were about to let go the hold they'd had on me for the last couple of months. I'd changed being here. Yes, I was older, but more importantly, I was wiser and more seasoned.

This trip, from the time I landed in Luxembourg until today, had been life-changing. Had the time on Formentera, especially, created a new version of Paul? I was certainly tired now of how I had lived on that rock of land, but there is no doubt I left more confident. Matter of fact, if I had thought I had life and this world in my pocket previously, I knew now I had started out with a very soft grip on what life really is and what it could be. In hindsight, my past thoughts were pretty shallow. I was a different person. I had lived a life recently that I had never imagined living. I'd spent two months without the assurance of a roof over my head each night. I'd thought about and dealt with money as I'd never had to before. I'd learned to navigate with and from people from all over the world. I'd traveled hundreds of miles with my thumb. I'd learned to communicate with people in languages I didn't speak. I'd thought about things in groups and by myself—either in caves or on mountains or on isolated beaches—that most people have never thought about. I left the Mediterranean Sea with interesting tales, but I also left, if I was any type of person, with the ability to benefit from these unusual experiences. I had to admit Formentera was not one of the most stupid and most uninteresting places

And When I Looked Back...

I looked up, because, I thought I heard a voice from the sky,
Was it her, no, only the wind about to cry—

And when I looked back, she was gone.

I could still imagine her holding my hand,
But, alas, it was only a memory of this strange, strange land—

And when I looked back, she was gone.

I heard her voice, coming from where she once had been,
But it was only the whisper of a very foreign wind--

And when I looked back, she was gone.

I thought I heard her clear and loud,
But as I looked, I knew I'd never find her in any crowd--

And when I looked back, she was gone.

I thought I could still feel her hair brushing my face,
But it was only the wind teasing me with thought of her embrace—

And when I looked back, she was gone.

I looked down that dusty road, and for a second hoped she had turned around,
But it was only my imagination, then I knew she might never be found.

And when I looked back, she was gone.

As I walked back, by chance again I thought I heard her like before,
Was it only a dream, but maybe, again, I had to look just once more—

And when I looked back, she was gone.

Written June 25, anticipating leaving Formentera and thinking of Olivia on earth. I was totally wrong about that. I knew then my life, my world, would never again be the same. After this, would I ever want it to be?

Barcelona

If you ever wondered whether there are such things as angels, there are, and Gabriela and Augusto were two of them. I hardly knew them; they didn't know me; we mostly spoke different languages, yet they held out their hand because someone needed it, well beyond what normal people would ever do.

12.

Los Colores

9:00am, Monday, June 29, 1970

The Ibiza-Majorca-Barcelona passenger ship departed the port of Ibiza on the afternoon of June 28th and arrived with the rising sun the next day at the historic city of Barcelona, which centuries ago sent Christopher Columbus to find the New World. Finally, back on solid ground, not island dirt and sand, would I also find a new world as I contemplated in what direction to head next?

I was so glad to be off the high seas. My ticket price barely afforded me the ability to hang on a side railing flopping over the sea as we navigated the Mediterranean. It was rough. I didn't see Bert at all. I hoped his travels in the future found him happier than when we parted. Although the morning sun was still shining, already it felt like afternoon heat. I was somewhat in shock as I walked the pier to solid ground, especially seeing what lay before me: the hustle and bustle of a very large city; the craziness of one of the world's largest and most inhabited cities thrown at a guy who had lived on a small, fairly uninhabited piece of land out in the sea for the last two months.

After spending two months on islands with populations that numbered fewer than most college campuses, I was getting a real wake-up call as I walked toward buildings that looked as high as mountains and a noise level that was almost debilitating compared to the quiet of my little Formentera. Yes, each step brought me closer to chaos and the fearful thoughts of trying to hitchhike out of a large city.

The huge Columbus Monument appeared to be waiting to greet me as I walked to the edge of the harbor. Already I was tired and hot just from walking the incredibly long dock area from the ship. My land legs were taking a while to replace my sea legs. The cooling island breezes had left me, and the big city felt like a lion ready to pounce.

I stopped for a second to think what my next move might be. Every direction looked busier and riskier than the other. No one was going to pick up a hitchhiker during this traffic. While on the boat I had pledged to myself to only spend money on food, liquor, or cigarettes for the rest of the trip. I had to avoid spending any pesetas for travel or shelter. I was a hitchhiker, end of story.

As I was scratching my head trying to visualize the best direction to head in, I noticed a bench. I sat down, sliding to the shaded part. Not long after, a nice Spanish couple I had met very briefly on the ship came by and stopped to chat. They were attractive and stylish but in a quiet way. The woman's bright pink lipstick matched her scarf; the man wore a dark, button-down shirt and had a beard.

After a couple of pleasantries, I asked if they had any idea where I could go to hitch a ride heading north up the coast. They looked at each other and then at me, and their faces said everything: it would be an impossible task. They told me I had to walk ten or twenty miles to the best highway or buy a ticket on the train going north. They added that as the day went on, Barcelona would get more hectic as the Spanish dictator, Franco, was in town. I don't know exactly what kind of face I made at that point, but it stirred compassion. Gabriela looked at Augusto, saying something in Spanish and then asked me if I'd like to come to their apartment and think out my next move a little more thoroughly.

If you've ever wondered whether there are such things as angels, there are, and Gabriela and Augusto were two of them. I hardly knew them; they didn't know me; we mostly spoke different languages, yet they held out their hand because someone needed it, well beyond what normal people would ever do.

We walked to a very quaint and old part of Barcelona and up to their third-floor, one-bedroom apartment overlooking a small but busy street filled with restaurants and shops of all kinds. The apartment was nicely appointed and presented a crafty feel, which was apt as both of my hosts were artists. Gabriela, in her early twenties, was Barcelona born and bred, a true artist and photographer. Augusto, maybe a little older and from the Spanish hills, was an excellent and accomplished photographer. I looked at his pictures on the walls and we talked about artists we admired.

As the day went on, I realized I was feeling more relaxed and clear-headed than I had in months. The atmosphere and hospitality that the two of them provided were immediately healing. Though my odyssey on the islands was meant to be the ultimate rest stop, in hindsight, many of those days were filled with suspense, drama, anxiety, and bewilderment. Augusto and Gabriela were educated and cosmopolitan, counterculture in their interests and sympathies but living productive lives.

That afternoon, after a long shower and some of Gabriela's homemade punch, we all sat down to talk. My look, as well as my unusual composure and demeanor, identified me as a traveler who had navigated many miles. Gabriela wanted to hear about distant cities. Augusto was especially interested in my sketch/wordbook. Besides being some of the nicest people in the world, each was smarter than the other and noticeably more intelligent and creative than most.

Augusto seemed to be especially taken by one of my long poems. My original title was "Color has Appeared in the Middle of White," but he dubbed it "White Turns to Color". There were lines he kept on asking me about repeatedly, and then finally he said, "These words deserve music. Have you ever written any songs, Paul? This to me is a song waiting to take flight."

"No, not really, even though sometimes I wonder if…"

"Well, Paul," he continued, "I have an idea. We know a group who is looking for English lyrics for songs. Would you be interested in showing them your words as a possible song for them?"

It was so nice of Augusto to think of that, but really, what chance was there of any of it happening? I needed a path out of Barcelona. Did I want to spend time with some local group of young guys with whom there would presumably be a language barrier?

"Augusto, thanks for the thought, but I really don't…".

He ignored my objection and continued, "Their name is

Màquina! and they are to play at The Isle of Wight Concert later in the year," as he continued to flip through my drawings and poems.

Immediately, I sat up and looked around. Did I hear that correctly? Although no one else was there, I still looked around to see if anyone else had heard what he had just said. The Isle of Wight! I knew the Doors were going to be there, as well as The Who, Jimi Hendrix, Jethro Tull, and many more. This group was not some high school group; they were big, and I needed to find out more.

Augusto made a call to the group, but they weren't available until Tuesday or Wednesday. It didn't matter how Augusto had a connection—possibly photography, I thought—to Màquina! (In English, that's "Machine.") I mentally pinched myself a couple of times.

While lying on a couch in the living room trying to fall asleep, I thought once more how strange and wonderful life can be. I started the day standing alone before a huge metropolitan city, lost as to what to do next or even how to think of my way out of this threatening predicament. And before someone could tell me to click my heels three times and say, "There's no place like home… There is no place like home…" my predicament changed to exhilaration and excitement. What a day. I couldn't wait to see what tomorrow would bring.

The next morning, Augusto and Gabriela checked in with their bosses and organized some work. I rose and felt like I should explore a little outside their apartment. Almost immediately upon reaching the street, I was drawn to the smell of some pastries that wafted out from a little café. I entered. There were no other customers, just a very cute young girl behind the counter as I sat down on one of the stools. She was probably eighteen, with shining eyes and long dark hair.

"Señorita, buenos dias," I said as I looked for a menu.

She replied with the greatest, warmest smile. "Buenos dias, senor, que le gustaria comer?"

I know she said good morning, but I didn't know the rest. It didn't matter; I was just staring at her. I was in love. We had that moment that sometimes happens in life: Out of nowhere, a stranger walks into a café looking rough, rugged, and weathered. A beautiful, innocent young Spanish lady asks what she can do for him. Their eyes meet; they stare; they are quiet; there is a feeling between them, and they are both caught in the moment.

I walked over to the jukebox and chose "Good Morning Starshine," returned to my stool, and saw her face light up as Oliver started to sing. The moment was unfortunately interrupted when her father appeared through the back kitchen door, took one look at me, then her, slid over, and nudged her out of the way. He said some things loudly that I didn't understand, but it didn't matter. He had pierced the daydream and was now in front of me, tapping his fingers on the counter.

The angel came back as if she had read my mind, bringing me a piping hot café con leche, a glass of orange juice, and a freshly baked pastry with blueberries and white icing on top. As I fished to find the correct number of pesetas, her father watched me carefully to make sure I was not shortchanging him. I again looked for the angel, and as I saw her taking a quick peek at me from the kitchen, I whispered silently, "I love you."

I eventually walked to the Ramblas, the very long quadruple-wide walkway from the harbor, which is tens and tens of blocks long and stretches west into the city. It's filled with shops of every kind imaginable as well as street vendors and street performers of all types and sizes. There were even some who dressed to look like stone statues, and it seemed they could stay stationary forever until their moment to surprise you came, and they moved. The Ramblas is Barcelona's answer to the Champs-Élysées. After some time walking and visiting a few stores, I found a quiet bench in the shade and sat down to write about some feelings I was having about Barcelona and, of course, continued to tweak the song I would take to Màquina!

Augusto had become even more excited when I mentioned the day before that if I thought of the poem as a song, then I saw the beginning as a number of spoken sentences before the singing started. He loved the idea even more when I told him that.

The rest of the day passed without event. My mind was consumed by the prospects of my meeting with the Spanish group, which I hoped would happen in the next couple of days.

I worked the song over in my head almost all night, and after very little sleep I wandered into the café again for my café con leche and to stare at my morning angel. I punched in "Good Morning Starshine" once again and headed to my counter stool. Unfortunately, her father was waiting for me, most likely having decided that if he served me, there would be less chance of me coming back.

The day seemed to stretch and stretch so that I thought the evening would never come. Augusto finally touched base with the group. They were premiering their new album that night at a big nightclub, Bocaccio, in Barcelona, and we were invited to come, not only to hear them play but to also sit down and talk to them for a while.

We took the bus and finally arrived an hour later. I was totally surprised. I had imagined the venue would be a beat-up warehouse, but I was 100-percent wrong. Bocaccio was like the Playboy Club in Chicago in its heyday. Glitz! Sexiness! Housed in a beautiful contemporary building, the entire atmosphere of the club was money. The line of people waiting to get in looked like models from Paris and rich playboys from all over the world. Everyone was dressed in the hippest clothes, and here I moseyed up to the front door in my rag-tag jeans and lived-in Spanish work shirt. Everyone started to mumble in Spanish things like, "What is he doing? Get in back of the line! Who is that guy? Get that bum and throw him in the street!"

Regardless of the comments, Augusto said something to the bouncer at the front door. He immediately opened it for us, and we walked right in. As I entered, I turned to look at the line and felt now instead of derogatory comments, there was more of the aura of *Who was that guy? Should we know him? Hey, Carlos, is he someone?* I smiled and was amazed at the sexiness of the interior. It was wall-to-wall people seated at tables with white tablecloths and velvet-covered banquettes with fleur-de-lys flocked wallpaper behind. Many others were standing around a couple of bars. The word was spreading about this group; they had a hot new vibe that was catching on fast.

As we entered one of the back rooms, their manager greeted Augusto with a big smile and a lot of laughs. It seemed Augusto had taken some photos of Màquina! before, and everyone thought they were great. Augusto had brought his camera. Introductions were made all around, and one of the band members, París, who spoke the best broken English, sat down with me and rubbed his hands together, smiling, waiting for me to take the song out of my pocket. Handing it to him, I started to say the title, but he interrupted me and said, "Blanco se Convierte en Color."

"Yes." I stopped him, holding up my hand and continued, "But in English... *White Turns to Color'*...say in English."

He did and smiled, as if he liked the way it felt to say and hear it in English. Now it was his turn to hold up his hand, to hush me as he continued to read the lyrics silently. After a couple of minutes, he asked me if I had thought of what feeling the music should have, upbeat or slow. Before I could answer, a guy yelled into the room that it was time for them to take the stage.

I stood in the back with Augusto and Gabriela, each of us with a beer in our hands, and we watched Màquina! play three or four songs. All were heavily instrumental with just a touch here and there of English lyrics. The crowd was waiting for this, and it seemed they got their money's worth.

After their set, we all went backstage, and París and I sat down together again, but we were interrupted again in short order. This time a TV film crew burst in, and five seconds later the newscaster was interviewing all members of the group. There were also some radio guys with mikes trying to record the group's comments. One person with a microphone spotted me and walked over, asking me something very rapidly in Spanish while holding the mike up in front of me. I turned to look at Augusto, and he just smiled and shrugged. I started to say something to the radio person, and as I got out my first couple of words in English, I could see it surprised him. For a minute he didn't know what to do. Should he cut me off quickly? On the other hand, I could be someone of importance. But after more thought and glancing at me carefully head to toe, I believe he decided there was more chance I was part of the cleanup crew than anyone important. Hence, he turned his head and was off, trying to get closer to the group's real members.

Hoping to continue talking about the song, I grabbed my

fill of numerous gourmet delicacies made available for press and friends as I waited for the commotion to subside. I found out that Màquina!'s manager was also the owner of the nightclub as well as numerous other nightclubs in Spain. He had big plans for the group. I really wanted to talk to him. Augusto sensed that, and while he was taking tons of pictures of the night's event, he informed me that, unfortunately, the manager didn't speak English. Gabriela came over to me and handed me another beer and told me Augusto had sold more of his band photos to the group. The way this night was going, it looked like it could be a very nice payday for him again.

After a couple of hours, most of the press had left. It was well into the next morning, and everyone was exhausted. At one point, París grabbed me and said the more he thought about the song, the more he liked it, but we needed to talk more—they were going to play at another club about 100 km from Barcelona in three or four days; could we meet again there?

I was concerned that this adventure might be too difficult to navigate. I'd already imposed on Gabriela and Augusto beyond my initial invite. But as I was trying to figure out what to say, Augusto agreed for me that yes, we would come; we could get a ride in the car of one of his friends.

As we walked to catch our bus back to the apartment, Augusto asked me how much I would charge the group for the song.

Immediately I answered, zero pesetas. If they'd use the song, that would be payment enough. I told him this experience so far had been so exciting and inspirational, and I was enjoying every second. He smiled and nodded. It was the correct answer.

We didn't get back to the apartment for what seemed like an hour or two, and all of us ended up sleeping through most of the day.

On Friday, the 3rd of July, I decided to go exploring and walked and walked until I was hopelessly lost. Eventually, I followed a small, curvy street that opened onto the Plaza de Cristo Rey with its beautiful, large old church. I entered the church and immediately was taken by the atmosphere. So old, so cold, so damp—but a place calling to me to find a seat and feel the history. I found a pew off to the side and listened to a choir practicing for Sunday's mass. I'd lost count of every church I'd walked into during my trip in Europe. If there had been one, there'd been twenty or more. I didn't try to attend Mass. Since I'd been traveling, I felt a mysterious pull to enter and maybe, odd as it seems, just feel. Was it the history of old buildings in Europe? Was it the quiet from the bustle of life outside? Was it only in my mind that I felt something—or was there a real spiritual vibration, something physical that touched my body in places like this? I don't know, but I was drawn to enter and feel. No one implored me to come in, and usually no one told me to leave.

I finally left and through walking the old part of Barcelona came to the Ramblas, found a free bench, and decided to write some thoughts in the sketchbook that I carried each morning when I left the apartment.

On the way back, I splurged and bought some bread, honey, tea, wine, and pastries for Gabriela and Augusto, my thanks for their efforts and help in the last couple of days.

Word came that tonight was a good night to see Màquina! again. Augusto arranged with a friend of his, Jack, to drive us to another nightclub called Maddox. Màquina! was one of several bands playing and, unfortunately, they were not going to play until around 1:30 a.m.

During our drive, Augusto again brought up that Màquina! was going to play the Isle of Wight Concert. He was trying to figure out a way to get there. Not only because of Màquina! but another group he had really enjoyed, a group called The Doors. He asked if I had ever seen them, and he was amazed that I said I had, as many as six or seven times. I continued talking and told Augusto that, unfortunately, about half the times I went to see them, the Lizard King (Jim Morrison) would inevitably start a riot and end the show way too early. The dude just couldn't make it through a concert. I went on to tell him that while I was in college, I had this idea to bring The Doors to Drake University where I was going to classes. I said I tracked down their manager and after a hundred phone calls finally got him on the phone. I told him I had the idea of ideas for The Doors. Drake had a bunch of dorms around a huge reflecting pond bordered by a hilly lawn to the water. My idea was to turn the water blood red and have the band alone on an island. Then I hit him with the idea that The Doors' last song would be "Light My Fire," and just as they were about halfway through, Jim Morrison would light a torch and throw it in the water, which then would explode in flames all around the island. The manager liked the idea and asked what I had been smoking as he might like some himself. But he added he would be worried about the fire laws in Iowa. He caught himself and said, "Let's not worry about that yet—there's always a way around things. Then he threw out that for him to go any further with this idea, I'd have to wire $50,000 up front.

I said, "OK, I'll get you a check in the next week or so." I thought I was pretty quick to fire that back to him with a good amount of confidence, but alas, there was no way I was getting my hands on $50,000. Everyone in the car laughed.

After a two-hour drive and hearing two different songs by Màquina! on the radio, we came upon another crazy scene. We arrived to crowds spilling out everywhere in front of the nightclub, but we couldn't even get in the club ourselves without paying something like $50 – $70 each. No way was that going to happen. However, we discovered the band was hanging out in the apartment next door, and we arranged to get up there.

París immediately greeted me with a smile and said that they felt the first half of the song was interesting and that they would work on some music in the next couple of months. They were just too busy right now to act on or even think about anything besides their publicity tour. It looked like all the effort had succeeded. Augusto said he'd keep track of the progress and keep me filled in, no matter where I was in the world six months from now. I left París my address in the States, and later that night, we saw them perform again. Afterward, we sat down with the group, and while we were drinking and talking, Augusto told París the story of my efforts to get The Doors a gig while I was in school. París asked me if I knew Jim Morrison or any of the band members. I said no, though I'd like to know them, of course. París then said they would be playing with The Doors later in the year and maybe he'd talk to Morrison, mention that I was a pretty good up-and-coming songwriter, and ask them if they would like to meet me. If so, he would get us together. Well, at that point I looked for another beer. I needed some liquor. No beer was within arm's reach, so I grabbed a bottle of wine, ignored any glass, and just gulped three or four big mouthfuls and said half out loud and half to myself, "Fuck, yes!" We finally left the nightclub around 2:30 to 3:00 a.m. and finally got to sleep around 5 a.m. on July 5.

Dreaming about the Doors & Màquina! all on the same night.

Los Colores

(Spoken, not sung)

I feel my life is changing, I start to hear a special sound,
I have to stop, I have to rest on this dusty ground.
Night is fading, so hard to see by such little light,
Then the wind comes by, lifts me, and I take flight.
The sun breaks through and I see everything covered in
white sand,
I can touch it, feel it, and breathe it like it was in my hand.

(Sung)

I can now feel colors,
Something is going to happen, Time has stopped,
And now color has appeared in the middle of white.

I watch my veins as they first start to pump my blood,
I watch until I am carried away by the flood.
The tide carries me into the earth and then back above,
I start to hear strange but soothing sounds, could this be love?

Something is going to happen, Time has stopped,
Color has appeared in the middle of white.

The sky now is the swirling white of my other life,
The change comes quickly with a cut of the yellow knife.
Now we are all seeing the most beautiful rainbow the world has ever known,
And all at once everyone now knows they are not alone.

Something has happened, Time has stopped,
Color has appeared in the middle of white.
As I watch my life turning
I know it will now never, ever, be the same again.

Composed June 5 on Formentera, Edited July 3 in Barcelona, Written and given to the
Spanish Musical Group: Màquina!

We caught up on sleep for the next few days and did little else. I did decide to send my almost filled sketchbook back to the States by mail at a cost of $10 US. That hurt. It only cost a couple of pesetas to buy another sketchbook. Although the page size was a little smaller, it would be easier to travel with.

One night we had dinner out at our favorite café down the street. The meat waiting to be served hung on hooks from the ceiling and was attended by an ample quantity of flies. It took a while, but as the saying goes, *When in Rome do as the Romans do.* I ordered from the hooks just like all the other Spaniards did. I remember grilled sausages served with fava beans and fried potatoes in a spicy sauce.

That night, Augusto said were all going to the movies. He wanted to see The Beatles movie *Yellow Submarine*. We did and had a great time.

Well, I finally decided for sure, I was leaving in a couple of days, on Saturday, July 11th. I'd stayed much longer with the unbelievable Gabriela and Augusto than I ever thought. They were more than good friends; they were forever friends. I could never repay them.

Augusto had made it his mission in my last days here to make sure I saw everything there was to see in this beautiful historic port city. Every day we'd hop on his motorcycle and he'd show me so many things. We stopped at the world-famous Gaudi Cathedral, called La Sagrada Familia, which was still not finished although it had been started over a hundred years before. A quick visit to the Picasso Museum was so interesting. He even drove on Las Ramblas and showed me parts that I had not walked before. We sped through the Barrio Gotico, the narrow streets and squares of the medieval part of the city.

He also was nice enough to take me to a number of record shops, so I could buy the song "Todo Tiene Su Fin" (Everything Has an End) by Los Modulos, a Spanish rock group. I'd been hearing the song multiple times per day and it just got to me as no other song I'd heard recently, and I had to have it. The song was very dramatic. I was starting to see a trend in my musical tastes: I liked big, dramatic songs and apparently, many of them were foreign. We finally found it, and I bought the 45 to send home with my sketchbook in an airmail package.

In saying goodbye to Barcelona, I had to say, I'd gotten to know her well. When I'd departed the boat from the islands, I had intended to leave and hitch out immediately. Instead, I'd stayed for almost two weeks and injected myself into the historic city to a much greater degree than in any of the other large cities I'd visited so far. How lucky was I to meet Augusto and Gabriela, then to stay with them, then to have the experience of a lifetime becoming acquainted with one of Spain's most famous rock groups? Because of the schedule back and forth to meet with the group, my stay was not hurried. There were days I watched life and became a fly on the wall looking and feeling like a local Barcelonan. Tomorrow, I would go for my last café con leche at my angel's café across the street. The last time I entered, the proprietor had already gone over to the jukebox and hit B −7 to have "Good Morning Starshine" playing for me as I sat down at the counter. He had apparently decided I probably wouldn't be the kind of vagabond or bandit to try and steal his beautiful daughter away, and so had let her serve me. After two months on those Spanish islands and the last two weeks in Barcelona, by no means did I speak the language like a local, but I did learn a surprising amount. As I was paying my bill and giving my Spanish angel a big tip, I started talking to them, and they offered me more to eat at their expense. Unfortunately, I had to go. I was already late to meet Augusto's friend, who would drive me to a good part of the highway outside of Barcelona to start to hitchhike north. Too bad, too late; it would have been nice to start my visits to the cafe the way I was ending them.

As I was walking out the door, her father walked around the corner, and I stopped and turned. She was watching me, and I said softly, "Goodbye, angel. I don't know your name, but I will dream about you every night until we meet again. You should come to Chicago and meet up with me..." And before I could say any more, her father jumped out from the hallway and gave me a dirty look. The door closed behind me strategically at that moment, and I walked away quickly.

Spain & France

Just then, I was elbowed in my ribs and looked down to find this woman, maybe a sixty-to-seventy-year-old Spanish woman, dressed all in black like the elderly ladies on Formentera, looking up at me.

My instinct was to elbow her back. What if she was an old lady? My side hurt.

As I was wondering about the ramifications of elbowing her, she palmed some kind of a card, then she motioned for me to look at it, sort of giving me a face like she was thinking...

"You stupid hippie, I'm trying to give you a train pass, don't look at me that way."

13.

Take Me Anywhere

Saturday, 8:00 AM, July 11, 1970

Augusto's friend Adrian drove me out of Barcelona to a spot on the highway pointed north, to hopefully get a long, straight ride up the coast. The weather was forecast to top 100 degrees Fahrenheit every day with no rain in sight and humidity readings off the charts for the next three to four days.

I started my new journey with a couple of quick rides, then nothing for a while. After two hours holding out my thumb, I got a ride from two young American guys to Arenys de Mar along the Costa Brava where the hot air was interrupted from time to time with the windblown salty air from the Mediterranean.

They let me off at a train station on the edge of town, as

they needed a part for their car and weren't quite sure where to go. I went into the train station to try to cool off. No such luck, but I did meet Andrea, a skinny twenty-five-year-old redhead from Australia with big brown eyes, patched jeans, and a purple backpack. From the moment I met her to an hour later, she had not stopped swearing at the heat. She had me laughing, so we decided to travel together and started hitching north again. But after two or three hours and no hint of a ride, we decided to give up and walked to the beach. We slept there that night: wind and flies, the smell of the salt air mixed with boat fuel. On the way to the sand and water, we met the two Americans who had dropped me off, and they came with us to the beach. We were all tired and fell asleep very quickly.

Although Andrea and I were getting along famously, I decided not to wake her as I got up around 5:00 a.m. the next day. She had said she really wanted to sleep and maybe to hang out at the beach that day. I was too antsy; my mind was going a mile a minute… what was my plan? Did I need a plan? Where was I going? Why, where, who, what and when. . . everything constantly running through my mind. In any case, I got up quietly and walked to the highway, thinking maybe this was going to be my day. I got a ride immediately.

However, after about fifteen to twenty minutes, the driver said he had to turn off the highway and, as best as I could translate, visit his sister. He left me off in a terrible location just coming out of a curve in the road. Most vehicles wouldn't see me until they were almost on top of me and inevitably then wouldn't stop. Actually, no one stopped for the next five or so hours. I had no idea where I was or if there was anything like a town or a gas station anywhere around. For all I knew, if I started walking to escape the sun, I might have to walk for hours to find anything.

At one point, I opened my new sketchbook and made a sign to hold up that said *Take Me Anywhere!* Unfortunately, it was so hot that almost everyone had decided to stay inside. There weren't any cars coming or going. There was only the sun. It was too hot to stand. As I was lying down by the side of the road and leaning on my bedroll, I accidentally slipped, and my hand hit the blacktop. Although I only made contact for a second to catch my balance, I burned my hand. There were places on the blacktop that were bubbling from the heat. Over the years I've heard stories that sometimes the heat in Spain can be so bad it can kill. If this wasn't killer heat, I don't know what would be. Luckily, I was young and healthy. But already I felt my body telling me, *You have perspired all you can. You are reading empty. You won't be losing any more water; you'll be losing brain cells.* My head felt like it was shrinking.

I debated walking into the woods for shade, but then for sure no car or truck would ever see me.

Around noon, four to five hours later, a bus slowly came by, passed me, and then started to back up.

I wondered what was going on. Maybe the bus driver thought I was dead lying there by the road. Instead, he allowed a tourist to get off the bus with his movie camera, and then he told me to stand up with my sign so he could take some film of this unusual wildlife in Spain, the crazy hitchhiker trying to hitch in temperatures well over a hundred. I did stand up, hoping he would give me a tip or something. I kept looking at him with my sad, help-me-please face, but instead, he just yelled to his wife in the bus, saying it was hotter than hell out here and this stupid ass is half-baked and more than half-melted. *Glad I got him now, for in another hour or so he's probably history*—and all this as he continued filming me. Though

I couldn't quite hear his commentary, I'm sure he felt my plight was amusing. He was especially interested in getting my sign on film. I heard him say, "You won't get any rides here, you dumb-ass hippie, you'll just collapse and die here on this road." Finally, he got yelled at by the bus driver, but by that time he had gotten all he wanted to on his camera. As Francis Ford Coppola Jr. was getting back on the bus, I asked the bus driver if he knew of any café or gas station anywhere near here. He said a half-mile down the road, turn right for another couple hundred yards, and there you'll find a gas station/café.

I made my way there, went inside and sat down at the counter for one of the most needed and best-tasting beers in my life. Of course, if there was any air-conditioning—undetermined—it didn't work very well, but at least I was out of the sun.

Though I had only been traveling from Barcelona for two days, I felt like I was morphing because of the heat and the traveling. So, after a couple of sips of beer, I made a trip to the men's room to look at myself in the mirror for the first time in a while. I was startled to see how much my appearance had changed. I had been cooked and baked to done. I was already very tan leaving the islands, but now standing in the hot sun almost all day each of the last two days, I was becoming a different race. I was not tan anymore. . . I was almost black, and my hair was bright golden yellow from the sun. It was startling.

When I walked out of the restroom and back to the counter, a guy and a girl were sitting in my area. They were American and had tried hitching north also and had given up, deciding the only way out was to take a train to the Spanish-French border.

We talked for a while and found out about each other. I found it a little strange that she was almost ignoring him and concentrating on me entirely as we talked. I thought the two of them were a couple. As they ordered three more beers, the guy went to the restroom, and she came closer to me and asked, "What's your deal? What's your trip? And who are you? You look like some type of Road Knight. I'm nobody. I'm a travel neophyte, but you have that kind of worldly look that says *been there done that*. You obviously have a story." She ended by saying, "I need one too."

She was curious to know more about my story and where was I going. I told her I wasn't sure. I was headed north to Switzerland but didn't know what I'd do there or where I might go next. I could immediately tell she was intrigued by my travels and what I was saying. She had just flown into Madrid, taken the train to Barcelona, met Jack there, and decided to try hitching, but they had failed everywhere. She said Jack seemed to be afraid of everything, with no adventure in his soul. When she heard that I had been hitchhiking since I left Rome more than two months ago, she started to beg, "Take me with you! This guy I'm with is a dud, the worst in every way." Her name was Allison; I guessed she was probably about my age, and as she was talking, I could see every Spaniard in the café boldly looking her up and down. I could see it bothered her, but she pretended not to notice.

Just then, Jack came back and said he had gotten directions. It was not a long walk to the rail station. On our way out, he said he'd pay my bar bill and walked to the register. I looked at her and said, "I really don't have the money to take the train; I can't go with you guys."

"That's unexpected," she said, looking kind of sad, and looking to see where Jack was.

I'd have gone with her in a second if I'd had the money. She was very attractive; she was an actress in New York City and had done some off-Broadway stuff. She had long blonde hair, was about five feet five inches tall with what looked like all the right stuff in all the right places—looking, well, like an actress should look.

I wondered, is she a successful or a starving actress? Would she pay for my ticket?

I leaned on the bar, brushed my now shoulder-length blonde hair back, sort of like a female model might do on a television commercial, and said, "Well, if you had the money, you could always pay my…".

And before I could finish, she looked up and said, "Yes, you're right, we'll fool the train conductor with my Eurail pass."

"No," I said, "I didn't mean that. That's not possible. What do you mean fool the conductor?"

She said, "Trust me." Then she got up, picked up my sleeping bag, and threw it to me and indicated it was time to go.

The three of us walked about two kilometers to the train station, then waited two hours for a train to come. Fifty or so mostly Spanish men and women of all ages were also waiting for the train. While we were waiting, she let me in on her plan for me to ride on the train without paying. It sounded pretty half-assed to me, but at this point, I was sort of committed and decided to go with the flow.

The train rolled in, and everyone got on. As I entered one of the cars, I found out it was already packed—standing room only, and there was almost no way to walk in the crowded aisles. As I pushed myself towards the middle of the train car, I turned to see how far behind me Allison was only to find that she wasn't there! I grabbed an upper berth suitcase rack and lifted myself up to look for her, but to no avail. The train began moving, and

I realized I was screwed. A conductor began moving through our car to collect tickets and fares. Perfect! I was dead; I'd have to pay a good number of pesetas for a ticket, which was exactly what I was desperately trying to avoid. Thanks a lot, Allison, for your great idea. As I was pushed and prodded by all the people in the aisle, I was wondering how many pesetas I had in my pocket. There was even a chance that I might be short, and then what—would they throw me off a moving train?

I thought I better get a look out the window and see the landscape I might be thrown into. It looked ominous. We were moving through stark-looking valleys and mountain cliffs. Just then, I was elbowed in my ribs and looked down to find this woman, maybe a sixty-to seventy-year-old Spanish woman dressed all in black like the elderly ladies on Formentera, looking up at me. My instinct was to elbow her back. What if she *was* an old lady? My side hurt. As I was contemplating the ramifications of elbowing her, she palmed some kind of a card. She motioned for me to look at it, giving me a face like that said, *You stupid hippie, I'm trying to give you a train pass; don't look at me that way.*

She pushed it into my hand just as a conductor was punching tickets two or three people away from me. It was Allison's Eurail pass. Wow! Where was she? This had been our plan, for her to get checked first and then somehow pass it to me, well away from her, so I could use it also. I looked up and, at last, saw her by the door. She had somehow passed it down the train car ahead of the conductor. Holding it higher, I freaked out because it was too obviously a beautiful woman, clearly not some guy with a beard. Then I noticed again the old woman next to me. Looking at her face, I could almost hear her thinking *Don't get your hopes up because it will be futile for you, hippie. This conductor will spot immediately that you are some dumbass with a beard and this Eurail pass has a beautiful young woman on it. You are dead, dead in the water. You might as well jump off the train right now.* I looked up and the conductor was right in front of me, saying, "Okay, Senor, no tienen todo el dia, Donde esta tu boleto!" I quickly put my thumb over the picture on her Eurail card. Seeing me, he made a face, barely looked at the card, and nudged me as he continued on.

It worked; I was okay. I marveled that none of the people handing the pass down to me had minded that I was cheating the Spanish rail system. I don't think that would have worked in the States. When she judged I was in the clear, Allison made her way back to me and held out her hand for the pass and then leaned into me and whispered in my ear, "I've ditched Jack; it's just you and me now, Chicago."

We left the train at Cerbese just past the French border. Hitchhiking was a lot better in France, and we got a couple of rides very quickly. Then two young Canadian college students who were driving around Europe for the summer picked us up. We immediately hit it off. At first, I'm sure it was because of the way Allison looked, but after talking with them for a couple of hours, we were all getting along well and decided to camp out together that night on the beach.

We picked a spot not far from a beach town, very secluded and quiet except that we could hear French rock on someone's radio blasting skyward from the outskirts of the town. Hunter and Ethan said they had enough food and wine for all of us. The night sky was beautiful and so peaceful. We ate and drank and talked and laughed until late into the night. This was one more lucky, in fact perfect, hitchhiking experience that I hope I will never forget as long as I live. I'll remember the perfect weather with the exotic fragrance of the pineapple and candelabra sages and the beautiful but lonely warming breeze coming in from the ocean. I'll remember city lights reflecting off the water and the lonely but hauntingly beautiful female voice coming from the distance. Whoever she was, she reminded me of Marie Laforet, whom I saw live in Paris. I'm sure each of the three guys lying on the beach that night was imagining what might have happened if the other two weren't there and it was only him with Allison. We all went to sleep imagining that, I'm sure.

As we rose the next morning, the guys said they could take us as far as Avignon, as they had planned to stay there a couple of days.

They left us off by the Rhône River, which runs around Avignon with a great view of the Papstpalast Avignon, which was the papal residence in the 1300s. It was definitely not one of your typical views while hitchhiking. The structure was huge and majestic, always at our backs as we tried to circumvent the town.

Allison decided I had been giving her too much responsibility for getting rides by having her be the more visible body and thumb sticking out. I was no fool. But at Avignon, she said it was time for me to go to work, and of course, we didn't get a ride for a while because of that. It had cooled down considerably when we crossed into France, although I'm sure it was still in the 80s, with bright sunshine. Allison found some shade from a nearby tree and was almost napping, leaning against her backpack while I stood in the sun.

Finally, a couple of French guys picked us up. Then we got another ride with a very young French guy who was too interested in Allison. He just wanted to have her in his car, at first saying he only had room for one. Eventually, he acquiesced and picked us up. He left us off in a terrible small access road off the main highway.

It was now getting later in the afternoon; I would have guessed between 6:00 to 7:00 p.m. As a hitchhiker, you always start to worry as dark approaches. Where are you going to bed down?

Not far away I thought I spotted what looked like an orchard, which could very well be our hotel for the evening. But I couldn't see any sign of a restaurant, and we were both desperately hungry. We had not eaten all day, just a snack or two from her backpack. We had pushed the hitchhiking to put some miles behind us.

As our stomachs were growling like hungry bears, we started to walk to some broken fence posts to enter the orchard. Allison walked down the road as I took a closer look at the orchard. She bought some fruit from an odd lonely fruit stand and talked the proprietor-farmer into splitting a long loaf of French bread for us as he was being yelled at by his wife to come up to the house for supper.

We waited until he was in the house before we crossed the street and made our way into the orchard. We found a low area that was somewhat hidden from the road and the house. We laid out our sleeping bags next to each other and started into our fruit. We also tore off some bread as Allison said she'd almost do anything for some meat or cheese to make a sandwich.

I looked at her and said, "Anything?"

"Where, what—do you see something I don't see? Where's some meat or cheese?" she fired back.

"Well, if you squint your eyes, you could imagine that we were eating steak or lamb from this jar," I said as I pulled out my half-empty peanut butter jar from my time on Formentera.

She yelped with glee. "Looks like a big, beautiful hamburger with lettuce, onions, tomato, and ketchup to me," she said excitedly as she waited for me to pull out a knife.

I responded, "Since we're imagining already, imagine your finger is a knife and dig in."

We laughed and put our dirty fingers in the jar to scoop out the peanut butter and spread it on our pieces of French bread. The night slowly enveloped us as we finished all the bread, most of the fruit, and emptied a half litre of some lemon soda Allison had been carrying.

She carried a part flashlight/part nightlight cylinder so we could still see each other's faces as I offered her a cigarette. I lit one myself as I lay back, looking at the stars.

She poked some of my smoke rings as we lay there, and then she ventured, "So here we are in France. We haven't talked about where we are headed. I know you're done with Spain, but Europe is a big place. What are your thoughts?"

"That's a good question. I'm running out of money, so it's almost like every day is a new experience or possibly my last experience. All I can say is my immediate goal is discovering Switzerland. I want to see the Alps. I've seen the Rockies, and I want to compare them. I think I've already told you I don't have enough money to get back to the States unless I get to London and there really is a famous bulletin board with cheap tickets for sale back to New York as I've been told. Otherwise, I'm stuck over here forever."

I figured I had about $140 left, and I was not traveling, as the book said, "Europe on five dollars a day." I figured it would be closer to $7 to $10 a day, as I was traveling now through or around big cities. If I skipped one or two meals a day and slept every night under the stars, I probably had another week before I had to get to London to try to get that plane ticket for around $100. That was a lot of ifs, and any problem, even a small one, could kill my entire plan.

She could tell I was thinking about bad things, so she punched me in the arm and said, "Tell me about what you were like as a kid. Were you good, were you bad? Tell me something about—you know, something about girls or one particular girl."

For some reason, the first thing that popped into my head was when I was—oh, I don't know how old but still young enough, I guess, barely to have a babysitter. It was midsummer in Cincinnati, and Connie, a babysitter who had watched my brother and me a time or two before, let me stay up past my mother's designated bedtime.

I was at an age when I was noticing girls and women. They were still a mystery to me—not the good stuff, but more how to get to the good stuff. Connie had been on the phone most of the night—typical babysitter. I was watching TV but wanted to be in the kitchen, sitting at the table looking at her and listening to her on the phone. I strained over the sound of the television to hear what she was saying. Then I heard her swear to her girlfriend, "I'd kill for a cigarette. I smoked my last one just before I got here."

Well, that was my cue. I came around the corner and said, "I've got a deal for you. I've got cigarettes. You want one? And I want to hang out with you here and not go to bed yet. Deal?"

She looked at me, for a moment, perhaps wondering, *How old are you again? Oh, who cares.* "Deal," she said.

I flew upstairs to my room where I usually had cigarettes hidden away. This night I had an almost full pack.

I hightailed it back downstairs and turned on my transistor radio. She lit my cigarette and hers with a great-looking see-through lighter. After a couple of puffs, she noticed that I was more than a casual smoker and asked me how long I'd been smoking.

"I don't know. A while," I said casually.

"How old are you again?" she fired back.

"It's not that big of a deal. Kids smoke more these days," I said. I wanted to find out more about her and—well, you know, things, information I could use in the future. Even though she was a student at Seton, the Catholic high school for girls, she was an older woman to me.

I felt I had a good start on my desires tonight, but I needed to do more.

"How about a beer," I threw out as she took a bottle of pinkish fingernail polish to do a touchup here and there.

"What! You drink beer?"

"Yeah, you know. Kids do that more these days."

She laughed and said, "You use that line a lot it seems."

Well, I'm not sure how many kids drink beer, there in Cincinnati or anywhere else in the rest of the country at that age, but I had gotten started a while ago. My parents bought a small two-bedroom house and soon made it into a four-bedroom house as my father finished the second floor for my brother and me on one of the best streets in the entire universe. Seibel Lane was just an average-sized dead-end street as dead-end streets go. What made it perfect for someone like me was that there were about twenty to thirty kids of varying ages living across from each other on that part of the street. As families moved in and out, I was often the oldest. As the saying goes—first to learn mischief, first to be admired. I had somewhat of a following. I don't know who started it or how it started, but the street kids started camping out in each other's backyards with a blanket thrown over a clothesline and some pillows and some pop and of course, comic books. I also don't quite remember how my type of backyard camping started, but after a time or two, I felt the experience was missing something. Soon that something included cigarettes, liquor, and sometimes beer. Sometimes, I would grab some empty drugstore plastic pill bottles from around the house and go down to our fruit cellar and fill a couple of them with different liquors that my father thought he had hidden secretly down there. Included would be some *Playboy* magazines if my friend Allen Peters could safely get some out of his father's secret hiding place. I can still remember some of those nights. We never went to sleep—good times, talking and finding out about life in different ways.

I felt pretty secure pulling a can of beer out of the fridge as I had done that before once or twice and knew that the timing was right. There were more cans of different types of beers than usual, which gave me some built-in confusion to work with—no danger my parents would know how many beers were in there.

We poured the can evenly into two glasses that had a stained-glass motif on them. This was new for me; my experiences happened mainly on the run with bottles or cans.

My parents' phone rang again. Connie picked it up and almost immediately made a face. Her friend couldn't talk anymore, and she hung up the phone.

I took the opportunity to ask her about more juicy stuff. "Have you made out with many guys?"

"What? That's kind of personal, isn't it?" she fired back.

At that age the concept of blackmail was not something I could have put my finger on, but I knew how to work it. I nonchalantly looked down at the table holding the beer and cigarettes and started shaking my head a little. I had her dead to rights giving me cigarettes and beer while babysitting. I could imagine her thinking, *Why, you little shit.* She sat back and answered, "Yeah, some."

I followed up, "What kind of kissing?"

"What do you mean, what kind of kissing?"

I wasn't sure. I had recently overheard a high school guy telling his friends how he had hit the jackpot with this girl. I didn't think it was wise to repeat the details; it was a guy thing.

On the other hand, we did these things with girls, and she was a girl. I felt this was too good an opportunity not to be bold and dig a little.

I thought one of the guys was talking about tongues, but that didn't seem right to me. "You just use the lips, right?"

"Have you kissed a girl?" she asked, reaching for the cigarette pack.

"Well, yes. No. I guess. Just sort of wrestling with some girls. I tried to kiss them, but not, you know, in any romantic way. Do you like kissing?" I threw back at her.

"Yeah, with the right boy."

Okay, this was good. I was getting her to talk. Kissing was okay, I guess, but I had seen enough copies of *Playboy* from my friend Allen's house. His old man had a whole closet full. I had seen all the good parts of a girl in those magazines. What I needed to know was how do you get to those things, and exactly what happens then. Again, I'd heard conversations, but I hadn't had my parents give me any of those educational books yet. (That would happen the following year.)

Then it hit me like a bolt of lightning as Connie got up and was looking for something to eat. Connie wasn't just a babysitter; she was a girl, and the closer I looked, she had a lot of good stuff herself. She was as pretty as anyone I'd seen on TV. From that point, I couldn't take my eyes off her, and she was realizing that as each minute passed.

I kept looking at her breasts. Was life changing for me? Was this the way life was going to be from now on for me, like every other guy in the world: spending my life just looking at girls' breasts?

"Do you think about girls all the time? Why so many questions?"

Just then the transistor radio started playing the song "The Garden of Eden."

I hadn't answered her yet about girls, but she didn't wait for an answer. She went right on and asked me, "I bet you like this song, don't you?"

I knew the song, but I really hadn't heard it so much. The fact that she mentioned me in reference to the song made me respond, "Why, is it talking about a lot of sex?"

"Sex. . . well, no. Well, yes. Wait a minute, so now you've gone from kissing to sex. What's next?"

Well, she had me there. For a moment, I was stumped. What was next—more sex, different sex? I thought I knew all the parts— you know, *Playboy* knows everything about those parts.

I think we were making each other nervous to some extent, as we both reached for another cigarette. As I took a couple of puffs, I was trying to think of something else to ask her, you know, good stuff. I didn't know when I'd have this opportunity again. So, I thought, *Go for it! Don't hold back, be a man.* So, I took another drag and purposely blew a smoke ring. I knew that would surprise her and maybe give me a little more credibility in my next move.

Okay, it was now or never to go on to the next level. "So, sex. . . have you had it? Have you had any?"

She coughed a little cough, gave me the evil eye and was about to, I believe, use a lot of swear words in response, but just then we saw car lights flash across the kitchen as my parents entered our driveway. The only swear word used was the one that came out of me. "Shit! They're home."

I was young but had been in enough trouble and scrapes of different kinds that I didn't panic. Instead, I jumped up, pushed the beer can down deep in the garbage, and grabbed the two glasses and splashed water in them as she opened the kitchen door and was waving a copy of the *Cincinnati Post* as hard as she could to get the cigarette smoke out of the room.

Then there was a second, only a second, but a second I've never forgotten. We both stopped and froze for a moment and looked at each other. Our hearts were both beating so loud I'm sure you could hear them across the street.

As I looked into her eyes in that second, I wondered, *What would've happened if my parents hadn't come home?* She liked me, I could tell, and here we were, just starting to talk about sex, the jackpot. This was the first time I was maybe talking about sex to a girl. I was on a new level; I know she thought I was somewhat cute. Shit! Why now? What could have happened?

As for her thoughts in that moment as we were looking into each other's eyes, she certainly might have been thinking the same things as me. But as I look back on it, it's more likely she was thinking, *Fuck! Fuck!* Maybe the look she gave me was the ultimate evil eye and she was really thinking, *You stupid little shit! I need to babysit. I need the money. I don't need to have your parents explode at me for keeping you up and oh, yeah, I almost forgot, you little shit: smoking. And smoking with the little shit I'm supposed to be taking care of and getting to bed on time. And oh, yeah, besides that I've got my feet up on the table, sharing a beer with this little jerk. They could have seen that. I need the money.*

Well that moment—full of life for both of us, I'm sure—passed as I heard my mother coming in the door and saying to Connie, "Now how much is it that I owe you, honey, for tonight?" As she walked from the living room into the hall and stepped into the kitchen, looking in her purse for some dollars, I quietly edged my way into the dining room and around the other way into the living room. I crawled slowly and quietly until I reached the stairs and then up the stairs, making sure my father didn't see me from the driveway, and slipped into my bedroom on the second floor. As I snuck into bed with all my clothes on and the sheet pulled up to my chin, I had a big smile on my face. I heard my mother yell to Connie downstairs, "Mr. Casper is waiting in the car to take you home, Connie. Thanks, good night. Say hello to your parents for me." At least I was learning how to make progress with a girl, and I bet she was thinking about me as she was going home.

As I heard my father's car drive away down below, I really needed a cigarette and unconsciously put my hand to my shirt pocket to feel for my pack. Shit, no pack. We took care of everything, everything except the cigarettes. Shit! Shit! *I'm dead*, I thought. My father will find them, and that will be the end of me. I stayed up most of the night thinking about Connie and getting grounded the next day for, let me see, probably forever and a day.

I told Allison that I figured Connie had grabbed the pack of Winston's and put them in her purse before anyone saw them. As far as how my plans for future adventures with Connie went, well, that was the last time she babysat. I had gotten too old to need a babysitter, or she had decided that driving down the street blindfolded would be safer than babysitting for a little gangster. We never saw each other ever again.

"You made up that story, didn't you, just to try and get to me. You're such a dick," Allison said.

"I swear almost every word is the truth. Give me a little leeway because it happened thirteen or so years ago, but I've never forgotten that experience. Look, I'll prove it to you. Look at me and stare into my eyes. If I made it up, you'll probably see me break into a smile, but…"

"Okay, look at me," she fired back. We stared at each other for a long minute.

"See, I knew it! You liar, you shit, I almost believed that story, and you were really getting to me," she laughed as she hit me and threw one of her shoes at me.

"Just because I smile doesn't mean it's not a true story. You're smiling now. See, people smile."

It was now very dark, and though we looked for a smooth a place to lay our sleeping bags, there were rocks everywhere. We continued to reach under every so often and grab one and throw it away.

"Well, what do you think? We're out of food, out of drink, out of cigarettes, and out of stories. Just for the record, that was a true story. Should we call it a day and turn in?"

"I don't think you're out of stories, but it is late. Remember earlier you asked me if you produced meat for our sandwiches would I give you anything? Well, it's time for anything." She leaned up on her left elbow, looked at me for a second, pulled back the top of her sleeping bag, and then grabbed my shirt to pull me to her.

As we began to know each other better, I had to smile and think back thirteen or so years ago to Connie and that night, though nothing ever happened other than fodder for a young boy's dreams. I have to say Connie did come through for me, albeit years later. Thanks, Connie.

We woke up to Bastille Day, the 14th of July, and soon found out that the entire country and every store was closed. But it did turn out to be our best day for getting rides so far. We got ride after ride and ended up around noon close to Grenoble and a crossroads sign just east of the city. Someone could continue east into Italy and the town of Turin, or west, staying in France to Lyon, or follow my plan to keep heading north, cross over into Switzerland, and eventually hit Geneva.

We met a few other travelers as we waited for a ride. Others were getting in and out of vehicles as they traveled one way or another from this obviously important crossroads. Some people wanted to get to Paris for tonight's partying; others were jealous of Allison's and especially my tan as they were coming from the north and were looking for the sun and its rays.

As we waited for a ride, Allison decided we needed at least one meal a day with some good nourishment and walked down the road to try to find something. That gave me some time to sit back and reflect.

Here I was, running out of money in a foreign country and about to cross into a new one. As I put my arms behind my head and lay back, looking at the clouds, more feelings were emerging. Many people would never want to be in my position. Most people would avoid the possibility of running out of money in a foreign land and think of it as a true disaster and failure. Why didn't I? As I wondered, I pictured myself arriving in Paris, green to the gills, cocky as a frat guy but untested and totally innocent as a traveler. What a contrast to who I was now, just three and a half months later. Sure, I looked different on the outside; anyone who knew me before, I guessed, wouldn't recognize me now—not even my family. But more significantly, I was very different on the inside, both heart and mind. I had seen things most people had never seen; I'd done things most people would never do. I'd lived by the side of the road with no roof over my head. I'd gotten on boats, trucks, trains, trolleys, cars, motorcycles and bikes—and either jumped off of or fallen from many of them. I'd tried with varying degrees of success to speak different languages, and in some cases carried on conversations with people who spoke no English at all. I'd tried to fight nature in making sand candles. I'd slept in a cave or two. I'd washed my clothes in numerous restaurants' bathroom sinks. I'd been handcuffed and arrested in one country and nearly in another. I'd run and hidden from police in different countries. I'd traveled through and experienced twenty or so countries. I'd walked the small, dark streets of Paris, the streets that Picasso, Toulouse Lautrec, and Voltaire had walked. I'd sat in a café or two where Bridget Bardot sipped wine. I'd been knocked over aggressively and picked up, the dirt brushed off softly by a Catholic priest who didn't know English but sure knew soccer. I'd slept and walked through a train out of history, one that had carried kings and queens, movie stars, politicians, celebrities. I'd sat in a train car with men who spoke different languages, men with big knives asking me how much money I had in my pockets. I'd walked in the footprints of Socrates, of Napoleon, of the Crusaders, and walked down the path of Saladin. I'd sat on the same edge of water that Columbus did before he set sail. I'd walked in and felt the Holy Spirit in the church of churches in Rome; I'd knelt with Muslims in the Blue Mosque and been awestruck by its beauty. I'd sat and looked at the most famous ceiling of history that Michelangelo painted, and though it had been weeks since I strained to look up at those glorious figures he painted, my neck still hurt. I hoped to keep this and the other memories. I hoped my neck continued to hurt and make me remember for the rest of my life.

I wasn't expecting the stop, this crossroads intersection of Europe, to get to me so much. I knew if I changed my plan, I could possibly hitch directly to England by the end of the next day and be within steps of getting on a plane to the States. I must admit I was tempted. But ultimately—regardless of things I'd seen, the adventures I'd had—I'd always felt I had a guardian angel watching over me and that there was more to see and one or two more adventures to be had with my angel.

As I lay there looking at the Alps, that old saying popped into my mind: If you've seen one of a thing, you've seen them all. Yes, I'd seen the Rockies and I'd seen the Pyrenees, but they don't compare to the Alps. I was hypnotized by the grandeur and by the massiveness of this mountain range. It seemed to go on as far as the eye could see. Even the cloud formations around some of the peaks seemed different. Of course, clouds are clouds, but the clouds in the Alps appeared to speak and sing. I'm not sure I wasn't hallucinating, hearing those strange sounds coming from somewhere above. They were hypnotizing the more you stared at them. I wondered what it would be like to be up there, not necessarily at the top but up among the clouds.

Allison came back, unfortunately empty-handed, and we immediately started hitching again and got a ride to Chambery.

I can't remember the look and feel of every town that I traveled through, but I knew as soon as we were dropped off at the edge of that small, picturesque Alpine village that I would never forget it. If there ever was a storybook street or town, Chambery was right out of central casting. Anywhere you looked, it was a picture, especially as you looked east with the snow-capped Alps as a backdrop.

We walked to the town center and the Fountain of Elephants, with its life-size sculptures of elephants honoring historic feats in India performed by one of France's adventurous noblemen. Although it a holiday, we did find a food stand and devoured some large, just-baked soft pretzels and some Alsace mountain beer.

A young French couple picked us up and took us to Geneva on Lake Lausanne just into Switzerland. Unfortunately, we were dropped off in an impossible place to get a ride, and even though it was five o'clock by the time we walked to a better spot (the time most travelers start to think about whether they will have a roof over their heads that night), we still tried to get rides. The blowing wind and the darkening clouds gave us pause as we had no plans for the night, but I talked Allison into another last ride or two before it started to rain.

It was dark by the time a young Swiss guy dropped us off right in front of the youth hostel in Montreux on the far eastern edge of Lake Geneva. We each got a bed for $1.50 that included a much-needed shower. Though we were late to arrive and most of the food was gone, we did talk one of the chefs in the kitchen into making up something for us. All he wanted in exchange was some American cigarettes.

It rained throughout the night, and even though it cost me a couple of dollars, it was well worth it. Montreux is absolutely beautiful, the Riviera of the Swiss countryside and the home of the world-famous Montreux Jazz Festival. There was no doubt we were in a different place now. This was not Spain; we were in the mountains of the moon. The beauty of the mountains with the lake and the town—this was different from anything I'd seen.

The Road

It's always before me,
Tempting me with the treasures I could find.
First it appears long and straight,
Then after the hill, it turns into dangerous curves,
Bordering one-thousand-foot cliffs.

But the road is always before me,
Tempting me and asking me what do I have to lose?
And asking me to think about all I could discover.
It tries to entice me with cooling winds from time to time,
As it does today, pushing a cooling sea breeze my way.

And that road always before me,
Tempting me with stories of ancient cities to the east.
Of finding forgotten books holding the secrets of time,
All the riches of exotic, mysterious lands,
And the surprises to come as I constantly sense the far horizon awaits.

And the road always before me,
Tempting me endlessly questioning my intentions.
Do I look for pleasures or do I search for riches?
I wonder day and night of what I could find,
Will I be led to an inevitable end or to another new beginning?
And always before me,
Tempting me, is
The Road

Written July 14th, while waiting for a ride at the crossroads to Geneva or Grenoble

We got up early, talked our chef into some more food to carry as we left the hostel to look around. But we didn't get very far before the skies opened up again and we were trapped under the awning of a large building for a while. Then, as quickly as it started, it stopped, and the sun came out. We walked and talked along the promenade around the lake. Even with the on-and-off again weather, I could sense Montreux was too touristy for me.

I started talking about leaving and mentioned that I had a plan to meet a Swedish girl here or in Saanen, not far away. Allison got very upset. Who was Olivia, and didn't I like being with this actress from New York City? Wasn't she enough for me? This was a no-win situation, especially when I went to the American Express office and there was a letter addressed to me but written in Swedish. It was from Olivia in Spain. It didn't make any sense unless she was writing two letters, one to me and one to someone else and mixed them up when she sealed them to send.

The rest of the day rained on and off, and Allison and I remained somewhat distant, albeit together. The next day it rained even harder. I thought it was never going to stop raining. I almost left but became ill and decided to stay another day. Then Allison said she was tired of dormitory living and the keeping of boys and girls apart and asked if I wanted to pay for a hotel. I couldn't afford that. More and more the handwriting was on the wall; we were going to be going different ways.

Switzerland

The Alps were breathtaking and beautiful
As we drove closer to them,
we also continued to climb higher.
I couldn't help but observe there were hardly
any other cars on this road.

What was I getting myself into?

And besides that,
thick ice was forming on every window
as we drove higher on this mountain road.

14.

The Kindness of Strangers

8:00 am, Friday July 17, 1970

The day broke first light with an ominous sky. I wondered if that was a sign for the rest of the day. Deciding to leave Allison was not easy. Besides the fact she was getting a little frustrated with me, mostly with the state of my finances, I had no idea really what I was doing—sure I was traveling, but where and why?

The only thing I was a little sure of was traveling alone was going to give me more flexibility, and I'd be able to move faster. That seemed like something I should have at this point in the trip. Whether I liked it or not, these days appeared to be the last of my adventure. Not that Allison was a difficult travel mate; she wasn't, and the benefits, let's say, were great albeit minimal since after our first night we'd been housed separately in the youth hostels. There was no doubt she wanted to stay together, but I thought I needed complete freedom and the ability to travel light. I might have felt differently if this were the beginning of the trip, or if I weren't still thinking about Olivia, but as it was, I wasn't sorry to leave Allison.

It had rained the night before, and it looked like rain now, but I had committed to leaving, and so I walked to a spot that looked like people were actually driving out of the area, not just from spot to spot within the town.

I got lucky and was picked up right away. A ride or two later, I was high up in the mountains. It seemed at every turn we took it got a little colder, and though there wasn't any snow on the road, snow covered all the grasslands up and down as we climbed higher. I continued to look at my map during a drive with a Swiss doctor who had picked me up on the way to visit a patient. We were quickly approaching a turn south I would need to take if I wanted to try and meet Olivia in Saanen. South of that was the Matterhorn, one of the tallest mountains in the Alps and for that matter the world. I wanted to see the town of Zermatt at the base of the mountain. I had seen enough mountain-climbing movies to figure that going into that town had to be a great new experience for me—not to climb but maybe to drink with some real mountain men.

As we passed areas with more snow on the ground, I thought about Olivia. To see her would be great; there was so much unsaid between us that I believe needed to be resolved and understood. I wanted to tell her that she'd made an impression on me greater than any other person I'd ever known. That she'd changed me. That I wouldn't forget her. Europe wasn't my home, and we didn't have a future—I was too young to be thinking about that anyway—but she was an indelible part of my life already.

And, for sure, I wanted to know what she'd say, what she was thinking now, what she'd written to me that had been sent to someone else. "Paul, I love you. Please come meet me."? "Paul, I'm marrying Jack."? Not knowing was frustrating.

I just couldn't make up my mind. If I knew for sure that she'd be there, I'd go in a heartbeat. But her plan was created in haste, with less than a promise or strategy. Would she come at all? And if she did, when? I didn't have the resources to wait around very long.

The only semblance of a plan I had for myself was to get to London with around $100 to find a cheap, orphaned ticket to New York City. Starting to go south again from here into the unknown could cost me crucial dollars that might inhibit my ability to get to England with anywhere near the amount of money I would need to fly to the States.

One minute I had decided to go south to find Olivia, and the next to be conservative and go north—to where, unknown, but at least in the general direction of England. Just then, my driver, the doctor, said this was his turnoff and that I should stay on main roads to continue towards Germany. He was sorry he couldn't take me any farther, for he had a sick patient who was waiting. But he did give me an old discarded men's skiing scarf and a pair of gloves as he said it looked like it was going to snow.

I knew it was getting colder as each ride took me higher and higher into the Alps, but I had no idea how cold until I exited his car and watched him drive off. It hit me like a punch, the cold wind carrying snowflakes. Snow in July. I wasn't expecting that. In addition to the newly falling snow, there were huge patches of ice and snow everywhere you looked, luckily not on the streets yet.

The doctor said I could get a cheap sandwich at a small hotel-boardinghouse just around the corner, and then it was just a mile walk to hit a major road going north. He was right, and I had a nice big sandwich with two meats and tomatoes, onions, lettuce, peppers, and even sauerkraut as well as a nice big hot cup of tea for less than one-dollar US.

As soon as I walked in and sat down, I was a celebrity. This place didn't get many walk-ins from Chicago. A smiling, round-faced elderly woman came over with the menu. I told her all I was looking for was a simple sandwich and some hot tea—how much would that cost? I took out a pocket full of Swiss centime coins and looked at her with my by-now patented sad, helpless, nice-little-lost-boy face even though I was looking more like a mountain man from the Rockies or the Andes or Siberia. She looked at her husband behind the counter of food not twenty feet away. He shrugged, and she said, "Un Swiss Franc," which was at the time roughly one US dollar. Perfect! As I was eating, they both came over to me to ask all the typical questions about where I was from, where I'd been, etc. They were nice, and the husband kept filling up my teacup with more hot water.

As we were talking, one of them mentioned the Matterhorn, that I wasn't so far away and that I should go there. I told them I had thought about that but didn't want to go so far south as I was running out of money. Then they suggested the Eiger, another of Switzerland's highest peaks that was almost directly east of here. They said it wasn't as well known as the Matterhorn, but it was very famous to mountain climbers and was very, very dangerous.

I thanked them for their kindness. Just before opening the door, the woman came out from behind the counter and handed me a liter bottle of Coke and a couple of cookies in a bag, such a nice gesture towards someone they would never see again. We both had that moment where we wanted to hug each other goodbye, each a little awkward in our attempt, but instead shook hands and said our farewells.

I'd say I had walked about a mile, maybe halfway to the road I needed to reach to have a better chance of getting a long ride north. As I had been walking on this isolated mountain road, I'd been watching clouds below me in the valley. Switzerland was so beautiful with its mixture of some of the world's highest and most beautiful snowcapped peaks and visions of painterly green valleys dotted here and there with little towns below. The scarf and gloves were a godsend, but it was getting so cold that I stopped to open my sleeping bag and get out my sweater and another shirt to put on.

Just as I started walking again, it began to snow, and then I felt something behind me. There wasn't any noise, but I had the feeling that something was lurking. I stopped and looked behind me. There wasn't anything—anything, that is, but a dense cloud coming straight for me. I was being attacked or embraced by this huge, slow-moving cloud. I tried to pick up the pace, but it soon enveloped me. It was freezing inside the cloud. I didn't know what to do. Should I stand still and let it pass? I didn't know how big it was or how long that might take. Should I run? But to where? There was only the slanted side of a mountain ridge above and an even steeper mountainside leading to a valley a long way below.

I continued to walk as I cursed my situation at the top of my lungs. If it wasn't bad enough just a week or two ago to have had to hitchhike in 100° temperatures with no rides for hours, now I was walking in a snowfall high in the Alps with a mean cloud streaming all around me and through me to my bones. It really was almost too cold to move.

Then I heard a car coming up behind me. I needed a ride desperately, but the cloud was so dense that the driver might never see me until he ran over me. The road was narrow, and there was very little shoulder. Just then a small car came bursting through, not slowing down as he passed me swiftly. He was either running away from a row of Swiss police cars or it was Evel Knievel trying for a new record on driving in a cloud high on a narrow mountain road without killing himself.

I decided to sit down on a huge rock by the road rather than risk being hit by the next vehicle to come racing through this cloud.

The cloud finally moved on, but unfortunately, I could see even more clouds below me, heading my way. I was getting scared. I was already freezing; I didn't need to be in more clouds and snow. I needed some luck.

Luck came in short order. Between cloud openings a passing car occupied by a young Swiss couple saw me and stopped just as the snow turned to rain.

As they drove on, I wondered if I still had a chance to get out and hitch towards Saanen and possibly meet up with Olivia. But the rain continued. I wasn't getting warm very fast, and the thought of going out into the rain just didn't seem right. I kept my mouth shut and wondered, as I have many times since, how my life would have changed if I had gone to Saanen and met Olivia. I'll never know. Instead, I just gazed out the window as we drove through majestic valleys and Alpine mountains on our way to Basel.

The Swiss couple left me off at a youth hostel, but unfortunately this hostel would only take in people who were members.

I walked around for a while, not knowing what to do as the evening and the unknown grew closer. As I walked by the Rhine River, I scouted out a tree-covered spot on the other side of a berm from the road as a possible place to bed down. Because the skies continued to worry me, I decided to try and give hitchhiking out of Basel one last shot. Within minutes, I got a ride. My ride let me off in a less-than-satisfactory place to hitch, and since I had napped in the car a little, I wasn't sure if I was still in Switzerland or had crossed over into Germany.

I walked for quite a ways until I saw a bank. The manager had just locked up and was getting in his car. I begged him to change some Swiss francs for German marks. He couldn't open the bank again, but he did help me out of his pocket with the equivalent of about $1.50 US.

It was after 9:00 p.m., but I was still trying to hitch when a car intersected the crossroad I was standing by and let out two young hitchhikers from Amsterdam returning home after having traveled in Italy. We talked and decided to hitch together. I felt very unsure that three guys hitching together would ever get a ride. They figured we'd better get something to eat if we were going to travel at night. We found a little place, and I spent two marks on a sandwich and a beer.

As we were leaving the café to try to start hitching, a German policeman stopped and told us that hitching was not allowed in the area. We had no choice but to go on walking, and by ten o'clock there was very little traffic, so we decided to bed down in a field not far from the road.

As we woke on Saturday, July 18th, and tried again, we were prevented from hitching by another police officer, who told us to walk a half mile east. When we got the area, there were twenty to thirty young people already trying to hitch. Hours went by. I had had enough. My two fellow travelers and I decided to go back to the Swiss border to get away from the pack and see if we couldn't get a ride faster.

I had hitched rides with almost a hundred different people on this trip, and I'd about reached my wit's end. I was so tired of hitchhiking.

Finally, a car stopped and could only take one of us, luckily it was me. The ride lasted for a while and I was let off but picked up quickly again, this time by a VW bus with four other hitchhikers already in it. We were all glad that we were on the road to Frankfurt. All of us were from different countries, and I was the only one who spoke any English. Eventually, we were all let out not far from Cologne. Two people went east, and another guy and I kept trying to go north as the sky again was threatening rain.

Finally, a German guy going to Düsseldorf stopped, but he only wanted to pick up one of us. We had to answer about twenty questions each that he asked in German and English. He eventually picked me. He was a strict, middle-aged man with more rules for car riding than the Army has. I asked to borrow a cigarette, but he said no and gave me a cookie instead. However, after an hour of talking back and forth, he finally gave in and handed me a couple of German Kim cigarettes. But again, as happened too much lately, I was let off at a very bad place in the dark. At about 9:00 p.m. I did get a lucky ride with another German, an elderly man who also was giving me orders like I was in the Army. But after I related some of my stories, he loosened up and told me when he was young he had hitched also, but hadn't had anywhere near the adventures I had experienced so far. As we were driving, he would occasionally tell me he'd soon have to turn east and drop me off, but each time he mentioned that he worried I'd be in no man's land as a hitchhiker in the dark.

As the day flew by with numerous rides and hassles, I had decided, regardless of money, I was going to go to Amsterdam and then quickly over the channel to England. That was it; mentally I was exhausted and ready for a change from traveling.

Finally, my driver swore in German, "Ssheissekopf. I guess I'm going to make my wife mad. I'm going to go out of my way to take you to another highway where you can get a good ride to Amsterdam."

An hour later we approached a rest stop, and as he pulled in to drop me off, he asked if I was hungry. I'm not sure I'd had anything to eat all day, and I said yes but that I didn't have very much money. He said he'd buy. Inside he ordered ham and eggs, salad, and potatoes and two beers for me. He was so jealous of my travel experiences and wanted to continue talking all night, but he said his wife would be fuming already at the time he would be getting home. As we left the table and he paid for the meal, he also told the waitress to give me two packs of Marlboros. I couldn't thank him enough for all his generosity and kindness.

I waved so long as he drove off and then considered my prospects. I was in a pull-off from the autobahn, very well lighted, on a hillside going down to a four-lane highway. As I stood there, I saw very few cars or trucks going by. I guess it was around 11:00 p.m. As I walked onto the grass hill alongside the parking lot, the restaurant's lights were turned off behind me. I found a spot at the top of the hill and turned in, exhausted.

Amsterdam

Only a couple of minutes later, she came out again, this time with a guy who looked like he could have been her brother. Same blonde long hair, bandanna also around his head and also wearing sunglasses. They stopped behind me as I sat on the wall. She said something to him, and he walked more to my side and said in broken English...

""Bonjour, man, mon nom is Pascal and this...this woman est Maya. She wants to ah...paint your picture."

"She wants to paint me?" I was surprised.

15.

A Place Called Paradiso

Sunday, 5:30 AM, July 19, 1970

I was roused early by honking horns and trucks lumbering by below me on the highway. It was a very cold, breezy, and misty morning. This was no good. I had hoped Holland would be warmer than Germany. It was so cold I had to get into the rest stop restaurant fast for the bathroom and a hot cup of coffee. The coffee was good, but as I paid for it, I also got a cold slap in the face as I realized I only had a couple of German marks left and no Dutch guilders. We were close to the border; I would soon be crossing into the land of windmills on a Sunday with no banks or money exchanges open. After paying, I went back to the bathroom to brush my teeth and wash my face and even other parts of my body a little.

When I walked out of the restaurant, I was surprised to see someone already hitching in the only sensible place to get a ride. As I walked down the circular driveway to where the exit lane identified the start of the autobahn, I nodded to a young man about my age and stopped thirty to forty feet behind him to give him right of way.

I guess just like in America, people like to sleep in on Sunday mornings in the land of the Dutch. There were few cars flying past and, remember, this was the autobahn. They really were going so fast they were almost off the ground.

We would look at each other from time to time, but we both stood our ground. I'm sure he knew he had the catbird spot. I just had to wait my turn until he got a ride, and then I would move up.

After about an hour and a half, he started to look back at me. I guessed he was trying to make up his mind about something, but I had no clue. Then he picked up his backpack, swung it over his shoulders, and started walking back to me.

The first words out of his mouth as he approached were, "Guten morgen, zu kalt und keine autos."

Well, he wasn't American. The time I spent in the car last night with my wonderful new friend Siegfried had prepared me somewhat as he spoke some German in the car. This guy was German, and he was either complaining that there were so few cars on the road, or he was indicating we might as well try to steal a car in the restaurant parking lot or wait here all day.

"Good morning, man," I said, as I shrugged my shoulders, adding, "I don't speak any German. Do you speak any English?"

"A little, mon," he threw back at me.

I could immediately tell he meant what he said about his

English. This meeting of minds would not last long unless he learned some of my language or I picked up more German. But regardless, he opened his coat and pulled out a pack of foreign cigarettes and offered me one. We lit up, cupping our hands close together to start the cigarettes in the growing morning wind. As I took two quick big drags, I felt I tasted a little bit of a Turkish flavor. Not that I was an expert in any way, but I did remember that distinct flavor, as I had smoked some Turkish cigarettes in Istanbul.

I held it up and said, "Turkish?"

He showed me the pack quickly, but I didn't recognize it and then he said, "Nein, sie kommen aus dem Libanon."

With his German accent I wasn't sure exactly where in the world he was indicating, and with both Arabic and Western words on the front of the pack, I guessed the smokes were from the Middle East somewhere. And I thought I was a traveler. We each took some puffs, always looking and hoping more cars would drive by. Our peeking at each other continued. We were each trying to get some feeling, good or bad, from the other. He was probably a year or two older than I was. We were both wearing sport coats; most backpackers or hitchhikers never wore sport coats. I knew why I did. Why did he? He also wore jeans, as I did, but there was an aura about him as if he were a professional on a business trip. His hair was black as the night, not very long, and his face was clean shaven.

As I flicked my cigarette butt into the air towards the barren autobahn, he tapped me on the shoulder, nodded up to the restaurant's driveway, and said, "Bist du hungrig? Lasst etwas zu essen. . . is that a good ideas?"

His gist was, "Fuck hitching, no cars, let's get some breakfast."

My first impression had been that his English was almost nonexistent, but his question to me ended with pretty good English, except for the plural on the word ideas. Odd.

As we started walking up the incline, I said, "Maybe just coffee for me. I am out of German marks and don't have much money."

I don't know how much he understood of that, but without looking at me, he said "No, no…wir…wir verwenden…meine Deutschmarks."

He seemed to be saying he'd pay for breakfast.

As we sat down at one of the tables by the big windows looking out to the autobahn, he ordered for both of us: eggs, potatoes, and bread and jam with orange juice and coffee.

"You Amerikaner?" he said as we both were acting like we hadn't eaten in days.

"Yes, I'm from Chicago, and before you can say it, no, I'm. . .". I tried to get the line out before he came back with that typical response.

He muttered, "Ah. . . du müssen ein gangsters," and then looked up and gave me a little smile. Of course, I agreed with him, smiled and pointed back at myself and said, "Yes, gangster. Bang, bang," and smiled. I looked around to see if anyone was following this part of the conversation.

He held out his hand to shake mine as he said, "Gerrard, from Munchen—oh, how you say? Munich."

Again, I pointed to myself. "Paul."

"Paul, you traveler?" As he held out his hand with his thumb up.

"Yes, many cities in Europe, but I am running out of money, and I'm tired. I've been on the road for about four to five months. I go north now to Amsterdam."

I wasn't sure out of all that what he understood, although I did feel he understood English better than he spoke it.

"So, Paul, wo wurst du Bleiben. Ah, merde, you. . .". He tried to get something out with some frustration and then put his hands together like in prayer and turned his head to feign lying down or sleeping and then added, "Amsterdam?"

"Good question," I said. I shrugged my shoulders and shook my head a little, indicating I had no idea where I would sleep. Matter of fact, I should be very worried about that. Amsterdam was another big city, and I was running out of money.

We finished our breakfast, and as the waitress was pouring more coffee for us, he indicated we should get going if we were going to hitch to Amsterdam together and get there before dark. As he was counting his money to pay the bill, I grabbed his arm and said, "We can't go together. Thanks, but two guys. . . we'll never get a ride together. People don't like two guys. Looks too dangerous. Do you understand?"

"Ja...Ja, I know. How do I say...ich have Platz fur Sie Bleiben... Merde..." He was looking around, not to see someone but to find the words he needed. Then he again put his hands together, miming sleep and pointed to me and then himself and smiled. Now, it was only fleeting, but since he'd talked about my sleeping twice, he was either going to be a very good friend or I was being invited down a street that is not my street in life. I think he sensed that I was having that thought and said, "Nein, nein. Ich mag auch Frauleins."

I guess he had been indicating that we would now become travel buddies. I would come with him, and he had a place for both of us to stay.

Okay, I thought, maybe he is the kind of friend I need now. I was hoping this place he knew of was the house of a friend that wouldn't cost me.

He started looking around again, but his intention was different. Then he spotted a young couple across the room. He said, "Ya, dis good."

He got up, walked over to them, and started talking, and then the male of the couple looked back at me for a second. I had no idea what story he might be telling this couple, but I could tell they were German. I heard both say "Amsterdam" a couple of times.

Gerrard came back and indicated we had a ride all the way to Amsterdam. As we waited for them to finish, I thanked him profusely for being so kind as to buy me breakfast. I had no idea how much he paid, but it was more than I could have afforded.

The German man and woman were an obviously well-off young couple. We followed them out and got in the backseat of what looked like a new BMW. The driver spoke pretty good English and indicated they had to make one quick stop on the way. The ride would probably take about two to three hours.

The three non-drivers mostly napped during the ride. There was very little conversation. Every so often I'd open my eyes and look at the Dutch landscape going by. The morning started cold and misty, and the sky, the farther east we drove, looked more threatening. I had a million questions concerning what we—or rather what I—was doing. Gerrard was a mystery, but I'm sure to him so was I. Something smelled funny; he just didn't seem like a traveler. He had other purposes right now. I kept wondering what those purposes were and how I fit in.

As we got to the outskirts of Amsterdam, it started to rain. It couldn't have rained for the three hours while I had a roof over my head in the car. No, no. I believe the rain purposely waited to come down until I was out in the open.

They let us off at a huge subway station that gave us easy access to all parts of Amsterdam.

Gerrard, however, felt we were close to the address where he was going to meet some friends, so we started to walk. And walk and walk. And let me remind you, we were walking in a constant rain, and it looked like the rain would continue.

Every so often he'd walk into a place and ask if anyone knew this address. Unfortunately, no one did. We continued to walk, and as we walked, he asked if I had heard of a place called Paradiso.

I had heard that Paradiso and its architectural and ethereal sister, Fantasio, had wild reputations. I'd heard some stories about drugs, women, and rock and roll. As far as I was aware, they were world-famous hangouts for travelers from everywhere. Both places were supposedly housed in large, abandoned churches or factory buildings in the heart of Amsterdam. And Amsterdam was probably the only town in the world that could accommodate and put up with the activities of both Paradiso and Fantasio together. It was hard for me to believe the leniency of Amsterdam's drug laws, concerning both selling and using. Nothing like that existed in the USA.

Gerrard said he believed we were close to Paradiso. We should go there and regroup, and maybe he could find out where his friend's house was located.

So, we continued to walk for what seemed like a couple of hours, mostly in the rain, but for a while it stopped as we turned down the street on one of Amsterdam's famous canals. In all my travels, I'd never seen any city that had this kind of design and land usage. Very beautiful. We walked down many different quiet, narrow streets next to the canal, which usually lay about three feet below the street level. Every canal block I'd been down had beautiful, large trees that framed the canals perfectly.

As we got closer to the northern part of the city, we encountered many more canals. Some of the canals had boats tied up and docked, using nearly every available inch, usually along one side of the numerous waterways. As we slowly walked by different kinds of houseboats or barges, I wondered what they were like inside, especially as the rain started again and I was so cold, wet, and tired. Besides, we hadn't eaten since daybreak, and it was now mid-afternoon. I almost felt like breaking into one of these houseboats. Many seemed like they had been closed up for some length of time with tarps covering them.

Finally, we turned a corner, and there was the massive building that housed Paradiso. Unfortunately, it was still closed, it seemed, as they were taking out garbage from almost every doorway. We found out we couldn't get in until 7 o'clock that night, so we walked to the other famous international Amsterdam hangout for young people, Fantasio.

Gerrard told me to wait on the steps leading into Fantasio. He thought he had just seen one of his friends walking way down the street and wanted to catch up. He took off, and I sat on the stone wall leading up to the steps. The loud sound of aggressive bass guitars would escape periodically from the front doors as they were opened and closed, letting longhairs in or out. In only a couple of minutes of observing, I saw what appeared to be hippies from all over the world. Gerrard told me young people came to either Fantasio or Paradiso as a specific destination. The more I heard and saw, the more I realized this just might be the drug capital of the world. To one who wanted or needed drugs, this was nirvana. Though not every drug in the world was legal here, many were. Gerrard said the police had other, more important things to do than chase down drug violations—I suppose like murder and robbery investigations. There were just too many people using drugs to monitor them all.

As I sat there, a few people nodded at me. My sleeping bag told them that I was a traveler. Those who did try to talk to me, unfortunately, mostly had little English.

A couple of minutes turned into a half hour, and there was no sign of Gerrard. I was worried, but then I wasn't. Even though we had only met this morning, I had a good feeling about him I pulled out my sketchbook to pass the time. The sun had finally come out, and I was tired of just watching people going in and out. I decided it was too chaotic to write, so I was going to draw. I started to draw a couple of kids obviously belonging to some travelers like me as they were clothed in bright-colored fabric pants and what looked like Indian or Pakistani tie-dyed tops in varying motifs and colors.

I had a pretty good start on one of the kids and was about to start on the other when a very innocent and striking girl wearing a bandanna around the top of her long, flowing blonde hair and sunglasses walked by and stopped for a second to look at what I was doing. I said, "I'm just waiting for a friend, just passing time. How are you today?"

She looked somewhat surprised and said, "Bonjour, je ne parle anglaise. A mal, je voudrais que vous me tracez." The only part I got was that she didn't speak any English. She was obviously French and there was something about her, something I was drawn to other than her looks. She kept looking at my drawing, then at me and then shrugged and walked inside, turning as she opened the doors to say, "Au revoir."

Oh well, que sera sera; that might have been interesting. I

looked around and then thought I might as well go back to my drawing. The kids were still playing out in front of me when Gerrard appeared from the side of the building. He indicated he had made some progress. I think he was going to meet someone who could write down the real address for us. He asked for a cigarette but immediately left to find the guy.

Only a couple of minutes later, the bandanna girl came out again, this time with a guy who looked like he could have been her brother—same long blond hair, bandanna around his head, also wearing sunglasses. They stopped behind me as I sat on the wall. She said something to him, and he walked closer to me and said in broken English, "Bonjour, man, mon nom is Pascal and this. . . this woman est Maya. She wants to ah—paint your picture."

"She wants to paint me?" I was surprised.

"Non, non—you her picture. She will give you francs."

Maybe I should have taken the money, but I couldn't. There was something about her. "Oh. No, no francs. But I'm not a portrait illustrator; I just sketch and have fun. And my name is Paul."

He translated to her, and she said, "Bon" and opened the door for us to follow. For a minute I thought it wasn't a good idea to leave the entrance but quickly decided Gerrard would look inside if he didn't see me out front.

It was dark and loud. This was a strange kind of meeting place for young people. There were rock 'n roll posters on the walls everywhere. The music was emanating from some kind of sound system, though as we walked down one hall after another, I saw a glimpse of a bigger room with what looked like a stage. We passed many tables with longhairs selling all kinds of things including drugs, mostly pot or hashish. As we walked, it seemed we were walking in a cloud of pot. It seemed to follow us.

Finally, we came to a room where some girls were selling clothes that smelled like they had bought them in and lugged them from Pakistan or Afghanistan. There were no lambskin coats, but I thought for a second what could have been, if only. . . oh well. That was before; this was now.

We went to a quiet corner of the room where there were some large, ornate, fluffy pillows laid out haphazardly. Maya pointed for me to sit on one leaning against the wall as she lay down on a couple about five or six feet from me.

Pascal asked if this was okay and could I paint her. I opened my sketchbook to a blank page, looked at her, and wondered how I was going to draw her. Should I be detailed, or should I draw her loosely, with some sketchy feel? I didn't know how much time I would have before Gerrard came back. I was sure he would want to leave quickly.

I think she thought I should have started drawing by now. She caught my eye as she turned her head and gave me a little shrug, imploring me to get started. Then she puckered her lips and gave me an air kiss.

As I put pen to paper and positioned her face, Pascal lit up a fairly large joint, took some puffs, and handed it to Maya. She took six or seven long drags and held each for a while before letting out. You could tell she was serious about what she was smoking. Pascal took it from her and moved closer to where I was and handed it to me. I wasn't in the mood and shook my head no. But he seemed persistent and said, "This is different, s'il vous plait."

I accepted it and took a couple of big drags, hoping that that would be enough and I wouldn't have to appease him anymore. As I was handing the joint back to him, I noticed he had also taken out a pack of cigarettes and was trying to get one out. Again, it looked like a pack from the Middle East. Did everyone like Turkish cigarettes, or had everyone recently been to Turkey and beyond?

I didn't know how many joints of different drugs I'd had since I started my trip. I guess if I'd had one, I'd had a hundred, but as I continued to draw, I realized this joint was different. I could certainly taste some Turkish tobacco in the inhale, and I assumed they had made the joint with either marijuana or hashish or both. As I've said before, smoking cigarettes was part of my life, but smoking dope never was, not in college nor now. My imbibing was in the spirit of camaraderie, to fit into the group. If I could draw on acid, I could certainly draw on this, whatever it was. As I continued to draw Maya, they continued to pass the large joint around to the point that I really couldn't tell how many puffs I'd had, which was a little unusual. Time was passing, and for the most part I wasn't conscious of that passing, but after a half hour or so, I realized I hadn't seen Gerrard. Suddenly, I started to get a little concerned. I needed a place to stay tonight. It was a rainy week here in Amsterdam, and I needed a roof over my head.

Pascal got up and said he was going to get us some drinks. I had to smile a couple of times as I was drawing when a string of oldies from the US blasted to all parts of Fantasio. First, there was "Be My Baby" by The Ronettes followed by "The Duke of Earl" and then "Denise" by Randy & The Rainbows. I had loved finding out about foreign rock in the different countries I'd visited, but hearing these songs brought back great memories.

As Pascal brought us some drinks, he indicated we should take a break. I think he worried Maya was getting tired being in one pose all this time. He sat down beside her and urged me to come over to them. He handed me a bottle of Coke as he

314

took out another joint, lit it, and passed it to me. Usually, I would have turned it down, but for some reason, my ability to make that decision wasn't there. I couldn't say no. That was a different feeling. I wasn't worried about it, though; my body and mind were floating a little, and I felt that everything was okay in my life and in the world. That was very strange for me, to say the least. It seemed all three of us were now in a kind of twilight zone.

Another oldie, "Monday, Monday" by The Mamas and Papas, came on. I guess I was subconsciously mouthing the words and humming or even singing softly. Pascal said he loved American rock and someday he'd like to own a lot of those records.

I asked him about his traveling, and he said both he and Maya played in a band; she was the female singer. The group was called "Les Couleurs de la Nuit" which translates as "The Colors of Night." They were here in Amsterdam trying to get a gig to play in the bigger event hall at Paradiso. As he was describing the band and its name, the song "Louie Louie" by The Kingsmen came on, and he stopped talking and started singing or trying to sing the words.

I watched him for a second or so and then asked, "Do you know the dirty words version of that song?"

He asked, "What, you say dirt words?"

"No, not dirt, dirty words. You know, like risqué. Do you understand risqué?"

"Ah oui, mots sales comme fuck. Vous know words?"

I listened for a second to get my bearings and then talked over the lyrics. As the song continued, I jumped in. "Each night at ten, I lay her again, I fuck my girl all kinds of ways. And on that chair, I lay her there, I felt my bone in her hair."

He laughed, although I'm not sure he understood all I said.

Then he leaned over to Maya to tell her in French.

She made no real response to what he said. She was now floating somewhere in outer space. Maya had had more drags on these joints then Pascal or I, but still—to be so far gone was a little strange. I wondered what other drugs she had been taking.

Maya did come back to earth for a moment or two and grabbed my sketchpad to look at her drawing. Without asking me, she ripped the page out and held it to her chest and then was orbiting Earth again, floating.

I looked at Pascal and said, "She really is floating. You know, I feel a little floaty myself. What kind of pot are we smoking— where in the world is it from?"

"Non, non, how you say? Not weed. It is brown that we are smoking."

"Oh, I don't know brown, never heard of that. Is that hash? I can taste also some Turkish tobacco. Did you cut the Turkish tobacco with hashish?"

He looked at me, obviously trying to come up with a word or phrase he knew in French but was having a little difficulty with the English. "Non, no hashish. Comment tu dis? Oui, L'heroin. Heroin."

It didn't register right away. I was expecting him to say some country's hash and instead—what he said was trying to register in my mind and then I blurted out, "Fuck, are you kidding, did I hear you right? heroin? What the fuck? You could have told me. Heroin?!"

"Non, non, petit. Just small. C'est different des se piquer à l'héroïne." He positioned his thumb and forefinger to feign injecting into his arm.

I started to feel different parts of my body. I'm not sure why—

maybe to make sure they were still there. Almost immediately again, I was at ease. There was, as I can still remember today, that different feeling that everything, everything in the world and in me was okay.

Evidently, we all fell asleep right there where we were lying. Gerrard found us an hour or two later. At last, he had had the correct address and indicated we should go. Earlier we had walked side by side through the streets of Amsterdam, but now, after the brown, I tended to walk five to ten paces behind Gerrard. He kept on urging me to catch up. Each time he did, I would mutter to myself, "Yes, easy for you to say that, but you can feel the lower part of your body. I can't."

Of course, even though he now had a good address, we still walked forever, and we were still asking people where to find that elusive street where we could sleep tonight. Eventually, we turned from a logical street where you would think we would find a young person's place onto a very busy street with a lot of foot and auto traffic. He stopped at a place that was flanked by shops left and right and said, "This is it."

I gazed around and gave him a quizzical look. There was no sign of a residence or anything like one. But before I could say any more, Gerrard was kicking a boarded-up doorway repeatedly.

A minute or two later, the bottom half of the door opened inward, and a hand and arm waved us in. We got down on our knees and crawled into a dark, junk-filled room that smelled stale. Gerrard shook the young guy's hand and said, "This is Chicago," pointing to me. We skirted garbage and junk to a stairwell and climbed to the second floor.

There we found ten to fifteen travelers like us sprawled out on the floor, some on sleeping bags, some sitting. As we approached, many yelled, "Schlie Blich, Gerrard. Hallo." I could sense quickly most were German. Of the fifteen or so, I'd say nine or ten knew Gerrard or were from Germany somewhere. There were no Americans or English, my luck. The rest I would find out were from France, Romania, and Ukraine. There were ten men and five women, all young, and though almost everyone seemed friendly and smiled at me here and there, I understood that no one spoke very good English and most not even broken English. It looked like I was by myself on this boat. And I wondered, is this boat a commune?

It'd been dark for a while when someone indicated everyone should try stealing outside to find some food now that the street was quiet. Most of us went downstairs, and one guy squeezed out to scout the amount of activity on the street. You see, we were homesteading in an abandoned, probably condemned building on a busy street. I'm not sure what they call it in Amsterdam, but in America, it's called "breaking and entering," and usually jail accompanies that activity. But even having considered that as we walked in the steady rain to a grocery store, I was glad I had a roof over my head.

We all bought different things and laid them out on the floor when we got back, and everyone ate and talked—everyone except me. Gerrard would talk to me here and there, but again, we had little common language.

Eventually, they all left to go to some bar. I passed, indicating I was too tired.

As I lay there in an abandoned building, alone, I wondered again what was going on. What was I doing? If Gerrard had told me this morning we were going to break into an abandoned building in the middle of Amsterdam, I would have given him some excuse as we entered the city. I certainly wouldn't have followed him on this path. But on the other hand, where else could I sleep? I had no money, and it was raining, and Amsterdam was a large city. There was no soft place to lie down and sleep.

I was feeling apprehensive being alone in an abandoned building that they obviously had broken into. I didn't know the laws here, but I guessed I was breaking four or five, and I was by myself. Not that it would be much better to be caught here with other people, but it would just be my luck to get caught alone.

I eventually dozed off. I have no idea what time it was or what time the gang got back. I was obviously very tired, because whatever noise they made coming back didn't wake me at all. Now it was early morning, and though no one was in sight, I thought I heard voices on an upper floor. When I finally got up, I followed the noise to see what was happening. Everyone was eating again, so I joined in. There was some jam, cheese, bread, and milk. I tried to eat as much as I could without being a pig. I worried when and where my next meal would come from. Mungo Jerry's current hit "In the Summertime" was playing on someone's radio. Europe loved this song for some reason.

After we finished the food, many in the group started lighting up joints of different sizes, filled, it seemed, with a virtual grocery store of different drugs. Besides not being my thing, it was way too early, and my body still didn't feel normal after yesterday's flirtation with heroin. I probably hadn't had that much. Regardless, it had been in my body, and it was unusual for me to be so lethargic and tired. The smoke was starting to get to me, so I went back downstairs, lay down, and without even trying fell asleep again.

Then—was I dreaming? I didn't know. I didn't even know if it was possible to feel pain in dreams. But there was pain, great

319

pain, sharp pain. I could almost taste it even though the pain was coming from the small of my back. What was I dreaming; where was I? It didn't make sense. Now there were voices, loud like when I'm awake and then the pain again. Ah, not dreaming, the pain was real, what the. . . I turned to see three uniformed Dutch policemen standing over me and yelling at me in Dutch. I quickly looked around to find my worst nightmare: I was alone and had been caught alone breaking and entering. In a foreign country.

I had no idea what these guys were saying, but by their tone and the looks on their faces, it sure wasn't, "Good morning, Mister, were you having a nice sleep, can we get you some juice and some breakfast?"

Those couple of minutes of yelling were enough for them, evidently, as one of them grabbed me and dragged me over to the wall and pushed me up facing the wall, kicking his feet at my feet to assume the position so he could frisk me.

Just then a guy came in wearing a raincoat. He seemed to be a detective. He asked in a couple of different languages and finally in English, "Are you alone?"

I said, "Yes, I'm alone." I wasn't sure if I was or not, but I didn't want to give the gang up, whether they were upstairs or out somewhere.

They turned me around and forced me to squat against the wall as they looked through my sleeping bag and my corduroy jacket and found my passport.

The detective looked at my passport and then down at me while shaking his head. I'm sure he was thinking, *You dumb ass, you're American; what are you doing breaking and entering in Holland? Don't all Americans have money? If you don't have money, then maybe you're a drug dealer or thief or worse.* Yes, I was sure that was how his mind was working. I was dead. I didn't think lying was my best move when he asked again if I was alone, but on the other hand, being a snitch wasn't my style either. "No, no one else. I'm alone." Just then, one of the policemen yelled something from the floor above. Then I heard many feet on the wooden floor up above. The detective looked at me and said, "You're alone? Right."

Then he was given my wallet by one of the other policemen. He opened it, looked at some things inside, then saw a closed secret flap that hid most of my money. His eyes opened wide as he counted. They then took me upstairs.

There were seven other people caught upstairs, and all of them also had to give up their passports, wallets, I.D. papers, and any money they had. I couldn't see how much money each had, but my guess was about $10 or so each in different currencies.

I was mostly watching the detective on my side of the room, but when the detective turned his head to a couple of the other officers who were searching the other travelers, I turned to see one policeman holding two big knives—they looked like switchblades— and then two pairs of brass knuckles and what looked like bags of different drugs. Two of the people, for whatever reason, had no passports. That couldn't be good.

We were all motioned to get up on our feet as one of the policemen came back upstairs with handcuffs for all of us. We were told to put our hands in front of us. He went down the line putting the cuffs on each of us. Another policeman yelled at us in Dutch, and everyone got their sleeping bags or and possessions together. I rolled up my sleeping bag and was going to put my sketchbook inside when the detective grabbed it and said, "Finish rolling your bag up. I'll keep this for the time being."

We all seemed to bump into each other trying to navigate the broken stairs, which was made more difficult by the fact that we didn't have full use of our hands.

One policeman pushed the guy in the lead of our criminal parade as we reached the half doorway to the outside. Immediately, all of us got down on our knees to crawl out as best we could.

Once outside, still on my knees, I found that a crowd had gathered to see who or what would come out of this old building. As I got to my feet, I saw two paddy wagons waiting for us. The crowd was mostly quiet, but there was some pushing and shoving amongst them to check out these criminals. We were divided and pushed into the wagons—wagons with bars. I had no idea of the seriousness of my—our—offense in Amsterdam. I knew the drugs probably weren't that big of a deal. The obvious lack of money concerned me. How could anyone enter another country, into a big expensive city, and not have some money? The police would assume they would have to steal to survive. I'm sure their solution would be to put us in jail or deport us.

Gerrard, unfortunately, was put in the other paddy wagon. Those with me talked together but in German, so I continued to be in the dark.

After ten or fifteen minutes, we stopped and were brought into a police station. We were in a large room with no windows and not much else but a couple of benches. I didn't know if they were processing the other group or if they were in some other jail configuration.

Not long after, the door opened, and we were again ushered down to the street, back in the wagons and off. We stopped about twenty minutes later and were dragged out, ushered in through double doors to more stairs and this time eventually to a jail cell. This time, all eight of us were together. They had taken our packs, and I didn't know to where or if we'd ever get them back.

We weren't alone in the cell. There was a hodgepodge of more sinister-looking men who were sitting on the floor with backs against the wall. They looked at us, we looked at them, and believe it or not, they appeared to be staring at me with special resentment. This was their cell; it wasn't good we were there. There was no communication. The police locked us up, took off the handcuffs, and put us in there, not explaining why or how long we'd be there.

I had no watch, and no clock was visible. I had completely lost track of time. We were caught much earlier in the day, and I had no idea if it was night now or what time it was.

During the hours of confinement, some prisoners were let out and more were brought in. It was probably just my insecurity, but I swear each new person who was thrown in looked meaner and more dangerous than the one before. For some reason, I felt that the new ones stared at me more than anyone else. After a while I saw a pattern. I really didn't talk to anyone or try to at length, but when I did talk, my English caught their attention. At first, I wondered why that was, but I realized that they figured if I was American or English, I inevitably had money—money they'd rather have themselves.

Gerrard talked often to the group that was brought from the abandoned building minus the girls who evidently were put in another cell. Curiously, though, as they talked in German to each other from distant parts of the jail cell, often one or more of them would turn to look at me with a funny expression, as if trying to figure out something about me or having to do with me.

I had been leaning up against one of the walls, but after a while one of the unknown cellmates got up from where he had

323

been sitting and moved over closer to me. If something was going to happen next, chances are I didn't want anything to do with it. I got up and moved to another bench.

Finally, a guard came and opened the cell door and asked for one of our group by name. He got up and the guard took him away. I immediately looked at the rest of our group. They didn't seem to care and didn't stop talking among themselves.

Then, maybe thirty minutes later, another call came out to one of our group, and the guard took him away also. Where? I wondered. To another cell, to a judge? When would my turn be and where would they take me? Also, it had to be getting late in the evening. Was the procedure going to continue? Would the interrogations last all night? I wondered if I'd be the last person called out. I hoped not. What were all these guys saying to the police, anyway? I wondered if this offense was worthy of having people work all through the night.

Then, as I thought everything would go as with the first two, there was a change—hours had passed since the second person had been called out. Had something happened? Did somebody say something he shouldn't? What was going on?

Finally, the third of our group was called out, and as he was being taken away, Gerrard got up and walked over to where I was. He didn't stop, but walked by, saying softly, "We have a plan to escape, to get out of here tonight."

"What!" I yelled to myself silently. I believe my heart stopped for a second or two. I looked around immediately to see if anybody had heard him. My mind was spinning almost as if it was trying to escape my body in its own jailbreak.

Did I just say to myself "jailbreak"? No, no way. . . impossible. How? When? Granted, my host and tour guide in Amsterdam was somewhat of a mystery. The few times we'd talked, we really hadn't found out much about each other. In hindsight, I had been happy to talk about me, my trip, my thoughts. Gerrard always seemed to avoid talking about himself. We just seemed to talk about things and not very interesting things at that. Who was he really? What was his reason for coming to Amsterdam? At one point, he had mentioned he'd been here many times before.

As I was trying to imagine what a jailbreak meant, my mind spun even faster and more wildly. Nothing seemed easy, and each time I tried to devise some plan that might be possible, I would get out of my body and look back at myself and say, "You stupid ass. Don't you remember what Woody Hayes used to say about passing the football at Ohio State? Don't do it, plain and simple, because there is one good thing that can happen with a completed pass, but the odds are with the two things that can also happen, and they would be very bad—an incomplete pass or an interception. An uncomfortable moment later, my alter ego proceeded to imagine a jailbreak. Yes, maybe in some far-out way escaping was possible, but also just like when passes are thrown, the fates get involved. We could be caught, and then we might go to a worse jail, a prison or we might be shot at, shot at! I couldn't believe my alter ego would actually say something like that as a possibility. Could that happen?

Every bit of clothing I was wearing started to feel like someone else's clothes. Everything was getting out of control.

Just then another one of our group got up to leave and walked by me. He stopped for a second to tuck his shirt in his pants and then winked at me.

No, no way. I can't believe that they have been talking about breaking out of here.

Again, I looked over to the remaining members of the group, and again they were deep in conversation. What were they saying? While staring at the group, I noticed movement in another part of the jail cell. That guy from before was making his way over to me again. He approached, smiling a big smile. I really didn't want to be his friend. Gerrard followed him and reached me first, grabbed my arm, and urged me to come with him.

We walked to an isolated corner and he said, "Paul, ihr müsst uns helfen, sorry. . . say in English, have plans to out from here." I looked at him like he had two heads. "Because of yous, my freund."

"What!" I looked around to see if anyone was watching and started to say something, when he stopped me and said, "Listen this plan." He proceeded to say in his broken English—or at least this is what I gathered—the biggest problem we had was lack of money. Too many of the group had only a couple of dollars each. The police would be concerned we'd resort to stealing or hurting someone to get money to live. They didn't care about our drugs. They didn't care we had broken into a house. Everyone in the the group was saying we just had to get out of the rain until we could find a legal place to stay. As I listened to him, he kept on going back to each one's bankroll or lack of one.

Then, this is where it got interesting. He needed a great idea to get us out of this, and after some time he said that he had gotten the idea. I couldn't wait to hear this. He grabbed my arm again and said I think it's all up to you because you must persuade the police that we have elected you banker and we've given you all our money because you're "die intelligentesten." I assumed he meant that I was the smartest one among all of them.

I was frozen. Did I really hear him just say this was their best idea? This best idea seemed really half-baked to me. No one would believe that story, let alone a detective on the Amsterdam police force. Matter of fact, I think if I told that story, they would say, "That is the dumbest-assed story we've ever heard. For that, we're going to put you in jail and throw away the keys."

Gerrard and I turned to see another of the gang being called out for questioning. And of course, like all the others, this one walked by me and winked also.

Then it hit me. This plan, which I had never okayed, was already in the works. Half of us had already gone and told that half-assed story to the police interrogators. My head was dizzy trying to imagine what the police thought. More importantly, I didn't know what I was going to say. I would be the last batter up in the bottom of the ninth. If I didn't get a hit, well, who knows? Nothing like feeling the pressure. It would be up to me whether seven of us would get out of jail or make this place our home, possibly for a long while.

At about that point, I started pacing back and forth in a corner of the cell. What was I going to say? Whatever I said, what was the chance they'd believe me? Yes, I knew I had a lot of money compared to the rest of my gang, but really, they voted me their banker. What could these guys have been saying?

As I watched Gerrard walk by and out of the jail cell, I knew the guard would come for me soon. I had no idea what I would say. I couldn't concentrate. I moved to one of the benches and sat down, hoping for a moment or two of clear thought. But just as I sat down, that guy who had been watching me nudged another guy, and they both got up, looking at me and coming in my direction. Perfect. Those two would probably try to get something, anything out of me, especially now that my gang had gone and I had no protection—as if any one of them would lift a finger for me anyway.

As they were about to sit on either side of me, the guard came in and pointed to me. I was relieved, and then I wasn't. I wasn't sure who was the more dangerous.

Out in the hallway, we walked until we reached the stairs, then went up a flight and down the hall until we reached a door that led to a small room. The room was pitch black except for a few standing lights angled toward a chair in the center of the room. The guard lead me to the chair and forced me to sit facing the lights. I didn't resist, but I was confused. Not because I'd never seen a police drama—I just never imagined I'd be *in* one. It only took a couple of seconds of that light before I couldn't see anything. The guard moved across the room and out the door and closed it behind him.

This I didn't expect. I knew the whole thing was not good, but, really, I'm not Machine Gun Kelly. Bright lights in my face as they interrogate me? Come on.

"State your name, age, and country of origin for us, please," came a voice from behind the lights.

"Paul Casper, 21, USA," I responded.

"Your passport says somewhere called Mount Prospect, Illinois. Is that a part of Chicago, which means you could be a..." but he either was interrupted or decided not to follow through with that thought and stopped talking in midsentence. Incredible, I thought, he was probably actually going to say that I could be a Chicago gangster! I wished I were from LA at that moment so maybe I would be accused of being a movie star instead.

There was some mumbling between two or three people behind the lights and then came, "I wonder, in America do they understand the difference between right and wrong?" Before I could answer, he added, "Well, in Amsterdam we just don't think anyone can open any door in any house at any time of day or night and just walk right in and make it your home. Is that the way they do things in Chicago?"

"No, sir," I answered quickly. "We were in trouble, some of my friends were sick, and it just never stops raining. We saw an open door, looked inside and thought since it was empty, no one would mind. We were only going to stay until it stopped raining, then find a hotel room or two."

One of the Dutch officers asked, "We found a lot of drugs on most everyone, everyone except you. That is somewhat strange. Why no drugs in your pockets?"

I hesitated for a second or two. I wondered if the question were a trap. Then I said, "I don't like drugs. I don't do drugs."

As I waited for the next question, I could feel my eyes going blind staring into those lights. I don't know if that was their plan, to make me feel as uncomfortable as they could and provoke me to say something incriminating. As I sat there, I felt more and more uncomfortable. It seemed it was almost five minutes of silence since their last question.

Finally, someone said from behind the lights, "Why are you in Amsterdam?"

"I have been traveling throughout Europe as you can see from my passport. Part of my wish list was to see the beautiful city of Amsterdam."

"How did you get mixed up with that group of people and when?"

"Let me see, yesterday or the day before. I've lost track of time. I've lost track of days also. I met Gerrard on the road traveling. I said I wanted to see Amsterdam, and he said come with me, I know some people with a house, and you won't have to pay."

He followed up, "Okay, I see that, but do you know what each of these people refers to you as?"

"Well, do you mean—maybe—" I hesitated, "—that I'm the group's banker?"

I thought I heard some snickering behind the lights as I said that, then again what seemed like a couple of minutes or more with no questions. I was fidgeting uncontrollably.

"And tell me, how did you get to be picked as the banker and what exactly does that mean?"

This was it. Our only chance to get out of this mess was at hand, but actually, I had no real plan of what to say. This was not my idea; I never thought they'd believe any of us, or they would never believe anything with a story like that. And then there was the unknown. I didn't know what any of them said, and what were the chances of any of them going off script?

"Did you hear me? We are waiting," came a little impatiently from behind the lights.

"Yes, yes, I heard you. Here's what I can tell you. When Gerrard and I reached Amsterdam, we met the rest of his friends at the restaurant. Of course, as you know, it seems like it's been raining for days and days without stopping. Everyone was very demoralized. As we tried to wait out the rain, we got to know each other. They were equally surprised and impressed that I had a college education and a four-year degree. They were also curious about how I'd traveled so much and spent so little money. They started asking me all kinds of questions about money and how to do it. After a while, one of them said, 'Can I give you my money and you advise me?' Then another one said that, and before long they all wanted to give me their money. And so, they gave me all their money, and they picked Gerrard and me to go out and find a place for all of us to stay. We left and started walking and tried a couple of places, but always the prices were too high. Just as we were about to give up hope and go back, saying we had failed, we saw an open bottom of the door in what look like an abandoned empty building. We thought we could stay one night out of the rain and then find a good place the next day. And so, as we were continuing to make plans to get out of there the next day, you discovered us. So, in a way, I guess I'm their—our banker, but really it's only because I said I went to college."

As soon as I paused to reassess my wild line to see if I could add anything, another question was thrown at me. "So, you are holding everyone's money. Can you tell me roughly how much money each person has and traveled into Amsterdam with?"

I didn't expect that. I was scrambling in my mind trying to outthink them and come up with some figures. "I'm not sure exactly. It's written down somewhere what each one gave me, but I'd say about $50 US apiece." I couldn't say too much more than that or else it would make me look like the worst one, the worst deadbeat of all, so far from home and not enough for a plane ticket back to the States myself. Because obviously what I did was divided the money I had by how many people were in the game.

"Do you realize that these offenses and laws you've broken are very serious? Maybe you do, maybe you don't. But you should realize that you, personally, have broken the biggest law of all; you are fraudulently acting as a financial executive with no experience. That is punishable with a long prison term. It is our job to protect the Dutch people. Matter of fact, just last week, this police office next to me put a fraudulent financial person away for ten years.

And I want to tell you, our prisons are nowhere as pleasant as our jails."

"What!" I couldn't believe it. Prison! I could feel sweat breaking out all over my body. And of course, I was the only one who had said that I was the banker. Prison! What a great day this was! Arrested, put in jail—actually, two jails, and now my future was in some prison. Then a thought popped up in my mind. All I could think was that my bad luck probably wasn't over. I imagined the guys stalking me earlier in our jail cell also getting a prison term. With my luck, they'd become my roommates in prison. I was dead, really dead.

Just then I heard laughing and one of the people knocking something off a desk behind the lights. And as that happened, there was more laughing. Then a comment from one of them in Dutch to another and a second or so later, the lights in the room came on, and the intense interrogation lights were turned off.

It took a minute or so for my eyes to adjust. I could see three men, two sitting behind a long table and another standing, all laughing and shaking their heads. I had no idea what was going on.

I could see that one of them was the detective who orchestrated our capture and the kick to my back in the first place. He stopped laughing, got up, and walked around the table, and sat down on the edge about three or four feet from me. He just looked at me for a second, then reached into his sport coat's upper inside pocket to pull out a pack of Dutch cigarettes.

"Have you tried any of these yet while you've been here?" he asked as he flicked one up and pointed the pack in front of me. I grabbed one and almost ate it. I needed a smoke very badly at that point. He took one and pulled a cigarette lighter out of his pocket and lit mine as we both took long drags. He started to chuckle a little bit, as did the other two guys in the room.

"Relax," he said. "You are not going to prison. Just relax, we were just joking with you."

I was still too nervous to really have an idea of what he just said. My heart was still pumping rapidly, but little by little, I could see this was a set-up. The entire interrogation had been for their amusement.

"Don't worry, no prison and no more jail. We are going to let all of you go. But there is a stipulation. And that is, you have to leave the country tomorrow and never come back or you will be arrested and put in jail for quite a while."

Finally, I could feel my body start to relax a little. One of the other guys asked me to explain why I was over in Europe in the first place. We talked for about a half hour and actually laughed with each other over some of my stories. They said a couple of times, you should write a book. And the detective said if you do, make sure you spell my name correctly as he proceeded to say it and spelled it out loud as the other two laughed.

He then stood up and said, "We will take you to one of either two places to stay the night. One of them is called Fantasio, and the other is called Paradiso. They are both state-sponsored youth centers. We'll call over there first to see which one has more room and opportunity for the lot of you. Also, we are going to have each of you sign your pledge to leave Holland tomorrow."

As we were walking out the door to the hallway to go down the stairs, he laughed a little and said that that story I told was one of the wildest they'd ever heard. "Just by that story alone, we'd almost have to let you guys go. I can't wait to tell my partner tomorrow he missed great fun on his day off."

But he also said, "Now, if you ever must tell that story again, just be careful to think it out thoroughly. You said they all gave you about $50 each, well I'm sure that was in Dutch guilders or German marks. You had nowhere near that in money as most of your money was in American Express Travelers Cheques with your name on them, originating in America." He was right that it was an obvious lie, but I—we were getting out.

As I was taken to an office to sign some papers and have my picture taken for my record, I wondered where all the others were. Had they already left and just gone their separate ways? But then one of the policemen took me down to the street level, and there everyone still was. They all crowded around me and were clapping and cheering. Gerrard put his arm around my shoulders and said, "Gut gemacht—how you say? Good, good work." A couple of guys raised me up on their shoulders as we walked down the street with the others still clapping.

The police walked us to the Paradiso Club, which of course wasn't ready to take people for anything, even a space on the floor to sleep. We had to wait. The police made us promise to stay here now and through the night. Of course, we said yes, but as soon as they left, so did we.

Gerrard wanted me to come with him to help him with some English translation he needed for a guy he was going to meet. Two more from the group came with us also, which didn't make sense; they knew very little English, if any.

We walked to the Dam Square, a sort of hippie traveler signpost and gathering spot. As soon as we turned one corner and had the square in full view, it presented hundreds of travelers from everywhere in the world. People were sitting on all sides of this national monument, a remembrance of the dead from World War II. The concrete pillar shot upward about 72 feet to the sky.

The monument was placed on a series of concentric cement rings forming steps around it. We walked through the crowds looking for the guy Gerrard was to meet. Some people were sleeping; some were talking and sharing information with others; some were like zombies just staring into their own minds, obviously on some drug or another. As we walked up and down the steps and around the monument, you could hear all the languages of the world.

I was just following Gerrard because I didn't know who he was looking for. After some searching, he said, "Let's try the Vondelpark." Whatever that was. We walked for a while and came to some water, a pond or lake; it was hard to tell in the dark. But what I saw was fields of tents and people. This was Vondelpark, another area where hippies congregated. But almost immediately Gerrard talked to someone, and we were headed back to The Dam.

After some time waiting, nothing was happening. One guy in our group met an American and brought him over to me. His name was Hugh, and not long ago he had gotten out of the Army and was traveling. He even had transportation. It looked like a bastardized car-truck combo with the top over the truck part. Again, Gerrard said, let's go back to Fantasio, and we got a ride from Hugh.

It felt like Hugh had come to me from heaven; he seemed to have appeared out of nowhere at just the right time. It was comforting to have another American in our rag-tag group, good to hear a familiar voice. As he drove us back to Fantasio he talked about some of the travelling he had done recently. He was originally from the west coast, he said, from northern California, just outside San Francisco. After knocking around for several years doing a variety of odd jobs he decided to shake it up and

The Road Knight

Rising with the morning's first light,
After another cold and wet sleepless night,

I make my way down this winding highway,
My thumb goes out and I wonder about today.

The road stretches out for miles and miles before me,
I feel I need to turn south to the Mediterranean Sea.

Many ask me why do I wander, why do I roam?
No kings or queens does this traveler find far from home.

This Knight is always listening to the call of the wild,
Most will never know for most are too scared and too mild.

Only on the road does freedom mean that you are really free,
To swim across rivers and climb where you want to be.

I've come from a foreign land and travel to other foreign lands,
There's a spiritual entity in me that this search commands.

It calls, "Come, come find your distant shore,"
I wonder how many more years will I be able to explore.

So many winding roads and unsaved streets,
Will my fates eventually carry me to my life's complete?

For whether I like it or not, it is my birthright,
For I am one they call The Road Knight.

Written May 25, watching the morning tides on the beach while on Formentera see the world; he bought a plane ticket to London. Immediately on landing, however, he saw that London was too much like the United States: everyone spoke English, just like home! He wanted to experience something completely different, a foreign country where the language, the customs, the history was all new. I found myself thinking, *if I wasn't running out of money and so tired of travelling, he could have been a great traveling companion. Oh well.*

As we drove through the dark streets of Amsterdam, I had so many mixed emotions. Each day forward was one day closer to my trip, my adventure, coming to an end one way or another. It would either end with a fantastic rabbit-pull out of a hat in London—or a tragically embarrassing failure, me the magician left on the stage with a runaway bunny and an empty hat facing a booing audience.

When we reached Fantasio, one of the guys went in with Hugh to see if there was any chance to get a bed in there. Gerrard, his friend Derek and I decided to walk around the building, still in hopes of Gerrard finding this guy. A couple of times I asked him the reason for the meeting, but he didn't answer or changed the subject. I decided it had to do with some free place to stay, a house or something, something that had to be legal after what we'd just been through.

Then, walking in an especially dark and smelly alley, Gerrard stopped and said, "Da ist er."

I didn't know what he said, but as he froze, I followed his eyes to two guys leaning up against the back of Fantasio. Suddenly, I realized Gerrard was not thinking about a place to stay; this was something sinister. The vibe completely changed.

We walked behind him until we reached the two guys. Gerrard positioned me next to him as he stood leaning against the wall next to the guy. Gerrard said out loud, "Das ist Paul" as he pointed to me and added, "Good English, you talk."

"My name is Rendor. Why are you here? Why is he here? Our business is fini…done." I couldn't tell what nationality he was, but he spoke English as well as I did. And he was big.

I immediately looked at Gerrard, wondering what business. Not the place to say that, that was for sure. Gerrard was giving the guy a death stare. I grabbed Gerrard's arm and said softly, "Gerrard, what business? I don't understand." He looked at me, but I didn't know if he understood. Still looking at me, he pulled a couple of small plastic baggies out of his pocket and then turned to the other guy saying aggressively, "Fick dich. . . Gib mir mein geld zurück; diese drogen sind scheiße."

I froze. I was right in the middle of a drug deal—no, not a drug deal, a drug deal gone bad. I got the fuck part and the money part and whatever the rest was, it wasn't, "How ya doing, pal?"

I looked around—for what I wasn't quite sure, because the tension here was about to explode. My mind was reeling.

"Tell that asshole everything I sold him is good. Tell him he's too stupid to know good or bad drugs."

Gerrard, without understanding all of that, exploded and yelled back at him, "Du scheißt Drogendealer, gib mir mein Geld zurück oder ich erzähle es allen."

Rendor fired back, "If you tell anyone anything, you'll be sorry."

It looked like Gerrard threatened to tell the guy's customers he sells shit drugs.

Just then there was noise coming around the corner and into the alley. A group of both male and female longhairs, laughing and talking, were approaching, and they were all high on something. It sounded like they were speaking French. We looked in their direction and hoped they wouldn't come anywhere near us, but they did. They walked right by us, singing and talking, oblivious to us. We were all quiet, letting them pass.

As they turned the corner, Rendor stepped out from the wall and said aggressively, "Don't even think about telling anyone about my business. What just happened is a warning to all three of you. I know your faces. Fuck off."

He and his companion walked away and turned the corner, headed away from Fantasio. Still watching him, I said to Gerrard, "What warning, I didn't—" But before I could finish my thought, I saw Gerrard was leaning forward in an unusual way. I touched his arm and said, "Are you all right? Are you sick?"

He straightened up a little, and then Derek and I saw him take his hand away from his side, and we saw the blood on it. A smallish knife stuck out in the middle of the blood. I couldn't stop staring. I was frozen, feeling like this was an out-of-body experience, but it wasn't. This was real. Derek said, "Was ist passiert? Hat er dich erstechen?"

I had no idea what he said. I couldn't take my eyes off Gerrard's side. His jacket was showing a growing red stain. As Derek put his arm around Gerrard to prop him up and get him ready to move, the knife grazed the wall and fell to the ground. He said to Gerrard, "Brauchen wir Sie zu einem Arzt zu bekommen."

I was dumbfounded. I didn't know what to do. Blood was leaking through his clothes; he had to be hurt pretty badly.

Gerrard turned to me and said, "Paul, bad thing. We go. How you say. . . du versteckst dich. . . ah. . . you hide. . . er weiß, dass Sie."

With that, Derek held onto him and walked out of the alley. I was left there alone, trying to understand what had just happened.

I tried to remember everything. What did that asshole say at the end? Something like, "Don't tell anyone. I know your faces. You will be sorry."

As I tried to relive everything, it hit me that I was in this alley alone. Alone! I started to walk away from Fantasio and realized I might be walking into something bad. I had no idea how long I had been walking. I had no idea of which way to go. I thought *The hell with this* and immediately started walking back to the entrance of Fantasio. As I entered, I saw three others who had been part of the group previously arrested. They saw me and came up to me along with another guy I hadn't seen before. I could tell by the look on their faces they knew what had just happened. They said something to the new guy, and he spoke to me in English. "They say this is all a bad scene. They want to leave Amsterdam as soon as they can. One of them knows a girl, and if they can find her, she owes them money."

Just about then Hugh came in, and we all searched for the girl who owed these guys money. We found her at some place called Espresso, which looked more like a legal drug outlet than anything else. Well, this was Amsterdam after all. But she had her own problems, having just broken up with her boyfriend. She couldn't help or was not willing to. It was a dead end.

We went back to Fantasio, and the guys from our group said they were leaving even if they didn't have any money. I felt they had to have something, so I gave them the Dutch guilders I had, and they were off. As I watched them disappear down the street, I thought about how I'd come to Amsterdam with such high hopes, especially for a free roof over my head. I didn't get the free apartment or house, but I did get a free jail cell. Everyone I met on my first day here was gone. I didn't know if I'd ever see

Gerrard again; I guess I had mixed feelings about that. He was a part of what would certainly make a great story, but I really didn't want to be involved, even as an interpreter, on any drug deals, especially ones that went south.

It started to drizzle, and I walked back into Fantasio and was immediately caught up in a crowd that was migrating to the music hall to watch a French rock group. The music was so loud that it was almost unbearable, and the psychedelic light show was almost blinding. Although I had no drugs at all in my body at the time, I was almost feeling high just by being there. It was wall-to-wall people, some just standing as if they were in a trance, others dancing and moving spasmodically, obviously not on one drug only but on many. I just stood there, totally lost, not knowing what to do next. I was in the middle of the huge room and fenced off from any way out by longhairs from what seemed almost every country on earth. This was Fantasio. This was what all these people wanted. They wanted that tribal beat and to be engulfed in clouds of hashish, marijuana, and who knows what else, able at those moments to do anything they wanted.

Somehow Hugh located me in the middle of all that action. He said I could sleep with him in his truck car tonight. He understood I wasn't looking forward to having to keep my eyes open all night to watch out for Rendor. There was no way I was going to be able to sleep in a locked hotel room. I probably couldn't afford it anyway. I would be vulnerable here at Fantasio or wherever I could lie down outside tonight. In his locked car, I'd be safe; it was a gift. I took his keys as he said he was going to meet an old friend and would see me later. Before he left, he walked me to where he had parked his car. It was actually very close to Fantasio, just an alley over behind another building. It was close, but it looked like a battlefield. There were bodies everywhere, some passed out, some propped up against the wall too stoned to even get up. There was refuse of all kinds everywhere. The smell was quite frankly the smell of death. Even clouds of hashish smoke floating through the alley from time to time could not dissipate that odor.

Hugh left, and I went back to Fantasio. I wanted to be with people even though I didn't know any of them. I checked in the small anteroom to make sure my sleeping bag was still hidden away there, and it was. I was exhausted and found an isolated spot in the back of the room to crash.

As I sat there listening to the band that was currently onstage at the far end of the room, I felt my body almost relaxing, maybe for the first time in the three or four days since I'd arrived in Amsterdam. Though my body was relaxing, my mind was reeling. In the last days, I'd had only one meal a day. I'd put a handful of different drugs into my body, most by just inhaling smoke. I didn't know how much sleep I'd had, and right now I was trying to stay out of sight because someone who knew my face had threatened me. I pulled out a cigarette, which I didn't really want, but I was nervous and needed to do something with my hands.

As this group played, I started to feel even more relaxed. It was loud here, and the light system was almost hypnotic. Even though I was somewhat hidden by a dividing wall, I was still looking left and right constantly to make sure Rendor wouldn't spot me—if, in fact, he was still looking for any of us. Though I didn't want to ever see him again, I did wonder how Gerrard was. I had no idea how bad the wound was. None of us saw how it happened, and there was a fair amount of blood on his hand as he tried to stop the bleeding. I wondered where he'd go to get help. Hopefully his explanation to the doctor wouldn't be, "I was in a drug deal that was going bad. The guy who sold me watered-down drugs stabbed me." The truth probably would get the police involved, and that was the last thing any of us needed as we had all promised to be good and leave the country tomorrow. In any case, I hoped Gerrard was okay. I'm sure my visit to Amsterdam would have been quite different if I hadn't met him—a much quieter visit for sure.

Just as I realized I was really starving, Hugh walked in with a girl he knew, and they brought sandwiches. I could've kissed him. His friend was Alison from San Francisco, on a semester abroad from college. We ate and talked for a while until Hugh said he wanted to find another friend who was supposed to meet him on Fantasio's front steps. Alison and I talked about where each of us had traveled so far.

After about an hour of talking, she started to get a little concerned Hugh wasn't back yet, so she went to look for him. It had to be three or four in the morning. I was totally beat. If I was leaving Amsterdam in the morning, I figured I had to get some semblance of sleep.

I made my way to Hugh's truck car, unlocked the doors, and totally crashed.

Lisle

He was quiet for a while as I was almost dozing off

It was about midnight and the train station was dead silent. But then he jumped up from next to me on the bench, yelling,

"Okay, okay. We won't go west to adventure, but how about coming home with me to Northern England and staying with my family for a while?

I bet you haven't done anything like that, have you?"

16.

Birdland

Tuesday, 6:00 AM, July 21, 1970

Moans and groans outside our vehicle accompanied by a soft morning sun peeking in the car/truck's windows got me moving quickly as I hoped to get a good early ride away from Amsterdam before the city got too congested. As I got dressed and got my stuff together, I continued to be serenaded by moans and odd noises orchestrated in all the world's languages. Looking out the window, I counted five to seven bodies just lying in the alley where they fell, probably after too many drugs, who knows what kind, the night before.

Although I was being respectful and quiet, Hugh woke up anyway. Neither of us knew what time it was, but the sun was now

345

just breaking the horizon. We had both heard the night before that the prospects for hitchhiking out of Amsterdam looked dismal. It would have taken me hours to walk to a spot that I'd heard about. Hugh decided to drive me to a better place. There were no rides to be had around here, so Hugh was a lifesaver.

As he left me off, he said all I needed to do is walk to the top of the ramp. The highway led south to Brussels. We exchanged addresses and a promise to stay in contact. He didn't know when he'd be back in the States. He said he'd like to visit Norway and Sweden next. We shook hands, and I watched him drive away. Knowing him in Amsterdam was a lifesaver. I wished him well.

I started to get a very bad feeling as I made my way up the ramp. Even before I got to the top and closer to the actual highway, I started to encounter hitchhikers waiting, and as I moved around what turned out to be the end of a long line of travelers, it was starting to look like gloom and doom. There were fifty to sixty people in line, and just as in other busy hitching places, you wait your turn.

I walked back to the end of the line. I didn't know how many singles or twosomes or threesomes were up ahead. But if they were all singles, it might take me ten to twelve hours to get a ride. I sat down, took out my sketchbook, and wrote the word "Brussels" on it for when I would get to the head of the line and start to hitch.

After two hours of waiting in the cold and rain, my position had only moved a little. I'm sure the dirty, rain-soaked hitchhikers wanting a ride did not interest most drivers.

I got off the highway ramp and started walking—to where I wasn't quite sure.

After walking a ways with no real game plan, the sky became

even darker and more threatening. It wasn't enough that it had been raining all morning; now we were going to add thunder and lightning to the party. I eventually walked by a tram station and saw some ads on the walls about taking the tram to the railroad station and a train over the English Channel to London for what I thought was a great price. I hopped on a tram and arrived at the rail station.

I made it to the right train just before it was to leave. I found a quiet compartment with an older Dutch couple. They were nice and bought me some coffee as the drink cart came around. They also gave me one of the sandwiches that they had made at home before starting their trip.

There was no doubt I could fill a book with my hitchhiking experiences and adventures, but relaxing on this train watching the countryside fly by was also a wonderful way to travel. It's not that I never would again stand by the side of the road and hold my hand out with my thumb position skyward, but there was no denying it: I was tired, very tired of hitching. Riding trains is a completely different world.

We talked about traveling, and they were very surprised that I had been able to travel so far all over Europe by using my thumb. They both were history enthusiasts and wanted to hear about my Athens exploration. They seem to hang on every word about the Acropolis; it was definitely on their bucket list.

Of course, I enjoyed sharing some of my experiences with them, but thinking about my journey through Greece made me realize that it seemed like all of that was a completely different trip than the one I was on now. So much had happened since then. So many countries. So many people met and talked with. The more we talked, the more I realized this trip was a very personal odyssey that I could have never imagined months ago as I flew over to Paris. One definition of "odyssey" reads: "a long series of wanderings or adventures, especially when filled with notable experiences, hardships, etc." As I watched the Dutch countryside go by, I had to smile to myself as I remembered some of those experiences. I had been incredibly lucky. As my mind recalibrated itself from that of an aggressive and determined traveler to a person floating back towards earth, I felt I would keep what I had learned as a lone hitchhiker as I continued on the road of life. The thoughts that I was now having were new. While traveling, I never had the time or the opportunity to think about anything other than where I would sleep, where I would go next, how I would get there, and if I could afford it. Life was starting to be different for me. I felt different. I felt it more each day in my body, mind, and soul.

We changed trains in Antwerp and then again in Brussels and finally arrived in Lisle, France, after seven hours of train rides. As I walked around the almost empty train station, I was told that they would kick everyone out at 2:00 a.m. My train to Calais wouldn't leave until the next morning. I had no idea what I would do in between. My finances did not allow me to spend any money on a hotel room, and of course, it was raining outside.

As I waited around to be kicked out, I double checked to make sure I had the two addresses I'd gotten in New York of girls who lived in London. I did have them, and that was my ace in the hole—to hopefully stay with them for free—because I would be in big trouble if I had to pay for a roof over my head in London.

I could hear what appeared to be distant thunder outside. No one was around, so I left my sleeping bag and walked to one of the doorways to the outside world. The wind was blowing harder than when I first arrived; it felt like rain was in the air. Just then a truck pulled up and out from the back was thrown a bundle of tomorrow's local newspapers. Two seconds later the truck was hurrying down the street and turning at the first corner. As I stared at that bundle, a little smile came over my face. Years ago, another bundle of afternoon newspapers had also been thrown at my feet.

It was the summer of 1960 in Cincinnati. That summer was the hottest summer in years in the Queen City. Everyone was complaining. Young and old both wondered if it would ever cool off again. I was twelve. I had a job delivering newspapers for the summer and was already perspiring heavily just riding my bike to my daily spot, which was only about a mile from my house. I was on my way to pick up my first of two bundles of the evening run of the *Cincinnati Post*, the city's late afternoon paper. I usually arrived just as the van was pulling up to throw me my bundles.

This Price Hill neighborhood was my route every weekday afternoon. For the most part, it was uninteresting except that it started off at the bottom of a street that continued to climb higher and higher. Unfortunately, by the time I crossed over to the other side and started to go downhill, I had already delivered most of my papers. Consequently, I carried the heaviest load walking uphill. Ted Sims, a guy who lived up the street from me, got me the job. I needed the money but was unsure if he was trying to help me or just wanted to watch me suffer each day on my route. Ted was both friend and foe. We grew up together on Seibel Lane. The street had a bunch of kids, and we competed daily in anything and everything you could think of. It was usually Ted as captain of one team and me the other. He tried harder than most to beat me, whether it was a board game, a card game, or any sporting contest, and on the unusual occasion when he didn't win, he tried to beat me up.

Anyway, back to delivering papers. I would hide my bike in the usual spot and then proceed to open two old, gray, smelly canvas bags to arrange my papers in. One side held the crisp new papers, and the other draped crisscrossed over the other shoulder to put my folded papers in. There was a complicated way to fold and tuck to make each a complete package approximately six inches by six inches, as thin as you could get it. You needed them to be that way because it was up to you to throw them as close to, ideally on, each subscriber's front porch.

As the summer progressed, I got very good at folding the papers quickly. I had started the job a pretty good thrower. In my first couple of days on the job, whenever I was a little off in my throw, I'd walk over to the house, pull out the paper from the evergreens, and toss it on the porch. As I became more proficient and hardened, I rarely attempted any reconciliation on an off throw; it didn't happen so much, and I realized they'd probably find the paper eventually, wherever it landed.

That changed one day in July. It had been a very good day: I was moving quickly, and the flow of folding and throwing was making me feel I was at the top of my game. I hoped I would finally finish on time and get to be picked up by the van with some of the other paperboys and driven to a Tastee Freeze to get a free ice cream soda. It happened a couple of days per week, but so far, I had never finished in time to be picked up when the van came by. I had been kidded about that mercilessly by some of the guys and especially by Ted, although recently even he had been trying to give me more tips on how to cut corners and get done quicker. He also acknowledged my hill was a challenge no other paperboy had. So, with all that, I was hoping that I could at least once this summer finish on time and get picked up for free stuff.

I was about halfway through my route when I accidentally tossed a newspaper on the roof of a house, attempting to finish quicker. I couldn't believe it; they'd never find that one, and I didn't want anyone calling to complain. On the other hand, even if I did finish on time, I'd also better have the right count of papers. We were given three extra every day, and we had better have at least one or two of them left and no complaint calls of any kind or no ride to ice cream even if I were there to be picked up.

That day I knew already I'd probably need an extra one as I often did during the summer when I approached Birdland. Birdland was an unusual house way back off the street surrounded by many big trees with all types of birdhouses and feeders and what seemed like thousands of birds flying everywhere. The birds weren't the problem; the problem was a big, vicious black dog that seemed to be always around, wanting to grab some part of me to rip off and take back to its den so it could gnaw on it all night. I had never done anything to that half-dog, half-monster, but our relationship was very consistent with the eternal, archetypal struggle of dog vs. paperboy. Before I was a paperboy, I used to see some cartoons on TV with dogs having happy dreams of chasing paperboys. I soon realized sometimes cartoons tell the truth. Eventually, through adversity, I had discovered that taking one of my folded papers and throwing it over part of the fence around the house drove the dog crazy. That forced him to go find it, and then I had my escape route.

Recently I had had an unexpected bad experience, although it wasn't due to anything I'd done. After I'd delivered a paper, one of the homeowners called after me, yelling that his paper was all smudged with bad printing. He needed another; he'd throw the first one away. I made sure the next folded paper was aerodynamically perfect to throw, threw it, and watched its path as I continued to walk up the hill towards Birdland. It looked good leaving my hand, but from nowhere a big wind came up as it approached the house and it glided onto the roof. I yelled, "Shit! Shit!" Now I had two problem papers and still the devil dog to deal with. Any other problem and even if I did make the van, I'd be yelled at and left sitting on the curb.

This was a new experience. What should I do? Then I saw that there was a tree close to the house. Could I climb up and get the papers? I wondered. After taking off my paper satchels, I looked around to see if anyone was watching me and then started to climb the tree. No branch went directly over the house, so I'd have to try and swing on one to get up on the roof. As I was about to do that with the folded newspaper in plain sight, a thought crossed my mind. It looked scary enough to swing on the branch I could reach and time my jump just right for the four-and-a-half feet to the roof. At that point, by the flat part of the roof, it was twenty to thirty feet to the ground. But suddenly, I had more concern about how I'd get back down. From the roof, there were no branches within reach. I'd have to run and jump and hope that I'd be able to grab the branch and hold on coming back. As I was hanging on the branch trying to decide what to do, I kept visualizing my lifeless body on the ground, clutching one or two *Cincinnati Posts* in my hand. I pictured the comments from the police, residents, and other paperboys: *At least he held on to his papers and didn't let them fly away even when he landed headfirst on the ground.* That made me re-think the idea. What if, once on the roof, I discovered it was impossible to get off? Well, it was one thing for a paperboy to goof up and not deliver every paper, but it was altogether something else for a paperboy to jump on top of a house to retrieve an errant paper and get stuck. I'd be up there probably for hours and not only miss my van ride for ice cream, I would have the ongoing reputation as the only paperboy who not only missed a paper or two on his route but didn't deliver half of his papers one day. That day would probably go down in infamy as the worst day in the gloried annals of paperboy deliveries; I'd probably be tabbed as the worst paperboy in all of history—that is, after the fire department came with a ladder to get me down.

So, with those thoughts, I decided, *Fuck it.* I'd have to hope the homeowners would forget to even look for their evening paper tonight. And in addition, all I could do was hope that the devil dog of Birdland was sleeping or had been taken to the vet for some reason. Not that I wished that dog and the inevitable horrific experience on any vet. I needed that paper desperately today, although I often used it as a last resort decoy.

I had lost some time climbing that tree, so I needed to pick up the pace. As I got to the top of the long hill, I started to hear the birds before I could even see the driveway entrance to Birdland. I don't know how all the homes around Birdland put up with the noise; it gave me the willies every time I approached. I walked slowly, turning my head left then right in hopes that the devil dog was not around. The coast looked clear. My heart was pounding more than usual, but I was sensing I might be okay; I wouldn't have to use the decoy paper. Although I would be short some papers in the end, I thought I could talk my way into hopping on the van that would take us to get sweets. I made my way down the long driveway, and although farther than usual from the front porch, I aimed and let my paper rip. As I watched it, it seemed to sail better than ever and found the front porch beautifully. I thought no NFL quarterback could have done that any better. This was all good; I'd make the van today. The curse would be broken.

As I turned to make my way out of the driveway, however, my heart froze. Ten feet in front of me was the devil dog, just sitting and looking at me. He seemed to be analyzing different parts of my body, trying to remember all the paperboy bodies he'd bitten and chewed on previously. Was there any part he hadn't tasted yet? I looked around for help, although I knew this was going to be between him and me. No one ever came to Birdland if they didn't absolutely have to.

Unfortunately, I was in new territory with the dog between the sidewalk and me. Usually, if I encountered him, it would be as I was walking in, not out. I would throw my decoy paper over a small fence by a vegetable garden alongside the house. There, the green leafy vegetables and tomatoes and rows of corn would hide the paper at least for a minute or two, giving me time to scoot out and down the street.

Now, I was trapped. The garden was too far, and besides, I was between the dog and the garden. I'm sure the dog would think anyway, *Screw the paper; I've now got the paper, boy.* I felt at one moment that I actually heard two hearts pumping wildly: I knew one was mine, and I realized the other one was the devil dog's. I could imagine he thought this situation just might be the trifecta of all time—his birthday, Christmas, and Easter—as he had me trapped only ten feet away. I was amazed I was still living. I looked around for some miracle. Then the dog wiped his saliva-gushing mouth with his paw. It was obvious; I was at the end of my rope. Instinctively, I reached for a folded paper, keeping my hand quiet inside the paper bag. I saw a small fishpond to the right about thirty or forty feet away. Could I? I wondered. If I could throw it that far and hit the pond, it just might surprise the devil dog enough to have him run in after it. I bent my right elbow in as much of a right angle as I could inside the bag, and then I just let it rip and threw it as hard as I could, yelling at the same time, "Go get it, boy. Get it!" He jumped up and watched it fly and bounded after it. As I was running out of the driveway, I turned and saw the dog jumping in the pond with a big splash and a howl that sounded like he had landed uncomfortably, to say the least.

I survived that day, but of course, my curse was still intact. I made the van even after all that—but not because I was faster than ever before. The van had a mechanical problem and was late coming to my stop. For a second I was all smiles, thinking that I had, unbelievably, made the rendezvous. That is, until the driver stopped and threw out a paper, saying that old man Wilkerson had already called and said he hadn't gotten his paper yet and they better get one out to him ASAP. The driver said we'd be going for ice cream sodas, but first I needed to deliver Mr. Wilkerson's paper in person. As I watched the van turn around and head to town, I thought about calling old man Wilkerson on the phone and telling him he'd already gotten a paper—all he had to do was get a ladder and climb up on his roof to get it. But surely that would identify me as the worst paperboy in history, so I got on my bike and started riding uphill to give him his paper. I toyed with the idea of telling him that this would be his third paper of the day since there were already two on his roof.

My walk down memory lane was interrupted by a clock in the station ringing in the late hour, and it broke the silence in a comforting way. For some reason, I thought of Olivia and started to write about how she was somewhat like flowing music from afar.

There were very few people either traveling or working at this hour in the train station, but I did notice what appeared to be two new bodies walking around with backpacks. I knew they'd spotted me also, but they appeared to be too shy to approach me to share stories about our travels. As they kept walking around me, it looked like they were arguing with each other.

Finally, one of the guys came over to me and said, "Are you traveling east or west? We have just left England a day ago and are undetermined where to go. We're arguing about it right now."

"I'm headed to London. I've been traveling for, let me see, about five months."

"Cool, where have you been?"

"Oh, a lot of places, really too many to talk about now. I'm kinda worried they are going to close this place and I'll be in trouble then," I said. "I'm running out of money, and I can't pay for any hotels or even youth hostels. What about you guys? Do you know if they are going to kick us out of here before morning?"

"No, didn't know that. But we have another big problem. My friend Mathias—even though we've only been traveling for a day and a half—wants to go home. Big brave adventurer he—so I'm stuck. Hey, do you want to come with me? I'll go anywhere, mate."

Just then his friend walked up and said, "Nothing is open. I'm starving." We all introduced ourselves. The guy wanting to travel with me was named Aaron. I guessed these guys were around seventeen or eighteen and as green as they come. They appeared to be much worse off than I was when I started traveling.

Aaron kept on pressing me to agree to travel with him. He even said he'd pay for things until we found a way to get me more money. He said he couldn't face going home so soon to his family or friends since he made such a big deal out of this adventure he

She Was Ancient Music Drifting In

It isn't often,
But when I'm alone,
In a strange place,
Then, sometimes
Only in my mind---
But, still, sometimes,
I can see her.

She was ancient music drifting in,
Long flying hair blown by the wind.
Wind that touched,
Wind that whispered,
Wind that silently spoke her name.
And now my life can never, ever, be the same.

Time stopped when she appeared,
Taking me away from the real,
Teaching me again how to feel.
Like a prism of color,
Wrapped in a spectrum of light.
Words had new meanings,
Words had a foreign rhyme,
Were my senses now real for the first time?

And she was ancient music drifting in,
Long flying hair blown by the wind.
Wind that touched,
Wind that whispered,
Wind that silently spoke her name.
And now my life can never, ever, be the same.

It isn't often,
But when I'm alone,
In a strange place,
Then, sometimes
Only in my mind---
But, still, sometimes,
I can see her.

Written July 21, while sitting alone in a Lisle, France rail station thinking of Olivia was going to have. For some reason, his friend thought traveling would be different, not so hard. Finally, Mathias walked away to see if there was a candy machine or something.

Aaron continued again, "Are you sure? We'd have a great time."

I said, "Traveling can be great; you need a lot of luck out there, though. If you are traveling on a small budget, there are no sure things. Sorry, I've run my race. I can almost see the finish line, and I must stay focused. But you should go. Just be careful out there."

He was quiet for a while as I was almost dozing off. It was about midnight and the train station was dead silent. But then he jumped up from next to me on the bench, yelling, "Okay, okay. We won't go west to adventure, but how about coming home with me to Northern England and staying with my family for a while? I bet you haven't done anything like that, have you?"

Well, that caught me by surprise. Hmm. I'd done a lot of things on this trip, but staying in someone's home in a foreign country did get my attention. Then he said, "You can come home with me, take showers, eat great food, and you can see a different part of England—and all of that for free! You look like you could use the rest, and the beds in my family's house are the softest in all of England. What do you say?"

If I'd thought about the pros and cons more—the cons including having to deal with my continuing anxiety about whether I had enough money to get home—my answer might've been different. But I didn't; I jumped at the chance. "Okay, let's do it," I replied quickly.

He was beaming. I've never seen a guy so happy about such a little thing as bringing a friend home. But as I watched him jump around with excitement, I could also see what some of his motivation could be. Maybe his thinking was, okay, I didn't really go on my big adventure, but I did bag a trophy animal for the wall. I've captured a world-class traveler, and he likes me. Now he's living in my house.

Mathias came scurrying back and said he'd talked to a conductor. There was another train to England, and it was leaving shortly. We needed to run now.

As we were making tracks to the gate, I saw some guards putting chains on the doors to close it up for the night. It was a little after midnight. We would take a short hour-or-two ride to Dunkirk and then change to a ferry. It would take four to five hours to cross the English Channel, then we'd land at Dover on the southeast coast of England.

Huddersfield

That's when one of the young English boys said,

"Hey, wait a minute, you mates are famous, aren't you?"

I was about to say no, not us, when my friend again touched my shoulder indicating don't say anything.

The boys couldn't figure out what was happening.

Then...

17.

Bang a Gong

Wednesday, 6:00 AM, July 22, 1970

All three of us dozed on and off during the voyage from Dunkirk to Dover. The passage was not restful. Without any beds or couches available, we sat up in chairs, and the sea that night was rough. We were being bounced up and down, and so were our stomachs.

I think I had finally turned and tossed enough to put myself in a secure position to fall asleep when there were three to four blasts of the ship's whistle alerting the city of Dover that we were coming in to dock. As I was grumbling to myself about the unnecessary noise, one of the ship stewards raised the blinds in the large room where most of the passengers were seated to display a bright, early-morning sun. Quite a difference from the previous week of almost daily, if not hourly, rain.

The big ship started to turn, and the majestic white cliffs of Dover slowly presented themselves as we passed. I don't know how white they really are, but they do reach like skyscrapers from the sea to the English countryside above. As I made my way out to one of the forward decks and looked up, I could immediately tell we were in a different land. This coolness was all English. I had experienced early-morning coolness in other countries, but this was different. It was both bone-chilling and a breath of fresh air, hopefully presaging new adventures to come.

As we disembarked the ship, Mathias decided he didn't want to hitch and departed to get a train north. Aaron and I grabbed a simple pastry and a cup of tea as we started to hitchhike out of Dover. I was hypnotized by the totally different landscape of beautiful, rolling green hills. Our first ride, unfortunately, took a long time to show up, but finally we were off. It was odd to see him hold out his left arm and thumb to hitch as we now were in the world of drivers driving on the left side of the road.

After a few short rides, we were dropped off in Canterbury. Aaron saw a quiet park with a couple of rolling hills, and not far away was the majestic Canterbury Cathedral. The last ride we got put us both in such uncomfortable positions that we just had to stretch before we got on the road again.

Aaron took out his guitar and started playing around with it as he walked around some trees nearby. Not long after he had disappeared from sight, three young English boys came up to me as I sat on a park bench. They could tell I was traveling and saw the empty guitar case and asked where we'd been. We talked a little bit, and they asked a lot of questions. These guys said they'd never been out of Canterbury, but each said they'd leave when they were old enough. Then one of them asked where I was from and what my name was. I was about to answer when Aaron came out of nowhere and grabbed my shoulder gently. As I looked at him, he shook his head no.

That's when one of the young English boys said, "Oh, I see, you mates are famous, aren't you?" I was about to say no, not us, when Aaron again touched my shoulder, indicating don't say anything. The boys couldn't figure out what was happening. Then Aaron started to play the opening chords of "Bang A Gong" by the English rock group T-Rex.

Immediately one of them yelled, "You're Marc Bolan, and you guys are T-Rex, aren't you? Whatta ya doing here? Are you going to play here?"

I guess if you squinted your eyes, you could almost convince yourself that Aaron did look a little like Marc Bolan with his frizzy hair and colorful shirt. Neither of us said yay or nay. We just let these guys talk themselves into believing that we were T-Rex.

As Aaron continued strumming the beginning of "Bang A Gong" with that rhythmic bass that the song starts with, the boys were dumbstruck. Then Aaron said we got separated from our tour bus. It wouldn't be back here for hours, and we were starving to death. We had left our wallets on the bus.

All that was music to the kids' ears. They offered to go buy us something to eat. Aaron orchestrated all of this quite perfectly. They ran off down the street yelling with glee. They were going to save T-Rex from starving to death. They were going to be heroes.

We laughed, and I had to give Aaron all the credit.

They eventually came back with some sandwiches and cookies and some soft drinks. They sat down with us and asked Aaron all kinds of questions about being a rock star. I knew Aaron was a huge fan of T-Rex, so impersonating them, and especially Marc Bolan, just rolled off his tongue like honey. He was good. Matter of fact, he was great.

About an hour or so passed. One of the boys said he should be getting home. "My mother is going to kill me." The others decided they had also had their fill of Aaron's made-up stories and decided to leave. We told them we knew the tour bus was on its way back and should come any minute. We all shook hands and said goodbye as they ran down the street.

We eventually got up and found a busy road to try and hitch out of Canterbury. First, a middle-aged woman picked us up, and then a young English guy drove us all the way to Trafalgar Square in the middle of London.

One of the reasons I wanted to go to London before heading north to Aaron's home was that I had the addresses for the girls I had met on the Orient Express who had said to look them up if I ever got to England. We tried to find one of them, but it appeared to be hopeless. London was way too big to get around cheaply, and I only had a partial address for both girls. As the day passed quickly, we decided we'd better leave. There was no way to hitch in the middle of a big city, so we took the Tube to the northern outskirts so we could find a ride.

We weren't doing very well. Nobody wanted to stop. It takes a certain type of person to pick up two guys hitching, especially if one of those guys has a large guitar case. So, the waits between rides were much longer than average, and by the time we had traveled to Dorchester, not far from Aaron's home, it was dark, and worse, it was drizzling. We picked a spot to set up Aaron's little pup tent under a sign next to the Blue Star Transport Café, which looked like a major truck stop and crossroads, although here in Britain the trucks were called "lorries."

We were hungry, cold, and wet but at least had some protection from the weather. That is, until about two hours later. The rains became torrential, and evidently we had set up on a slant. The rain eventually had nowhere to go but down, right through our tent. It was no use; we had to get out of there. We made our way to the all-night café and waited out the rain till morning.

In the morning we got a couple of quick rides, but then, unfortunately, a guy who gave us a nice ride remembered as he was making his way through Leeds that he had to stop off at his mother's, so he left us off in the middle of one of England's largest cities. We walked and walked; it rained and rained; we cursed and cursed. For three to four hours, we walked until we tried again to get a ride.

We were both freezing to death. The weather was attacking us minute by minute in different diabolical ways. At one point I thought my breath, which all day you could see when I exhaled, had solidified in midair.

Finally, we got a ride west to Huddersfield and a roof over our heads. Aaron's mother, who was probably in her fifties, always seemed to have an apron on and always had the friendliest and warmest smile you ever saw. She was an angel and sat us right down and made bacon and eggs with tons of toast and jam. I still couldn't get warm, so she told Aaron to go upstairs and run a bath for me.

The bath did the trick; it was heavenly. It'd been a week or two since I'd showered or taken a bath. In case you're worried about my hygiene, in that week or two I had probably been drenched five or six times from head to toe by thunderstorms.

After the bath I slept in a real, honest to goodness—and I still couldn't believe it as I looked at it—bed. It was heaven. I slept more than a couple of hours until Aaron's mom called us for tea in the late afternoon. Aaron's younger sister, Julia, about eight years old, couldn't stop asking me questions about where I'd been and the adventures I'd had. She was darling, and the entire experience was out of a book, quite different than the life I'd been living of late. The way I was embracing the comforts of a roof over my head, home cooking, hot baths, and normal people told me again that I was ready; it was time to end this journey. My body and my mind were one. However, it would end, it would end soon.

Later, Aaron said that we were going to a club in town called Builders. We took the bus and rode for a while because again, like every day, it was raining.

The club was smallish, with a bar and piped-in music. I understood on weekends they had live music. We already had plans to come back the following night. I could tell from the minute we walked in the club that Aaron wanted to treat me as a significant achievement to brag about, for he was the one had who captured me out in the world and brought me home as a trophy. He was beaming as many of his friends came over and asked question after question. Everyone wanted to buy me beers all night. I think I saw Aaron getting lucky with a cute girl, all because he was the guy who caught this wild world traveler and cajoled him into captivity here in Huddersfield.

We left the club about 11:00 and finally got home a little after midnight because we took the wrong bus from the club.

Finally, morning came. I continued into dreamland until Aaron's mother started yelling for us to get our butts downstairs because she had fish and chips waiting for us. Little by little I was feeling human again. It's amazing what sleeping in a nice bed can do for your bones and your mind.

We went over to the house of one of Aaron's friends and hung out for most of the afternoon playing records and horsing around. There were so many English groups I'd never heard of. I guessed most of them would never get bigger than garnering local attention there in England. Aaron and his friend went to pick up something from the pharmacy while I walked back to Aaron's house and watched television with his sister and father.

It looked like Aaron had a commitment to go into work on Saturday morning. His father said he and I would go and bet on the dog races.

That night we again went to The Builders Club, and again I was surrounded by guys and gals who wanted more stories about my travels. I did get some addresses of people to look up in London who might be able to give me a hand or maybe a roof over my head. Other than that, it looked like the evening would end the same way as the night before.

As we woke up Saturday morning, there was a completely different feeling in the house. For one thing, we got up earlier and as always had a great breakfast from Aaron's mom—not that different from an American breakfast, but then again, different. Just a little change or tweak here and there enhanced the feeling that I was eating in a foreign land. Another big change from this morning was Aaron's father, Don. Usually he left early for work, but today was for the dogs and the ponies. He got us to one of his bookies, off-track betting, which opened up an entirely new world for me. Aaron's father was a ton of fun to be with. He knew many of the other people betting, and they all kidded with each other in every way. For example, this one had a dream the night before, and when he woke up, he absolutely had to look for any dog with the name close to the name Red Queen. Another one only used numbers. He'd sit down with pad and paper, and as each race had a number of the day, he would take that and either add it or subtract it from something else happening in his life, like if his wife had a birthday, then he would add the last two digits in the current year divided by how many children he had.

Of all these guys and their foolproof methods to pick a dog, the one that seemed to work best was the guy who owned a bakery. He just closed his eyes and moved his finger up and down until he felt the vibe and then he bet on that dog. Nobody else was winning, but he did one once or twice.

I only bet on one race, and though I had listened to numerous races earlier, I still had no idea if I had won or lost when the race was over. The announcer's voice was very Cockney, and I only picked up a few words here and there. Someone standing with me looked at my ticket, which cost two and two to play, meaning two shillings and two pennies. He said, "Too bad, mate, you lost also." We spent three hours there. Aaron's father won twice but lost ten times that.

After the dog races were over, the horse races started. By that time there was a cloud of cigar and cigarette smoke floating barely above our heads, growing and destined to engulf all. After a couple of horse races, I decided to head back to the house. I ended up watching tennis on the TV with Aaron's sister most of the afternoon.

That night we went to Builders again. The band was different. This was my third visit, and I was feeling very comfortable as we all danced a little. People were still buying me beers because I was the foreigner, which continued to be a novelty.

Track Two

From the loud speaker came...
"For race number twelve ...
*Track One—***Queen of Twilight**
*Track Two—***GiveMeMoreMoney**
*Track Three—***Green Reindeer**
*Track Four—***My Wife Knows Everything**
*Track Five—***Honest Crook**
*Track Six—***Car of Idiots**
Came the field mumbled by the announcer
Then...
Another lost sentence,
"Did you hear that?" I ask.
Someone says, "A change on
Track Two, now running **"My Wife Knows Everything,"**
And
Track Four has **"GiveMeMoreMoney"**
But it doesn't matter,
Because before I can check my stub
the race is over, and the winner was not running on
Track Two.

Even though last night was later than usual, not back until 1:00 or 2:00 a.m., this time there were no bus problems; I got a ride from one of Aaron's friends. Aaron had left the club earlier, but as it was closing, a few girls said their parents weren't home and there was going to be a party at one of their houses. I was undecided. I was in uncharted territory without Aaron. But then Christine took my hand and said, "You're coming with me." I finally got a ride back to Aaron's early in the morning. It was all a lot of fun and there was some making out, but ultimately my mind was on the end of the trip. I could feel it in my blood; my body and my mind were consumed by it.

Sunday morning came quickly. It was raining as usual, and it seemed the family's plan was to have a restful, quiet day. I was treated to more good meals and just hanging around and listening to music. At one point, I was making a note of something in the smaller of my two sketchbooks, and Aaron asked if he could look at the drawings and read some poems. I wasn't paying too much attention to him, but after twenty minutes or so he said, "Mate, how'd you ever know you could draw, and how did you become an artist?"

That was a mouthful, and I wasn't sure how to start to really explain. I started to tell him that from an early age I would goof around and draw things. And I guess comparing my stuff to other people's in grade school and beyond, it was obvious I had some talent. I told him my father was a strict guy who had worked very hard all his life and was a businessman. When I graduated high school, he would have none of that art stuff. Artists don't make any money, and no one was sure if I was any kind of a real artist anyway. So, it was decided I'd go into Liberal Arts in college to start. I'm sure my father hoped eventually I'd transfer to a business curriculum. Well, things got very interesting in my freshman year at college in several ways, but alas, not very good for getting the grades I needed to stay in college. I was flunking out after my first semester and needed a miracle to stay there. To make matters worse, I had also decided to join a fraternity. It was a great thing to do and I had a lot of good times and met some great new friends, but I wasn't very good at juggling all those things. It was looking like I'd be saying goodbye to all of it unless I pulled a rabbit out of my hat.

To make matters even worse, my fraternity, Theta Chi, was holding Hell Week at the same time that final first semester grades came out, a double whammy of bad things. Aaron asked, "What do mean Hell Week? What the heck was that?"

I told him all fraternities had a final initiation to make it into the fraternity, and that was called Hell Week. Hell Weeks at certain colleges and universities were very tame or nonexistent, while at others they were scary, disgusting, and sometimes cruel. I told him that if you went through it as a pledge, you wanted to give it to future pledges as hard as or worse than you'd got.

Aaron sat up straighter and said, "What you mean disgusting? Tell me more."

I went over the concept with him and then proceeded to give him one example. During our Hell Week, the pledges were told to go into the basement of the fraternity house. As the twenty or so of us got down there, a good part of the area had been covered floor to ceiling with a cellophane-type material that got our attention immediately. This looked like something you might see in a psycho murder movie. Then we were to go into what appeared to be a smaller isolated room, something like a fruit cellar, and told to strip off everything. Then as we went back to the larger room, we were split into groups of threes by a crowd of actives in the fraternity. At that point, we lined up against one of the walls with one of us lying down face up and another kneeling over him to the side, and the third one positioned to stand over the head of the pledge lying down. It all seemed a little strange. Then the actives proceeded to give those kneeling a paper plate piled high with baking flour, and those lying down had to raise their hands above their heads a little to the rear and hold a basket of eggs as they opened their mouths as wide as they could. Then my pledge father, with a devilish look in his eyes, told us it was now time to play the Bombardier Game, and immediately the actives started betting on certain groups to succeed or fail. We then were instructed that even though we were a three-man group, the one holding the plate of flour was to work against the other two by creating a ridiculous smoke screen to impede the Bombardier as he pulled one of the eggs from the basket and cracked it over the head of the smoke screener and tried to hit the mouth of the poor pledge lying down with the yolk from the egg—through the smoke screen. The smoke screener was being covered with more flour every second, with blown flour over him from head to toe. It was a contest. We were told the last-place team would be very sorry, and the first-place team much happier. To finish, first the top guy had to get an egg yolk in the target's mouth. As soon as he did, then all three of us would switch positions and start again. Once all three were Bombardiers and all targets hit, we would be done.

Of course, there was no real reward; that was just talk to give us some hope of living through the torture. And it was torture. More than once, some of the actives had to jump in and throw a bucket of water on someone as they were lying down with mouth open and inhaling all the flour and gagging. I think one of my frat pledges actually passed out, as he couldn't breathe. Then at the end of this weird ceremony, they herded us in the anteroom, which was so unclean I believe city inspectors wouldn't even go in it, and brought out, believe it or not, a regulation fire hose. Though it was the dead of winter, they turned it on us full-force for about five minutes until we were near death with some guys forming icicles on parts of their bodies as they cleaned us off. And when I told Aaron that though all of that was disgusting enough, it was only the first night of five more days of Hell Week, he just rolled his eyes.

I felt it was time to get back to how I became so involved with the art world. Right around Hell Week, I was in an ever-deepening hole with my grades, and for some reason I decided to take a shortcut through the art building as I was going from one class to another. I was about to give up and accept that though I had had great fun and in its own way a very educational first semester, I wasn't going to last long in college if I didn't apply myself to my studies.

In any case, as I was walking down the hallway, a guy asked me if I had a match to lite his cigarette. I lit his and pulled out one of my own, and we started to talk a little. He mentioned some of the art hanging up on the walls; he wished he could someday create something as good as that stuff —what was identified as the best in the school. I wasn't paying too much attention as he was talking, but then I really took a second and looked at the artwork. Though I didn't say anything, I thought I could do just as well or even better. Too bad my father just didn't see a life for anyone who'd gamble on an art career. In another life, maybe I could have been a guy who not only was having a good time in college but also was getting good grades, maybe even excellent grades. That would be another world, wouldn't it? But then out of nowhere, a lightning bolt struck.

As I was daydreaming, he kept on talking about how he loved the fact that he hardly had any homework, that the classes weren't so tough, interesting and rewarding, but not tough if you had some talent. After that, the lightning bolt. I thought, wait a minute, I'm close to college death, but I haven't been kicked out yet. If I could pull off some magic somehow and get an A in an art course, I might be able to salvage and maybe survive this rocky road I was on.

What I'm going to say now is slightly exaggerated, but not much. I immediately threw my books down, ran down the hall to the first door to the outside campus I could find, and raced over hill and dale to my dean's office. As I approached the double doors leading to his office, I started sliding on my knees, and magically his doors opened, and he looked up from working on something at his desk in surprise. With my hands folded in a prayerful and begging scenario, I pleaded with him to let me change a couple of classes to art classes, even though the time to do anything like that had passed some time ago. As I pleaded my case, he tapped his fingers on the desk and finally said, "Do you think I'm a dummy, Paul? If you had any talent you would have gone into art in the first place. I've got your records right here. You look like you are on a fast train out of here."

Well, years later, some people have talked about me and some of the things I ended up doing in my professional life, and I have to say that I couldn't have done half of them if I wasn't a pretty good salesperson. I got my start that afternoon in my dean's office. I talked him into changing one class to an art class even though he would have bet any amount of money that all this was just a ridiculous distraction and I'd be out on my ass shortly. To make a long story short, I got an A in that course, stayed in school, and finished in the required four years. In my last semester in Advertising Design, I made the Dean's List. Too bad my original dean had left; the subsequent one didn't appreciate what a lucky shortcut can mean.

So, I said to Aaron, "Sometimes life takes you and you just go with it. I guess the future will tell me if that shortcut was really a good thing. Sorry to be so long-winded. Hopefully, that gives you some insight and answers your question."

As he was getting up, he was just shaking his head. He turned to me and said, "You are lucky, Paul." As he walked by me he asked if he could rub my head to see if any of my luck could rub off on him.

More and more, though, I was starting to feel itchy. The end was close, and each day the thought consumed me.

Now it was Monday, and Aaron and I helped his mother most of the day with some cleaning and chores around the house and yard. That night Aaron and I walked to the White Cross Tavern in town and stayed there until its close. After a week or so with Aaron, I could understand 95 percent of what he said, but in that tavern, I did a lot of pretending. I mostly had no clue. Their English language was a different language than mine. After the bar closed, we walked to Aaron's grandparents and had coffee and rolls, and they asked me questions about the States until around 2:00 a.m. Finally, we walked home, mostly in silence, but I couldn't help but think and imagine some storylines from past horror tales I'd heard or read or seen on TV—the things that can happen on lonely, dark, and misty English streets in the dead of night. A dark and rainy night in England is different than anywhere else in the world, I think.

Tuesday was mostly spent sleeping late and going to bed early as Aaron had talked me into one more side trip. We had watched some special on TV in the last couple of days about Loch Ness in Scotland and the Loch Ness Monster. Everyone watching in the living room believed without a doubt that it was real. They loved it when I said I wanted to believe also and thought that it would make an interesting story to go out in search of it. The next day Aaron did some research and presented me with an idea. He said, "We're going to Scotland. You and I are going to catch the Loch Ness Monster."

This caught me by surprise. It was right up my alley. Yeah, I bet we could catch that elusive monster, so I made the decision for one more adventure. Aaron told me we could hitch up north to Scotland in one day. I believed him, but the reality was more like three days. I had visions of swimming monsters in my mind, and I was ready to believe anything.

On the 29th, we set off about 12:30 p.m. His mother absolutely would not let us leave without our almost daily fish and chips. We got two rides quickly, and I have to say I was kinda excited to go after the monster in the lake. I had always been more interested than most in stories about aliens, the abominable snowman, and other weird creatures. I don't know why. The unexpected and unknown made real was something that I often hoped for.

After two rides, the road went cold. As darkness came and we were basically at the fork in the road—back to reality or possible adventure—we decided to set up Aaron's tent. We had reached the A-1, which led north to Scotland and south straight down to London.

Aaron's mother had made us some cold supper for the night.

We pitched the tent somewhat away from the road, but it seemed that instead of the bed of clover we were expecting, we had picked the Amazon jungle full of hundreds of insects. It was terrible, but Aaron was so tired he fell off to sleep almost right away. On the other hand, I laid there fighting insects and started to imagine the "what ifs."

What if when I finally did get to London, every ticket I could find was closer to the $250 the original flight across the Atlantic had cost me. What would I do? What could I do? I was thinking and thinking and looking at that eventuality from every side imaginable. How would I even survive in London long enough to find out if I could get a ticket or not? So many people had told me London is one of the most expensive cities in the world, but the more I thought about it, the more expensive it became. Where would I stay? What would I eat? I almost started thinking I needed to meet an English Gerrard who had friends, so I could stay for free somewhere. But then I snapped out of that line of thinking. I didn't need to see the inside of any more jails.

I'm sure I did finally get to sleep; I don't know for how long, but it wasn't restful. The sun was up now, and I heard the big trucks going both north and south just over the next hill on the A-1. For a time at first, those going north pulled me mentally, but the forty or fifty bugs on the inside roof of the tent watching me and planning their attack inspired me to go south. The south spirit would whisper in one ear, *Don't be a fool. You've been lucky over the trip so far, and now your luck is up. Go home.* A little bit later, the north spirit whispered in my other ear for me to pick an adventure. It said, *Let's go. Let's find the Loch Ness Monster. You'll be famous. You have had a lucky star over you from the beginning, so keep believing.*

Aaron woke up and we both lay there for a while. I think

we were both watching the insects and wondering how many of them could sting or bite. I could also sense that both of us were thinking, *Oh, fuck it. This wasn't a good idea.* It was just a matter of who was going to say it first.

I decided I would be the one to say it first as a couple of the insects started buzzing a warning to break camp. I felt that Aaron didn't need another adventure where he made big promises and again it was all talk and no action. I decided to take the blame, so he could save face and have a good excuse why he was home again so soon. We said our goodbyes as we packed up. I owed him and his family a lot. I will never forget the experience and will treasure it always. I wish all of this family only the best in the future.

Aaron said he wanted to walk a ways. As I walked the other way to where I could hitch at the entrance of the A-1 going south, I watched him until he was out of sight.

When I turned around, I saw an unusual sign post that gave the distances, from standing at that spot, to a random selection of far-off places in the world. How strange, but so apropos for me at that moment. They were listed in no apparent order:

Kilometers to:

Paris, France: 769 Kilometers Madrid, Spain: 2,001 Kilometers Rome, Italy: 2,064 Kilometers Berlin, Germany: 1,393 Kilometers Stockholm, Sweden: 2.190 Kilometers Athens, Greece: 3,432 Kilometers Helsinki, Finland: 2,656 Kilometers Moscow, Russia: 3,163 Kilometers Cairo, Egypt: 3,696 Kilometers New Delhi, India: 6,736 Kilometers Johannesburg, South Africa: 9,280 Kilometers

Note: There are 1.60 Kilometers to 1 mile

About an hour later, a guy picked me up and took me halfway to London. Then an old Beatles-themed BMW painted entirely front to back in the style, characters, and colors of the movie *The Yellow Submarine* picked me up, and the driver said he'd take me all the way to London. I must tell you when he stopped his car, I almost told him that I was mistaken in putting out my thumb out at that moment. Could I really enter the end of this trip riding in a cartoon car like this? What a way to enter the streets of London! I had to laugh. He handed me a joint and turned up his radio loud. Appropriately, Mick and the boys were singing *Give Me Shelter*.

London

"I heard there was a bulletin board behind the door with people selling the return half of their airline tickets home after deciding to stay in London instead."

"No, no such thing as that here." she said

I'm dead. This is the big one. I really am dead. I have no way home now.

18.

Extraordinary Circumstances

Friday, 3:00 PM, July 30, 1970

For the most part, London is a very flat city, but there was one hill as we got closer that gave me pause for just a second. I caught a glimpse of the breadth, depth, and hugeness of this ancient city on the Thames. My first time through London was very quick, lasting only an hour or two until I hopped on the Tube to get to a place at the far northern border of the city to continue hitchhiking north.

Philip, my driver, and I had gotten along famously as he drove me down roads where everyone who saw us stopped in their tracks and did a double take. You just didn't see a car painted like this, at least not in real life. On my door, all along the side, was a painting of The Yellow Submarine and four very prominent portholes with images of Paul, John, George, and Ringo. The front of the car had rainbows and images of cartoonish animals with the driver side full of music-hating Blue Meanies apparently chasing the Sgt. Pepper's Lonely Hearts Club Band and more rainbows. Every inch of the car was painted, even the hubcaps. As you were walking down the sidewalk, you wouldn't be any more surprised if you had seen a fire-breathing dragon.

Philip asked me if there was anyplace special I'd like to be let off. I was trying to remember what the guy said in Athens. Could I remember where the American Express office was? Of course, I couldn't. Philip started throwing out parts of London to see if anything rang a bell. "Okay, mate, what about Oxford Street or Mayfair or the Kings Cross area or even by Charing Cross Road in Soho in the Covent Garden district? Or maybe the Notting Hill Gate area of Kensington and Chelsea. . . ".

I stopped him there. "Yeah, Notting Hill Gate. That seems familiar."

"Right, we're not far," he said, giving me a thumbs up.

As we drove there, I got more and more worried. I could see nothing but stone, brick, glass, and asphalt. This was possibly the busiest and most expensive of all the cities I had visited. My goal to find a cheap place to stay and get a cheap ticket to the States looked more elusive each block we drove down.

"Chicago, there's your American Express office. It's getting late, mate. I think I remember a cheap hotel close by," he said, leaning towards me to turn left on the next street.

I wanted to jump out of The Yellow Submarine right there and then and run into the American Express office, but he was right to look for a bed for me. The afternoon was waning. I'd be dead in the water without a roof over my head. It looked like rain. Of course, it did—this was London, city of fog and rain.

We drove around in circles for a while before he pointed to a place down the street and said, "That's the place, look. They have a sign in the window, 'Room For The Night Available.'" I could barely see it, but I saw a sign, so I believed him. Then he went down a block and another and saw a restaurant with tables outside and an open parking space across the street. "Well, mate, you're home free; we got you to London safe and sound, and you saw the American Express office where you need to go tomorrow. Now let's get a coffee or beer and celebrate the end of your trip and the beginning of mine."

Philip ordered coffee. I felt I deserved a beer. I was feeling somewhat relaxed. So far, so good. Got a good ride into London— got a great ride. Philip was a gift. The odds of being picked up by someone who would take me around London until I found the place I needed to be and besides that found me a cheap hotel were a million to one. I was so lucky. Everything could have come crashing down around me. London was a mega-city. It could have eaten me alive. Besides all that, the clouds seemed to have left, and the sun was shining down on us. Lucky, lucky, lucky.

Philip came back from making a phone call and said it was time for him to go. His friend had a potential buyer for his car. Philip needed a good price to get an airline ticket to take him to South Africa and the start of his new life. It was nice to see him so excited about his prospects. Although I thought Philip was a gift from heaven, he said picking me up and hearing of some of my adventures gave him the boost of confidence he needed as his departure grew closer. I had re-invigorated his dreams. He couldn't thank me enough as we got up to shake hands goodbye and wish each other good luck. I gave him my address in the States, and he made a promise to contact me when he was settled in Africa. There was a second as we shook hands that I wondered is this my chance to see another continent. Should I say, "Fuck it" and go with him? It only lasted a moment; reality returned, and I picked up my sleeping bag and started my way down the block. I took a left-hand turn and there it was: that beautiful, cheap hotel in the middle of London. It was like finding buried treasure. As I approached, I noticed that the vacancy sign wasn't there anymore. I walked in and went to the front desk.

"Hello," I said, relieved to have a place to stay. "I'm here for the open room you have. How much is it per night?"

"No room, yank, last one just rented in the last half hour or so. Sorry, mate."

I stood there just staring at him. A thousand things immediately flashed through my mind, all of them disastrous. I was dead; I was done for.

As I walked out of the hotel, I had no idea of which way to go. The streets were full of cars and double-decker buses and the sidewalks jam-packed with Englishmen and women hurrying to their destinations. I had none, but this was way too busy a street to think a new destination would fall out of the sky and into my hands. I turned right at the next intersection. The new street was better. I kept walking down another block, then again to another, then left, all the while desperately trying to think of some idea, some way out of this enormous hole I was in. Finally, after an hour or so of walking, I turned onto the quietest street of the ones I'd been walking on. Apartments or townhouses lined each side of the street. Maybe this was a chance to sit down on one of the stoops and try to come up with a miraculous idea. I was tired, and though it hadn't rained, the London sky always seemed like it could open at any moment. That's all I would need. If that happened, I just might have to lie down in the street and wait for a double-decker bus to run me over.

I picked a set of stairs in the middle of the block, put my sleeping bag down, and was looking forward to resting when the door at the top of the stairs opened. A lady came out with a broom and started yelling at me and sweeping dirt off the porch in my direction.

She yelled, "This ain't no park, you bum! Get your bloody bag and get out of here."

As she looked like she was about to come down the stairs after me with that broom, I got up and scurried away.

After passing a house or two, I turned down another street and looked back. She was gone. I was almost at the end of the new block when I saw a guy sitting on some stairs in front of me. This street seemed to hold no promise of any answers, and worse, I thought I had just felt a raindrop.

I didn't even want to look at the guy sitting there. I had had enough of people yelling at me.

"Yo, mate, got a match?" he said softly as I walked past.

I looked at him; he held up a cigarette and gave me a smile. I turned to walk back and took out a match and lit the cigarette for him.

"You're obviously a traveler. Where have you been?" he asked. I decided maybe I'd have a cigarette with him. Couldn't hurt.

"I guess all over, some twenty-plus countries. I'll tell you, it's catching up with me now, though. I'm trying to fly back to the States from London, and everything is up in the air. I've got some real problems. No ticket, less money than I had planned, and right now walking around in circles in one of the biggest cities in Europe trying to find a cheap hotel to put a roof over my head tonight. Am I still in the Chelsea area? I've lost track."

"Yeah, we are in Chelsea."

"Good. I've got to stay close. By the way, do you know where the American Express office is by chance?"

"Sorry, mate, I'm not from this area. I have no idea."

"You wouldn't know by chance of a cheap hotel around here?" As I watched the sun setting, I couldn't forget that I was running out of time.

He didn't say anything for a couple of minutes as we finished our cigarettes and continued to watch the pretty sunset. But then as he threw his cigarette butt into the street, he said, "Well, mate, this might be your lucky day."

I turned my head towards him. What did he mean? I didn't feel lucky. I waited for him to follow up, and it started to drizzle. I looked skyward; there appeared to be just one dark cloud over us. Perfect. Raining only in the part of London I was in.

He started, "I'll tell you, I've been trying to come up with some excuse, some reason I didn't make it home last night. The reality is I got lucky at an office party and stayed out all night and now also most of today. My wife is going to kill me."

"I see. You do have a problem. And maybe I'm a possible get-out-of-jail-free card for you. But first, how could this be my lucky day?"

Now, the thought did cross my mind he was maybe talking about some Jane or Elizabeth or Dolores. Could he possibly mean he would introduce me to his girl from last night and there might be a place for me to stay? Of course, there would be a lot of ifs in that kind of thinking, and as I watched his facial expression, I didn't think that's what he was talking about.

"The night started with Veronica, but as the drinking continued for both of us, somehow I landed in a strange little hotel not far from Hyde Park, which is north of where we are now. I have no idea how I got there, and I have no idea where Veronica is now either. It wasn't the greatest hotel, but it was dirt cheap—as it should be since there are eight beds to a room."

Immediately I got an image of a skid row type of place with every floor filled with hopeless alcoholics, unclean drug users, and other types of bottom feeders. It was not a pretty picture. I was about to say that it was probably not for me, though my companion did look pretty normal, but before I could really say anything, he spoke: "And it's only—how do you say in US dollars? About $2 US per night."

That got my attention, both good and bad. But I wasn't in any position to argue or think I could do better as darkness was engulfing us. Many of the people I'd been around over the last few months were unclean drug users, and I was still kicking. Still, I worried that by the time I got there, there might be no beds left.

However, before I could tell him that I'd had bad luck with hotels in London, he reached into his pocket and pulled out a key with a number on it. He said, "Here's my key from last night. They won't sell the use of the bed until they find out about me. Only problem, I'm out of money. If you pay my last night's fee and an underground ticket for both of us for me to take you to the location, you've got a cheap roof over your head for tonight."

"It's a deal." I extended my hand to shake and consummate the arrangement. I also said to him, "Why don't you use me as a reason you were out last night. Say for some reason I was at the office event, that I had too much to drink, and you were worried about me, and ultimately you felt a responsibility to your fellow man not to leave me alone on the dark, misty streets of London late last night."

"That's pretty good, actually. You know, I don't even know your name."

"Paul. What's yours?"

"I'm Max. Glad to know you."

"I also have some piece of paper from America that I can give you as evidence you were with someone from the US. I'll write down my home address in the Chicago area as additional support for your story."

"Brilliant, actually, brilliant. That should work. Let's find a Tube station and get you to the Paddington Station and the hotel and then me on my way home."

We found an Underground station, hopped on the train going towards Buckingham Palace, and got off and walked a couple of blocks. As we were about to turn the corner to the hotel, he stopped and grabbed my arm. "Let's not take any chances. Here's the key. Right across the street is the Belmont Hotel. Don't worry; there will be a bed for you." We shook hands, and I walked down to the hotel. The front desk guy looked at me suspiciously, but as I held up my key, he just hunched his shoulders and said, "Okay, mate. As before, your bed is down the hall in the Kensington Room."

As I walked down the hallway to my room, I have to say I was pleasantly surprised. It was clean and well kept. This didn't look like a place for bums, thieves, or gypsies. My room was small, and even though there really were eight beds, there was room to breathe. All beds were taken except the lower berth on one of two bunk beds. I wondered who my bunkmate was.

I threw my sleeping bag onto the bed and decided to explore the hotel a little. The dining room was also very clean, exceedingly clean for that matter, and there was fresh coffee and some rolls and cupcakes lying around. I saw a menu for the following day—scrambled eggs, toast, and muffins—and all was included in the cost of the room. The first-floor bathroom had multiple toilets and four shower stalls. I couldn't take it anymore. I rushed back to my bed, opened my sleeping bag, and grabbed my makeshift dub kit and jumped in the shower. Heaven.

After my shower, I made my way to a living room and sat down in a quiet corner and ended up falling asleep. I awoke around midnight, tiptoed into my room and saw that everyone was out cold. I found my bunk, crawled in and fell asleep immediately.

As I opened my eyes in the morning, my room was abuzz with activity. My bunkmate was nowhere to be found; I wondered if indeed I did have a bunkmate. One guy from Germany was yelling at his traveling companion to get to breakfast before they closed it for the morning. I jumped up, put on my boots, and raced out of the room to get some breakfast.

While I was eating my eggs and seven pieces of toast, the manager brought in a tall guy who looked American and pointed to me. The guy came over, stuck out his hand, and said, "Hi, I'm Rory, I understand you are my bunkmate. I'm from the East Coast, Boston actually. Where are you from? Mind if I sit down and have a cup of coffee with you while you're reading?"

"No, not at all. Please sit down. My name is Paul. I'm from the Chicago area."

After securing his coffee, he sat down and said, "Well, Paul, there are guys all around us who have been traveling in Europe and other places. I've met some in the short time I've been here, but I have to say, you are straight out of central casting. You are a traveler. Anyone talking to or looking at you would know you have stories. You are brown from the sun, your clothes, though not rags by any means, tell a story of travel. It seems you have just the right amount of dust baked into your person. I see you're wearing a bleached cotton work shirt from either Spain or the Middle East somewhere. You have a beaded necklace, handmade it looks like, from some hippie or gypsy as well as a beaded wristband. You just don't find those things in a department store. What is your story? Where have you been? Who are you?"

"Yeah, I guess I have turned myself into a different animal. And I guess I do have stories. I'll have to take some time and sit down and think about this trip I've been on. I haven't done that in a while. Maybe tonight over a couple of beers. We'll see. But to answer your question, I've seen about twenty countries or so, something like that. I came over to Paris to work, trying to become a modern-day Larry Darrell. Have you ever read the novel or seen the movie *The Razor's Edge*? My dream, after working a year out of college, was to find riches and fame in Paris and become like Larry in the book—a well-traveled, confident, and interesting person of the world. My life at that point seemed to be always tempting me with the thought there is something else out there in the world for me. Something better. Something I needed to find. For several reasons, Paris didn't work out, and another American I met on the plane flying over here and I decided to go into business to find and buy and eventually sell exotic lambskin coats from the Middle East and transport them to some of the major cities in Europe. We took the Orient Express east with our destination Afghanistan and/or Pakistan. We never made it. Other things happened, and many countries later here I am finally in London, hoping to get my hands on one of the cheapest airline tickets ever available and fly back to the States. Supposedly, I've got a lead on how to get it; as a matter of fact, I better get going."

"Well, that was a mouthful. I thought I was having a great experience in my three weeks over here, but wow, I must hear more, Paul. Where are you going to get this ticket?"

"You know, this is going to sound crazy, but I met another traveler in an outdoor café in Athens months ago who told me to go to the American Express office in London. He said they have a bulletin board behind the door where people sell their return tickets to New York after falling in love and wanting to stay in Europe. They sell their tickets for what I understand is dirt cheap. Less than $100. Based on that short, chance meeting in Greece, I've decided to bet that his story was true. If not, I don't know. I don't have the cost of a regular flight back to the States. I guess if not, I'll have to stay over here forever. I know, kinda half-baked. Actually really half-baked. But it seems like I've had a guardian angel traveling with me the entire journey, so I guess I'm hoping my angel is still with me."

He just stared at me quietly for a minute or two then said, "I've got to hear more of your story, Paul. I'd like to buy you dinner tonight. What do you think?"

"Okay, thanks. As I said, I'm closer to moths flying out of my wallet than dollars or English pound notes. But now I've got to find that American Express office."

Rory stood up with me and said, "Mind if I tag along? I have to see if I have any mail there myself."

Our hotel was just south of St. John's Wood and north of Regent's Park. Someone told me they thought the American Express office was east of our hotel. We had to ask a few people along the way, but finally, we were about a half block away from that big white and blue signage. My heart started pounding wildly. I pushed the double doors open aggressively, twisting my head left and then right and then back left again, but to no avail. I didn't see any bulletin board. Okay, that must be the wrong door. I looked to every nook and cranny of the huge room. This appeared to be the only door bringing people in and out. My heart started pumping again. Maybe I was missing something. I bolted to one of the windows and nodded to the person behind the counter.

"Excuse me," I said, panting a little. And not even waiting for the woman sitting there to look up, I said, "Where's the bulletin board with all the personal messages and especially messages about getting a cheap airline ticket back to the USA?"

"I'm sorry, a board? What do you mean?"

"I heard there was a bulletin board behind the door with people selling the return half of their airline tickets home after deciding to stay in London instead."

"No, no such thing as that here."

I'm dead. This is the big one. I really am dead. I have no way home now. I looked around quickly for my guardian angel. I didn't see her. I walked over to one of the benches against the wall as Rory came up to me, sensing problems.

"What did she say?" he asked.

"She said no bulletin board. I'm dead. I'm a prisoner in Europe."

Rory replied, "Well, I didn't expect that, but I'm sure you didn't either. Come on, let's get out of here."

We walked for a while, both of us quiet. I had a million thoughts going through my head, all bad. Rory, I think, had no idea what to say to me. We passed a pub, and Rory grabbed my arm and said, "We need a drink, even though it's still morning. If we ever were going to drink this early for some reason, this is it."

Oddly, there already were a couple of tables occupied with people drinking alcohol.

We sat down at the first open table we came to. Immediately from behind the bar, the bartender yelled, "What will it be, mates?"

Rory jumped in, "Draw two beers for us please."

We were quiet for a couple of minutes just taking sips of our beers. Then reality started to creep into my head. I was in one of the most expensive cities in the world, and I was running out of money. What was going to happen to me? I imagined I'd probably have to wait a month or so, like in Paris, to be okayed for a work permit. I didn't think I'd make it that long on what I had in my wallet.

Rory asked if I could call home and have my parents wire me money for a ticket. I said no, I couldn't do that. I'd be classified as a failure forever if I did that. I knew this was my problem, and somehow, some way, I was going to ride it out to the end—what end was a good question.

We again became quiet, just looking off into space and looking into our beers. Finally, I had to become vocal about the stupid situation I had gotten myself into. I started lamenting, "Why me? Why have I traveled all around different countries just to end up in a huge, expensive city with no way home?" I was talking to no one in particular about my predicament, but I guess I was getting louder and louder with each passing moment.

Then out of nowhere, I felt an unexpected tap on the shoulder. I turned to see a middle-aged guy drinking a beer at the table next to ours.

"Been hearing you as you talk about your problem here in

London. I have to say, what I've heard, it does seem like a bloody big problem you have. But I live here in London, and I'll tell you, we care about people. People take care of each other here. There are organizations that help people with all kinds of problems. Why don't you asked the bartender to look up some of them in his phonebook and then call them on his phone at the bar?"

Before I could get up, Rory was already out of his chair walking to the bar. As I got there, the bartender had his phone book out and was talking to Rory. We found two numbers that seemed to have some connection to my problem. Unfortunately, the bar's telephone was out of order, so I wrote down the two numbers, got some change, and we were off to look for a pay phone.

About a block away, we found a phone booth. I called the first number of the two and they had no idea how to help. As I called the next number, I could feel my heart beating at an increased rate. Again, the feedback was, "Sorry, mate, no idea, and no advice." I stayed on the phone with the lady on the line for a minute or so, knowing if I hung up, my chances of a miracle were over. She was a nice lady, and even though she appreciated my situation, there was nothing she could do. As I was thanking her for trying, she said, "Wait a minute." I had no idea why she said that or what she was doing, but I said softly into the phone, "Please, please have her find something, something that will help me."

She came back on and said she remembered a call that had come into their office a day or two ago saying they had one, maybe two seats open on a flight to New York City. However, she said that no one in the office thought the call was legitimate. The male calling only spoke broken English and wasn't from a travel company or airline. He just said that he had a reduced-price seat.

After searching for the man's number on her desk, she found it—no company, no person's name, just a phone number.

I had no choice. I wrote down the number and leaned back in the phone booth, held up the last few pence I had and said, "Okay, this is it, my last chance to get out of London." Rory crossed his fingers.

I called the number, and it rang and rang. After about seven rings, a man answered, and in what I thought was a Middle-Eastern accent said, "Yeah, what is it? Who is this?"

Uh, oh, this didn't sound right. I was silent for a second, trying to make some sense out of what I had just heard. I couldn't. "I'm sorry, I must have the wrong number," I said.

"What? What you mean? What?"

"I'm sorry, I thought I was calling to buy a ticket, an airline ticket to New York City."

He pounced on that line quickly. "How much you have, tell me. How many pounds you have?"

I could hardly understand him with his accent, and besides that, no one, or at least no one legitimate talked like that. This sounded like a scam.

I responded, "I think I have the wrong number. I'm sorry for bothering you."

But immediately he shot back, "No, no. This is the place. We have ticket."

I said, "I heard a ticket for less than $100 US." I just felt I had to ask.

"Yes, yes. We leave in three days. You come today and give me money. You have pencil? I will give you address for you to come today."

Putting my hand over the receiver, I asked Rory if he had a

pen or pencil. He didn't. He jumped out of the phone booth and started stopping people.

Success! He came back in a couple of minutes with the pen. There was a discarded London newspaper on the ground inside the phone booth. I tore off a piece and told the guy to give me the address.

Wow, I couldn't believe it. Could I be this lucky? We started walking, and after a couple of blocks, it was my time to say to Rory, "Let's stop in here and drink to my good fortune," as we walked by another pub.

The bar was like the other one, and we sat down at one of the ten to fifteen tables in the old English decorated pub.

Rory toasted me, and as we were drinking our beers, I was feeling lucky, almost giddy. I had done it. I had done the impossible. I scored a plane ticket out of thin air. I pulled out the piece of newsprint on which I had written down the address to go to later that afternoon. I was staring at it, and Rory asked me to tell him again where I had to go and said we should ask the bartender how to get there. I guess I was talking loudly. Again, I got a tap on my shoulder.

"I've been hearing a little bit, governor, about your good fortune to get an airline ticket, but say again, where do you have to go to pay them?" I told him the Queens Park area. His eyes widened, and he shook his head vigorously no. He was dead serious.

"That's one of the poorest and most dangerous areas of London. I couldn't ever see that anyone would do that kind of business there. I live in London, and I never go there myself. It's a pretty risky part of the city. A lot of crime."

I was crushed, brought back to reality. Just as I was going to make sure Rory could come with me, he was walking towards a phone booth in one corner of the bar. As he came back, he said there was a problem with his airline plans. He had to go to the British Airways office to straighten out a mix-up that had him mistakenly leaving London later that day.

So here I sat by myself in the Sheep's Head Pub, sipping my beer, staring at but not paying attention to a soccer game running on the TV over the bar. Rory had left ten minutes ago. I was just trying to figure out what to do. I'd certainly been lucky; my guardian angel had stayed close many times during my trip since leaving Chicago in April. I was thinking I'd need some powerful luck here in London. What was going to happen? Now I had to take the Tube to a very dicey part of London to visit some iffy address by myself to buy an airline ticket back to the States. I would not be dealing with a reputable travel company but evidently with an Eastern European who bluntly and roughly asked me what I wanted in broken and not very good English. Those two things probably would have stopped most people in their tracks, but I didn't have the luxury; I was desperate and had run out of possibilities. As I continued thinking, something else started to creep into my head. It was one thing not getting a ticket and losing my money on some con, but if this neighborhood was so bad, there were other things I'd like not to lose, like my life.

After ordering another beer and the day's sandwich special, it was time for me to go. On my way out, I double-checked with the bartender which Underground line I needed to go to the Queen's Park area. He concurred with my notes from the phone call and the directions. But he also gave me one of those looks, a look that you don't like to see. Why is a nice guy like you going to the pits of London?

I found the right couple of lines I needed to travel on and arrived at a deserted Tube station. As I exited the Underground, I came face to face with what looked like the aftermath of an apocalyptic war. There were no human beings anywhere. The tall buildings look used and empty. There was only dirt in the grassy areas as I walked to find George Street, which I did easily. In the middle of the block was the address I was looking for. I stood in front for a few minutes, again wondering if this was something I really wanted to do. Finally, I decided that I didn't have a choice—I needed to go in. I was desperate for an airline ticket.

I walked through the front door of the four-story brick building, moving from bright sunlight into almost pitch dark. I saw a couple of ceiling lights, but they appeared to be burned out. Of course, why would life be easy here? There was no elevator, only a dark stairwell going up into more darkness. Again, I stopped. What was I doing? The situation had to be an ideal scenario for any robber. What should I do?

I started climbing the stairs. I was hearing imaginary noises on every floor, but, there was no one anywhere. I was the only one making any noise as I ascended from floor to floor and finally to the fourth floor. I walked to the end of the hall to room number 425. I had noticed many of the apartment doors, besides having suite numbers, also had the occupant's name. This one, number 425, didn't. Of course, it didn't; this person or whoever lived here probably wanted to stay out of the light of day. Who knows who or what I would find behind the door.

After a couple of minutes looking at the door and failing to conjure an ability to see through solid wood to tell me what lived behind it, I decided this wasn't working. I said to myself, *You're a fool to be here. Get out. Get out now.* Finally, I got the message; I turned to go. And just as I did, the door opened.

I froze and slowly turned back to find out who had opened the apartment door. It was a young man with dark olive skin, about twenty-five to thirty years old, somewhat surprisingly dressed in a black dress shirt, black tie, and black pants with his black hair combed back in what appeared to be an Elvis Presley ducktail hairdo. I didn't immediately say anything, but then the shock of seeing a 1920s-dressed gangster passed, and I said, "Hello, I'm sorry. I must have the wrong apartment." Whatever I had possibly imagined in that apartment, it wasn't him or that.

As I started to walk away, he said in very broken English, "Wait. What do you want? Tell me?"

"Oh, I'm sorry. I was looking for someone who had an airline ticket for me to fly back to America. Maybe I'm on the wrong floor."

"How much money you have? How many pounds?"

This wasn't good, a guy dressed like a gangster from old just caring about how much money I had, not asking my name or anything that I would expect a travel company employee to ask. It looked like I had decided to open door #3 where I should've opened door #2. This looked bad. How bad, I was afraid I was about to find out.

I continued, "No, really, I think I have the wrong place."

At that point, he opened the door to the apartment wider to show three other guys dressed the same in a smoke-filled room playing poker on a coffee table filled with chips, cards, and beers. One guy looking like that was enough to trigger an inner alert, but four guys set off sirens in every part of my body.

One of the guys inside said something in a foreign language I couldn't place, and the man at the door grabbed my arm and led me in and closed the door behind me. The two guys sitting on the couch got up and indicated I should sit there between them. I do have to say I was more than a little uncomfortable. In fact, I was freaked out. The radio played a Middle Eastern song, but as I sat there I swear it sounded like the song "Goodbye Cruel World" in a foreign language. If so, how appropriate.

"You have the money?" one of them said immediately upon me sitting down. "My name Sharif. You called me."

And without thinking—I was probably too scared to do anything else—I gave him almost all the money I had left.

I reached inside my corduroy sport coat and took out my American Express checkbook to sign the last of my Traveler's Cheques over to them. Then the one guy said, "You give us $120 US."

I froze and looked at the guy. He wasn't smiling. With every bit of money I had on me and selling my boots to these guys, I didn't have that much, plain and simple. This was not what was talked about on the phone. But should I start to argue with these guys in this position?

Although I already had the American Express checkbook out and was holding it, upon that comment from him, I put it back in my upper inside pocket, cleared my throat and said, "That's not what we talked about on the phone. We were talking about something under $100 US dollars."

"That was when we had three tickets. Now we have only one. You pay to me the money."

I couldn't tell him I didn't have the money. I had to say anything but that.

"No, that's too much. Ninety US, that's it. That's all I'll pay. If not, I will leave." I didn't let on that I wasn't sure they'd let me.

They looked at each other, and one of the guys whispered something to another guy. He really didn't have to whisper; I couldn't understand their language anyway.

I wasn't budging; I wanted to look resolute. That was my final offer. All I could think about while I waited for some response was *I'm dead. I'm totally dead.* This was my only, my last chance to get home. But what else could I do? I needed some money to pay my hotel bill, and although the Underground wasn't expensive, I didn't think I could hitch a ride on it.

They asked me where I was staying. I told them a hotel in the Chelsea area of London. Then one of the guys grabbed a piece of paper and wrote something down and handed it to me. I imagined it to be their final offer, probably an offer I couldn't accept. What could I say; maybe it was already too late? I opened the folded piece of paper. To my surprise, it wasn't another dollar figure for the airline ticket. It was an address, a date, and a time. I was confused. I looked up at them and met their expressionless faces. I started to say, "What is this, what does this…"

I didn't get any more out before one of the guys said, "Okay, give us the $90 and early Monday morning stand in front of this address and someone will pick you up and take you to the airport."

I just stared at these guys. I have to say, I was surprised. Hell, I was shocked. I'd done it. I'd gotten a flight back to the States.

There was some confusion as I signed over the last of my Traveler's Cheques to them. They owed me some change but didn't have any, so finally one guy went out and brought back the correct difference in English pound notes.

One of the guys in particular was getting antsy. It looked like he was losing big to the other two but wanted to continue the poker game. As I was putting the money in my wallet, one of them said, "Okay, now you play poker with us. We not good. You probably win lots of money."

That caught me off guard. I hadn't played a lot of poker in my life, but when I did at the fraternity house or at the dorm in college, I usually did quite well. Could I take the chance here with these guys and play? If I did win, that would be great. It would provide some protection money as I closed out this trip. But I wasn't born yesterday. Someone telling me they weren't very good at poker but really wanted me to play was an obvious setup. One of the guys got up to grab some more beers and gave me one as he sat back down. I took a second to look again at the paper that one of them had given me. There was no phone number on it.

"Can you write down a phone number just in case there is a problem?" I said.

"No, no phone number. Tomorrow is August 1st. We move out of this apartment. We will have no phone. Everything okay, don't worry."

Now that didn't sound so good. And just as I was going to question him more, one of them started to deal the cards. He dealt me in and said, "You put in $2 US or one-pound English."

Too much was happening, and I had a lot of questions. I put out my hand palm down and said, "No, I'm not playing," which won me a dirty look from the guy who was losing big.

"Okay, okay, then we done. You go now." As he said that he got up and opened the door. The mood had changed, and I had the feeling I'd better get out of there now. There was no shaking of hands, and they didn't even look up as I walked out the door, which swiftly closed behind me.

I was somewhat befuddled as I walked down the four flights of stairs and into the London sunshine. A strong breeze hit me immediately. It was like a slap in the face. I stopped walking and turned to look back at the building.

Was all that real? Did I dream this? I pinched myself as a strong blast of cold air hit me right in the face.

I examined the piece of paper with the pickup time and place on it again just to confirm that it was real, that I wasn't dreaming all this. Though I had read it just twenty minutes earlier, this time I took a second on each line and let it all register.

Today was Friday, and I was supposed to be at the address early Monday morning. Not perfect. That meant I'd only have a couple of days to spend in London to see all I could. I guessed I could live with that, especially given that I was now almost out of money.

As that thought brought a chill to my body, I also realized that I had just given these guys almost all my money, and I didn't get a ticket or receipt or anything except some stupid address somewhere in London and a promise that someone would pick me up and take me to Heathrow Airport. *Paul, you're a fool.* It seemed more likely that I had been conned than I now had a $90 ticket back to New York City. I had left my destiny completely in the hands of an incredibly dodgy group of wannabe gangsters who had no phone number, no known address, and seemingly no legitimate business. Now out of that smoke-filled room and into the fresh air, it was obvious to me that it had been a world-class con. Was that even a real apartment or some sham just for me?

I turned, feeling I should go back and ask. Just then, the door to the apartment building opened, and a bunch of skinheads came out punching and pushing each other around. That stopped me. One of them looked at me and said something to the others, and they all stopped to stare at me.

This could be bad, I thought. I looked around. There was nobody else in sight in any direction. I told myself to move, to get out of there immediately. Right then the lesser of the two evils was to assume the guys in the black shirts would deliver compared to the risk of walking into a gang of skinheads blocking the entrance to the apartment building.

I made my way back to the Belmont Hotel and saw Rory sitting in the lounge area, watching a soccer game on the TV. He couldn't wait to ask me how my meeting went. I told him what had happened and that when I left, I didn't leave with an airline ticket or receipt for a ticket and that the people I gave the money to now were moving out of their apartment and had no phone. All I had was an address and a pickup time. I just had to trust them.

Rory listened intently and then responded, "You're fucked! This is like something out of a cop show. They never find these guys no matter how hard they look afterward." He got up, stood quietly for a second or so, and then added, "Let's go get some beer. Let's find the closest pub."

We were getting pretty good at finding pubs. We wondered if we could start some kind of business doing this for a living.

As we sat down in a somewhat crowded pub and started to drink our beers, I couldn't help it—I guess I was somewhat loud again, lamenting if someone would really come and pick me up Monday morning and take me to Heathrow. Rory knew the drill. He let me get my fears out in the open; I think he realized it was cathartic for me.

Whether many Londoners like to listen to others' conversations or just those in pubs, as before, in the middle of vocalizing my apprehensions, I got another, now somewhat expected tap on the shoulder.

As I turned, a middle-aged man asked, "What is the address that you are supposed to go to Monday morning?" When I related the address, the man said he knew that area very well. He was trying to think of a reason why anyone would choose that area as a place to be picked up. He said there are no businesses anywhere around there, just different types of housing. It didn't make any sense to him. It was southeast of here and a long way from the airport.

Well, that was just great, yet another reason to worry, one more thing to play with my mind. Honestly, I already had more than enough things to worry about. He did say it was across the Thames River and was hard to get to on the Tube. I looked at Rory with a look of desperation that begged him to come with me. He understood that look immediately and said he was leaving for Germany about midday on Monday and there wasn't time to do both.

We left the pub and walked a while and stopped at a hotel restaurant for some dinner. It was still early as we left the restaurant. Since we couldn't come up with a way to spend the rest of the evening, we approached an English bobby and asked him for some ideas. He suggested a couple of places in Piccadilly Circus, so we found an Underground station and popped up after climbing the stairs to a crowded, noisy, popular nighttime area of London.

We finally picked a theater that was showing a variety of live acts. We were entertained by a very exotic snake lady, Princess Anastasia, who had many different and dangerous looking snakes climbing all over her. The thing that got her the most applause was that she not only was able to perform some fire-breathing at the same time, but unbelievably, so did one of her snakes. There was also a knife thrower, a couple of comedians, and some actors who put on odd little sketches. Between acts, different striptease artists performed, each apparently from a different country since each of their butts had the name of a different country written on it. We eventually made our way back to the hotel around 1:00 a.m.

Saturday morning brought another day of bright sunshine and the hopes of new adventures. London was looking her finest, and people seemed much happier in general because of that beautiful bright sun shining on them. We continued our practice of having a big breakfast, going back numerous times for additional helpings. Saturday morning, it seemed, was a travel day for many, and our hotel was somewhat empty. Someone had to eat all that food, didn't they?

We had befriended the Greek manager of the Belmont Hotel—actually, he had befriended us. I think he liked all the Americans staying there more than other nationalities with the exception, of course, of Greeks. He sat down with us as we ate and was very interested in what we had planned for the day's activities. He found it hilarious that I wanted to buy a stylized band jacket, something like the Beatles wore from time to time. He wondered where in the world I had gotten that idea. The idea just was hatched last night at dinner.

As we were eating, two girls from the north of England in London on business sat down at the table next to us. Within a couple of minutes, we started talking, and the beer started flowing. After more than a few beers each, one of the girls started looking at me with half-closed eyes. Then she said, "You know what you need?"

"No," I said. "Tell me."

"You are missing something. Your look is pretty good. It reminds me somewhat of that Beatles Sgt. Pepper look and...

actually, that's it: you need a band jacket. With your long hair and beard and suntan, you'd be a hit walking down any street in London."

"A band uniform. I have to say I never would've thought that myself."

Rory pointed out, "Actually, his look is more like a Beatle on the cover of their album *Let It Be*. On *Sgt. Pepper*, they only had mustaches.

I lay awake a long time that night thinking about many things, but one of them was picturing myself in a black or dark blue band uniform short jacket. I woke up the next morning thinking about that.

So, after breakfast, we made our way to the famous Portobello Road Market. Ads for the market stated, "If you lost it, it's probably here. If you can't find it anywhere else, it's probably here. And even if you haven't realized you need it, it will jump out at you like nowhere else, here."

We walked in and looked and looked and walked and walked for hours, but no luck.

That night for dinner we returned to the restaurant we felt so comfortable in previously. A part of that comfort was because it had a TV going all through dinner, and we continuously laughed at the shows.

When we finally made our way back to our hotel, Rory went to bed immediately, but I was wide awake and decided to try and write down some thoughts in my sketchbook, as my daily journal was almost out of pages. I sat on a bench not far from the front door of the hotel and was interrupted constantly by people wanting to know what I was writing. I couldn't believe the traffic; it was after 1:00 a.m. I finally gave up about 2:00 a.m. and turned in.

The Sunday morning sun again was bright and beautiful. Today was my last full day on this journey that was now well into its fifth month. I had traveled thousands of miles, experienced twenty-some countries, and met hundreds of people from the four corners of the world. As I lay in bed watching some puffy white clouds pretend to make pictures of some odd-looking animals for my amusement, I became sentimental. I was feeling a lot of emotions. I decided I'd have to write some of these thoughts down later that night after putting myself in a reflective mood or even maybe tomorrow morning before I left the hotel.

As we finished our breakfast, both Rory and I had things we wanted to see.

First, we made our way to Speaker's Corner in Hyde Park. It was and is famous as a place where you can hear all types of outlandish ideas from people from different places in the world and maybe some from other planets.

After a couple of hours listening and watching, we made our way to one of London's landmark concert venues, The Roundhouse. There was supposed to be a surprise group that was to play later that night; however, I wasn't crazy about paying for anything anymore except food, drink, and the hotel bill as I was leaving. But Rory had a feeling something very neat was going to happen, so we waited in line. Two hours later, I had had it, and so had Rory. We got out of line and left.

We almost went to the London Zoo as we walked south to the Thames, but for some reason at the last moment decided not to. Finally, we reached Westminster Abbey and spent time there and then Buckingham Palace. Then for a while we watched boats going up and down the Thames.

As I walked, I was cognizant that this was really my last bit of exploring on this trip, and the emotion was growing. I was walking and talking with Rory, but part of my mind was trying to have my body really feel where I was: the sights, the sounds, the smells. . . this was the last of all of it, the last of my trip.

When I landed in Paris, I wasn't sure how to get started. I was so apprehensive and big-eyed at everything I saw, and now I could barely identify with that person. It was not that when I was walking down the famous streets of London, I felt like a king. But I felt that I belonged here. There was something in my gait—if not confidence, something like it.

We made our way back to our hotel to get some dinner, and afterward we walked to our other favorite hotel with the restaurant that had a TV to watch some shows and relax. Unfortunately, I guessed we'd been doing that too much without ever paying for a room there, so they kicked us out. We eventually made our way to a pub and met a Canadian guy who in the next couple of days was going to ride his motorcycle all the way to Africa. The three of us immediately hit it off, and we stayed in the pub until 11:00 p.m. As we were leaving, the Canadian, Gregory, said he was hungry and invited us to join him as we walked to one of London's Indian restaurants. We were lucky that he offered to buy.

As we said goodbye to Gregory after the late-night meal, we wished him luck. Just for a second, I tapped into that electric feeling of the start of an adventure that Gregory must have been feeling. In a way I envied him. All the things he'd see, the people he'd meet, the adventures good and bad he'd experience. Any of those thoughts, though, were fleeting. I was totally onboard with where I was in life right now. I'd run my race. At this point I was not sure I'd won or lost or even finished that race. Everything seemed to be quickly coming to the end.

Both Rory and Gregory, though, were very concerned about my situation. Gregory thought my experience of getting this ticket for the flight back to the States was as wild a story as he'd heard in a while. He desperately wanted me to somehow let him know if I did make it back to the States or if everything was a scam and there was nothing left for me to do but try and get some job quickly in London. I think Gregory was very worried that I might be up shit's creek. Rory had mostly overcome his initial pessimism concerning my Middle Eastern acquaintances and come to feel that I had been so lucky throughout my trip that I had one more bit of luck coming to me and that this would all work out very positively.

Finally, back at our hotel, Rory said he was dead tired, and we said our goodbyes. I would have to get up at 3:30 a.m. to start my day. He wasn't getting up that early. I couldn't have done a lot of things on this trip without many of the people I'd met, and Rory would be one person I'd put at the top of that list. His generosity with me in the last few days would never be forgotten. He helped me enjoy my last days in Europe. I hoped he got his travel plans straightened out and that his last days were relaxing and interesting. We exchanged addresses, and I wished him luck as he started his senior year at Tufts University in Boston when he got back.

I don't know how long I lay in bed looking at the ceiling, but I guess eventually I did fall asleep. So much was going through my mind.

I woke up early. I'm not sure how much sleep I'd actually gotten. It didn't matter. This was it, the day I traveled back to reality. The adventure was over. It was now about 5:00 a.m. on the morning of August 3, and I was sitting alone in the Belmont Hotel's dining room, trying to put some last, closing words in my journal.

There is no doubt as I picture myself five to six months ago getting ready to start my trip that now I am almost a completely different person. Yes, I look different; most people would not even recognize me back home.

But that was surface and not really important. What was more significant was what is under that beard and hair. My mind and my heart had gone through a catharsis, a significant change. I would never be the same. I had never intended to have the kind of experiences I ended up having. I never imagined I'd see twenty-plus countries, and I would never have thought that I would feel so different from that guy who got off that jet prop in Luxembourg half a year ago.

I only had a couple of pages left in my journal, almost the perfect amount of space to put down my closing thoughts. There was no doubt I felt a certain way as I sat there that morning, but I still found it hard to believe I could be so, well, so relaxed. I was about to take the Underground to a part of London I'd never been to and wait in front of an address where someone would mysteriously pick me up and take me to Heathrow Airport. Most people would think I was crazy to feel calm at this point. No ticket, no phone number to call, no receipt. Just an address from four unlikely people who appeared more like 1920s gangsters than anyone I should trust. If I didn't get picked up later today, I would be flat broke with nowhere to stay and no money for even a meal.

The Paul at the beginning of this sojourn would have been scared to death and worried every second about what was happening. That Paul probably wouldn't have come this far down this road in the first place. I guessed we'd see which Paul won out in the end.

The Belmont Hotel

Eight beds,
in one room.

Eight beds,
full of doom.

Eight people,
sleeping without a sound.

Eight people,
better off lying on the ground.

Eight lights,
that don't help the darkened hall.

Eight lights,
to guide you as you fall.

Eight stairs,
leading to another floor.

Eight bodies,
and they all snore.

Eight guests,
have left today.

Eight guests,
have survived and gone their way.

Eight beds,
left bare.

Eight beds,
and you wonder, could I, another night dare.

Written August 1, while contemplating going to bed late at night

412

I found myself thinking about the beginning of my trip. I had dreams of a new life in Paris. It was going to be my new start; there had to be something better in Paris than in Chicago. Did I make the right decision to travel east as the story goes—Going East to Meet the Czar—or should I have tried harder to overcome the difficulty of a foreigner getting a job in Paris?

I hadn't been prepared to travel. I could, however, easily picture what my apartment would look like over the Seine. How different would I be now if I had been working in Paris for the last five and a half months? What Paul would I like better, this one who had traveled or the other who would have become part of Paris's day-to-day working class?

I say in my journal that because I really didn't know from the start what I was looking for, I didn't know if I'd found it. But I did find some concrete things to think and dream about, and that was at least a start. I would come back someday, and I would again, I'm sure, want to set off in search of that dream, that something, that something different that many young people think about. Maybe then I would find it. Maybe now I had found it. I didn't know. Maybe would become clearer to me back in the States.

I had learned new things about myself. I had surprised myself repeatedly during my trip. Although I was tired and had run my race, I could sense that once I rested up and recharged my batteries, I would take the experiences from this trip and have much more ammunition for the next parts of my life. I could almost sense that in the future, as I reread my journal, some of my abstract philosophical thoughts would start to define themselves and either dissolve or form concrete, positive ideas and directions.

I thought: *I should go up and start to pack.* Pack for the last time. It's now over; the trail has come to an end. There is no more.

A half hour later, I was on the Tube streaming to that questionable address that would end up as either a perfect, miraculous ending to my trip or the start of an impossible hole to climb out of.

From the moment I walked out of the Belmont Hotel for the last time until I was walking through a quiet London neighborhood in its early morning, the city had been shrouded in fog. In some places, the fog was a gentle lapping on the ground, rising only to my knees, but in other places it was thick and well over my head.

I finally found the address the four gangsters gave me. The guy in the bar was right: this did not make sense as a pickup point. This was such a quiet street, so nondescript. As the only sound was from my boot heels walking on the street, it seemed like the entire neighborhood was still asleep. After trying in vain to swat some of the fog away, I sat down on the curb in front of this large, somewhat ugly house I was supposed to wait in front of. It seemed so odd to me that they wanted me here. It would have made more sense to choose a commercial building, which would have been much easier to find.

I waited. My pickup time came and passed. The fog, luckily for me, appeared to be getting tired of just sitting around and doing nothing. It started to dissolve into fresh air and a cool British morning.

Because I was early to arrive in the first place, it seemed to me I had been waiting way too long, and each additional second was starting to drive me crazy. This neighborhood felt like a ghost town. Was there ever going to be anyone walking around? This was eerie.

Finally, after an hour beyond my pickup time, I was hit across the face by the apparent reality of the situation. I had been conned.

There was no one coming. I was a fool to be sitting here on the curb. *Get up, you fool. It's time to get out of here. Unfortunately, because you are a fool, you have no idea where you're going to go next.*

Out of the corner of my eye, I saw the morning wind blow a copy of *The International Herald Tribune,* which was open to the comics page that had Rip Kirby's column at the top. I considered going after it to see if Rip had found his treasure. I wondered, had I found my treasure? But what would my treasure be? Many, I'm sure, would say I'd been on a quest, but what had I been looking for? Would I find it back in the States, or would the quest continue? Continue to what? To where? How would I know where to search or how to search? Is that what life is, always wondering what's over the next hill? Where and what, I wondered, would be my next hill? A moment later the wind gusted again, and the newspaper— seemingly with a mind of its own—took flight and hovered above for a second and then flew beyond some trees across the street. I whispered, "Goodbye, Rip, until we meet again."

I turned to pull my sleeping bag closer to me so I could pick it up. That's when I finally heard a noise that broke the quiet in this ghost town: an odd noise, a strange noise. It seemed like some mechanical monster moving along a nearby road. It was curious. I looked in the direction it was coming from. What was it? The noise was getting louder.

A couple of minutes later, a huge bus turned the corner and veered onto the street I was sitting on and sped past me, almost hitting me. I had to fall backwards, yanking my legs up from the street not to have them run over.

Leaning back, I looked with a glare at the bus as it stopped a house or two up from where I was sitting. I was thinking *What the fuck?* Another big bus took the corner and again almost hit me and eventually stopped behind the other bus. Then two more turned and stopped right where I was sitting.

Almost immediately upon the buses stopping, loud noises came from behind me. I turned to see three or four of the large row houses behind me squirting out what seemed to be hundreds of twelve-, thirteen-, and fourteen-year-old girls running to the buses, each carrying their little suitcase. I was immediately overrun by many of them as they were trying to figure out which bus to get on. As I lay back trying not to get stepped on, I happened to look up at the driver in the bus right in front of me.

It was one of the 1920s gangsters who had sold me the ticket the other day. He was still wearing his uniform of black shirt, black tie, and pants. As I stared at him thinking, *What the fuck?* he opened his window and waved me on the bus. Immediately, I looked at the other bus. The other bus driver was also wearing that familiar gangster ensemble.

I walked around the bus, got on, and sat in the first seat by the driver. He proceeded to tell me that the four guys playing poker were the four bus drivers and that all four of them had pooled their money to create this special charter flight. All four of the guys had quit their jobs and were starting new lives in New York with the money they'd make from this charter.

I had to sit back and shake my head. In a couple of minutes, I would be on my way to Heathrow with 350 young teenage girls, a couple of adult chaperones, and my four new best friends. This gambit appeared to have worked. I would not find myself tonight walking the streets of London with not enough money for a roof over my head. It, this, everything appeared to have worked out. I was on my way back to the States. My angel of mercy was still with me.

I grabbed a pack of cigarettes from my jacket pocket and offered one to Shamir, the bus driver. As we lit up, one of the chaperones making a face at us and said, "You shouldn't smoke in front of all the girls," but honestly, I didn't care. I just sat back and blew some smoke rings, feeling very happy, very content. Yes, it did hit me that I was now going back to reality, going back to a very different life, to a very different world. It was fitting that as I returned to my previous world, one of the first things to happen was that I got yelled at for something I shouldn't be doing.

The bus caravan took its time as we fought a lot of unusually congested London traffic also headed for the airport. As I stared out the window not really looking at anything, I was feeling more than ever the pull of America and going back to reality. It was a funny feeling. I found myself thinking like I used to think before I took off for Paris. The feeling of making an important decision, the pressure we all seem to feel in the States, consumed by everyday life. In the last five months I had truly experienced a different world. Could I merge the two and make a new world for myself? What would that *new world* be? What would I do? What would my first step be?

Well, I knew I was going home to Chicago and, at least for a while, I would live with my parents until I could earn some money.

Talking about money, in various pockets in my pants and sport coat I had some loose change from different countries and some paper money. It looked like I would be landing in one of the most expensive and largest cities in the world with less than $10 to my name.

As I saw in the distance jets taking off from Heathrow, I started to wonder how I was going to make it home to Chicago.
I hoped my guardian angel was still looking after me.

Afterword

2019

*"My life will change this year
and it will never be the same again."*

My 1970 trip started me on a journey much different than the one I thought I was on. Yes, I learned about new countries and new cultures and met life-changing people. But I also discovered within myself new strengths and abilities and hungers. I wanted to be my own boss, chart my own path and create my own business. And now I had the tools to do these things. When I arrived back in the States, I realized that the many hardships I had encountered during my *"European Odyssey"* had made me mentally stronger, increasingly flexible, substantially goal-oriented, and more eager than ever to find success. Yes, my life did change—because I had changed.

My journey also made me examine my idea of success. Had my trip been successful? My original goal of working in Paris had been a failure. The next challenge, to go to India and Afghanistan on the Orient Express, did not happen—never got to either country. During my subsequent travels I would decide to go to a city, then often head in the opposite direction because of factors beyond my control. But against any measure I could set for myself my trip was successful beyond my wildest dreams: it is a cliché, but it really is all about the journey.

I learned that failure does offer opportunity. I saw that there are lessons to be learned that I didn't know I needed. I gained a lifelong appreciation for other cultures and ways of life. There were many "failures," but I had learned that failure, both literally and figuratively, was not the end of the road.

And so, when I returned my new adventure began. I started out as a graphic designer again, but eventually became an art director in a publishing company. Lightning struck and I was hooked...I loved publishing. I eventually absorbed enough to feel that I could create and publish myself and that's exactly what I did.

I knew very little about publishing but had to learn to do it all. As I had for my European trip, I looked to vintage cinema for publisher role models: Jimmy Stewart in the movie *"Bell, Book & Candle"* was a favorite. And as I had learned on many a road in many a country, I found I could manage and overcome the hardships, surprises, disasters and many unknowns I encountered along the way.

I am gratified to have built, with my wife and partner Kathy, three different successful publishing companies and to have produced numerous books, magazines and websites. During this time, I was able to work with individuals and companies around the world, and always felt privileged to discover all the wonders of a place I had not yet visited. I collaborated with other publishers large and small, good and bad, and it was another journey of which I am very proud.

My magical trip has provided me with hours of dinner-party anecdotes and tales to tell my sons, but in the end, it has given me a never-ending sense of wonder and joy. When sitting alone on a balcony enjoying an ocean sunset, or in my study watching flames crackle and spark from my fireplace while snow falls outside, I find myself beginning to smile as I remember the young man who set off to see Paris and went beyond to find the world—and the man he would become. He was lucky and so am I.

Postscript

2019

I met so many interesting people on my *"European Odyssey"*,
and they all changed my life in different ways. So, if you happen
to come upon this book,
recognize yourself in these pages and remember meeting me,
please contact me through the website below—
I'd love to reconnect and hear about your life after we met:
what you are doing now and where in the world you are doing it.

www.BeyondParis.info

Thanks for reading Beyond Paris. I hope you enjoyed the
story…
If you did, could you please leave a review
on the site that you bought the book from.

PPS:
Wonder how I made it home,
back to Chicago from JFK? Go to the
Beyond Paris website to read the final chapter:

And put in code:

PCBEYONDPARIS

www.BeyondParis.info

CPSIA information can be obtained
at www.ICGtesting.com
Printed in the USA
BVHW070812050819
555096BV00008B/189/P

9 781499 905632